Communication Strategies for Today's Managerial Leader

Communication Strategies for Today's Managerial Leader

Deborah Britt Roebuck

First published in 2012 by
Business Expert Press, LLC
222 East 46th Street, New York, NY 10017
www.businessexpertpress.com

ISBN-13: 978-1-60649-199-7 (paperback)

ISBN-13: 978-1-60649-200-0 (e-book)

DOI 10.4128/9781606492000

A publication in the Business Expert Press Corporate Communication collection

Collection ISSN: 2158-8162 (print)
Collection ISSN: 2156-8170 (electronic)

Cover design by Jonathan Pennell
Interior design by Scribe Inc.

First edition: January 2012

10 9 8 7 6 5 4 3 2 1

Printed in the United States of America.

Abstract

Given that communication is the lifeblood of an organization, managerial leaders need to understand how to use communication strategies to build their teams to achieve organizational objectives. Studies repeatedly point to the impact communication skills have on the ability of managerial leaders to succeed or fail. Too often individuals move into managerial leadership roles without awareness of the need to improve their communication skills. These individuals may be subject matter experts whose technical skills allowed them to succeed as individual team members, but when placed in managerial leadership roles, they fail because they lack the relationship building skills needed to foster teamwork. Therefore, this book provides the communication principles that are so critical for today's managerial leader. It builds a solid foundation while it guides readers in strategies to enhance their written, oral, and interpersonal communication skills. Most research has stated, and the author has found true in her own managerial leadership roles, a leader spends the majority of his or her day interacting with others. As managerial leaders, individuals face many challenging situations such as determining how to inspire a shared vision about goals and objectives, building trust within their unit, listening with an open mind, giving feedback, and encouraging collaboration, to name a few. The focus switches for the managerial leader from doing things to leading others. Therefore, this book is for anyone who currently serves as a managerial leader or for anyone who desires to manage and lead others. Most managerial communication books focus on the important written and oral communication skills. While the author believes these skills are critically important, she found in her role, as a managerial leader, she devoted the majority of her time to interpersonal communication. Leaders need to build teams and to maintain relationships with all stakeholders. The best way to make that happen is through skills such as listening, asking questions, and giving feedback. Therefore, this book includes an emphasis on interpersonal communication. As Chris M. Martin stated in a recent article, "The ability to communicate effectively may be the number one management quality." Therefore, this book will raise awareness relative to oral, written, and interpersonal communication skills so that individuals can become better managerial leaders.

Keywords

interpersonal communication, written communication, oral communication, managerial leadership communication, social media, teaming, crisis communication, virtual teaming, feedback, coaching, mentoring, listening, meetings, emotional intelligence, interviews, ethical communication, presentations, e-mail, blogs, business letters, memos, reports, communication principles, 7 Cs of effective business writing, proofreading, building trust, conflict, asking questions, nonverbal, direct versus indirect writing strategy

Contents

Preface ix

Foreword. xiii

Chapter 1   Building the Foundation of Managerial Leadership
             Communication 1

Chapter 2   Gaining Insight Into the Role of Interpersonal
             Communication Skills for Today's Managerial Leaders. . 63

Chapter 3   Understanding How to Communicate in
             Day-to-Day Situations. 129

Chapter 4   Developing Written Communication Skills 183

Chapter 5   Sharpening Your Oral Communication Skills 275

Appendix A: Crisis Leadership for the New Reality
Ahead by Barbara Gainey 333

Appendix B: Common Errors Found in Written Documents 343

Notes. 363

References 369

Index 381

Preface

Communication continues to be the lifeblood of all business organizations. No organization and its leaders can achieve goals, build the company's reputation and brand, or win friends and customers without effective communication.

Too often, individuals move into managerial leadership roles without an awareness of the need to focus on their communication skills. These individuals may be subject matter experts whose technical skills allowed them to succeed as individual team members, but who fail when placed in managerial leadership roles because they lack the relationship-building skills needed to foster teamwork. Therefore, this book will give you the needed communication strategies that will enable you to succeed as you manage and lead others. The book builds a solid communication foundation while it helps you enhance your written, oral, and interpersonal communication.

Numerous research studies have concluded, and I have found true in my own work experience, that a leader spends the majority of his or her day interacting with others. As a managerial leader, you face many challenging situations such as determining how to inspire a shared vision, building trust within your team, listening with an open mind, giving feedback, and encouraging collaboration, to name a few. As you move into leadership roles, your focus switches from doing things to leading others to accomplish tasks. Consequently, this book is written for those of you who serve others or who desire to move into managerial leadership roles.

Many managerial communication books focus on written and oral communication. While I believe these skills are critically important, I have found when leading others that I have devoted the majority of my time to interpersonal communication. Leaders need to build teams and maintain relationships with all stakeholders. The best way to make that happen is through skills such as listening; asking questions; mastering nonverbal communication; employing emotional intelligence; understanding conflict; using mentoring, coaching, and counseling; and giving feedback. Thus, this book includes an emphasis on interpersonal communication.

As Chris M. Martin, a writer for Yahoo Contributing Network, suggested in a recent article, "The ability to communicate effectively may be the number one essential management quality. Communication savvy will most likely be a manager's greatest asset." For this reason, I hope that this book will raise your awareness of the importance of your oral, written, and interpersonal communication skills and help you make the choice to enhance those competencies. With awareness and tenacity, you can make the right choices as you travel on your journey to become an outstanding managerial leader.

My Thanks

I wish to acknowledge the following individuals for their assistance in bringing this book from an idea to a reality. I could not have completed this endeavor without their support, and I feel blessed to have had their encouragement.

I must first thank the Business Expert Press team beginning with David Parker, publisher and founder, who believed enough in me to wait an extra year for the book. David would send an e-mail or pick up the telephone whenever I needed encouragement or a response to a question or concern. I consider him to be a role model of a managerial leader. Next, I am grateful to my collections editor, another outstanding managerial leader, Debbie DuFrene. She provided words of wisdom and spent countless hours reading and then rereading every word I wrote. She worked tirelessly to help me create the best book possible. Finally, I must thank another managerial leader, my production liaison, Cindy Durand, who was available whenever I needed help. When I would encounter difficulty on some issue, she would jump in to help and make sure I understood the process. All three of these managerial leaders enabled me to complete this book, and I am grateful for their guidance and faith in me. Also I must thank Bill Klump from Scribe Inc., who brought the manuscript to print. I think, at times, my manuscript was a challenge, but he rose to the occasion and made the book a reality.

Two special individuals, also outstanding managerial leaders, deserve recognition as reviewers for my book. First, my thanks to my father,

Aubrey C. Britt, who checked and rechecked my grammar and word choice. We spent many hours together discussing the content and working to improve each chapter. Dad, please note that I changed every "most" to "many." My second reviewer was my friend Kathryn O'Neil who kept right on reviewing while she retired from a corporate position, packed up, and moved from Georgia to Texas to accept a teaching position. I was often amazed at the things she would find that I thought I had already corrected. My work benefited greatly from both of these individuals, who provided objective perspectives and a keen eye for detail. I thank them for their dedication and for ensuring that my book was the best it could possibly be.

Next, I must thank my former EMBA students, MBA students, and business associates who provided stories, quizzes, and articles. I know their contributions enhance and validate the content of each chapter. My sincere thanks to Candace Long, Paige Yeater, Dom Crincoli, Pam Napier, John Boe, Nathan Kalb, Toni Bowers, Rebecca Warlick, Chris Festa, Kathryn O'Neil, Arky Ciancutti, Maggie Anderson, Jennifer Garvey Berger, Andy Smith, Paul McElvy, Rick Brinkman, Charlsye Diaz, Tony Hsieh and his team of elves, Jeff Haden, Julie Sims and Robert Half International, Joe Urbanski, Pierre-Paul Allard, and Vanessa and Carmine Gallo. Thank you for your kind words and encouragement as you read what I had written. Your feedback and belief in me kept me going. You will continue to be my inspiration as I strive to enable others to succeed and achieve their goals.

Finally, to Rob, my husband, who did not question where I was going when I headed upstairs to my office or else told me I better go upstairs to work on my book; to my daughter, Hillary, who constantly reminded me I was working all the time; and to my son-in-law, Rich, who would ask, "Is the book finished yet?" I appreciate their love, encouragement, and patience as this project did take time away from them.

Deborah Britt Roebuck

Foreword

By Anthony D'Angelo and Ray Crockett

In this time of economic turbulence, trust in companies and their leaders is now measured at an all-time low—substantially lower than it was a generation ago. Pete Peterson, chairman of the Blackstone Group, observed, "What matters is what the public thinks and the public trust is what has really crashed." Yet many organizational managers and leaders are not aware of the role of managerial leadership communication and how essential it is to trust. Managerial leaders typically get their jobs because they're smart and experienced. They are often less astute about managerial leadership communication than they are about finance, marketing, operations, product development, or strategic planning. Yet they are the de facto chief reputation officers for their organizations.

Many of these individuals suffer from a blind spot in the science of managerial leadership communication. Often the "soft skills" are not perceived to be as important as learning finance, accounting, and strategy. Thus, learning these vital skills is commonly omitted from a managerial leader's business education. Hence we have managerial leaders who underestimate the importance of their role as communicators and have not been educated on communication and how best to interact, motivate, and influence others. Often, these managerial leaders will avoid contact with the media, employees, community, shareholders, and other constituencies because they just do not know how to effectively communicate to advance their missions, to build support, and to gain the trust of their stakeholders.

A managerial leader must communicate, hold others accountable, and be transparent to influence people and build trust. A leader has to engage audiences in the messy give-and-take of dialogue and be willing to construct or alter a company's position or policy based in part on their input. Organizations must be unerringly ethical, transparent in policies and operations, and willing to invest—sometimes generously—in righting wrongs and fixing what's broken. Taking such actions requires a knowledgeable commitment to ongoing communication, transparency, and a long-term focus on results. A managerial leader who diligently builds his or her organization's reputation can have that work destroyed in an instant without disciplined caretaking. Witness Toyota, an enviable brand that symbolized quality and reliability, and how clumsily the company managed reports of its vehicles' accelerating and causing accidents. As Toyota's position seemed to shift week by week, the CEO was initially absent, then repentant, while negative news reports arrived constantly and were exacerbated by inadequate responses, a lack of clarity, and ultimately lingering questions about the company's and its leaders' competence. So don't follow that path, but instead choose to invest time in learning communication strategies to communicate effectively with all of your stakeholders. Learn how strategic communications can not only help avoid business disaster, but strengthen your brand and company, creating value and building respect and good will among customers and your business community.

Anthony D'Angelo and Ray Crockett lead the MBA Initiative for the Public Relations Society of America. Tony holds the position of Senior Manager, Communications for ITT Corporation, while Ray recently retired from Coca-Cola North America as Director of Communications.

CHAPTER 1

Building the Foundation of Managerial Leadership Communication

Studies repeatedly point to the impact communication skills have on the ability of managers and leaders to succeed or fail. "The ability to communicate effectively may be the number one management quality," stated Chris M. Martin, Yahoo writer, who himself holds a BS in Business Administration and a JD.[1] Managers and leaders need to use effective communication strategies as they build their teams and organizations to achieve organizational objectives. Too often, individuals move into management or leadership roles without an awareness of the need to improve their communication skills. These individuals may be subject matter

Photo courtesy flickr user World Economic Forum, CC 2.0

experts whose technical skills allowed them to succeed as individuals, but who fail when placed in a management or leadership role because they lack the needed communication skills to foster collaboration. If communication is so important, just exactly what is it and does it differ for managers and leaders?

Definition and Types of Communication

Simply stated, *communication is the glue or the life blood of an organization.* Said another way, communication can be thought of as the *gears that lubricate the machinery of the organization.* It involves sending and receiving ideas, feelings, thoughts, opinions, and facts to other individuals by using written, oral, and interpersonal communication. A managerial leader uses communication to get things done with and through others. Effective communication takes place when a meeting of the minds occurs and all parties have a shared understanding.

Managerial Communication

Managerial communication is often defined as communication between managers and employees that allows them to complete the work of an organization. You will note that in this definition, the focus of managerial communication is within the organization.

Leadership Communication

The focus of leadership communication shifts more to interacting with external audiences to project the image and reputation of the organization. For leaders, internal communication still takes place, but it is more strategic in nature; the day-to-day communication activities are left to the managers. Leadership communication is focused on how to lead change and inspire a vision. As you can see, this type of communication is more complex and serves a broader audience. Sometimes you will also see it referred to as corporate communication.

A New Form of Communication: Managerial Leadership Communication

With social media, up to four generations of employees in the work place, and a global economy, organizations and leaders need a new form of communication. This new form, *managerial leadership communication*, brings together the skills and competencies of managerial and leadership communication under one umbrella.

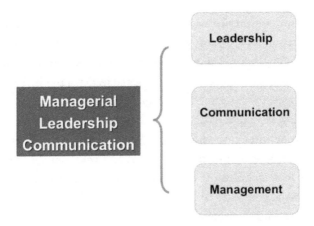

Managerial leaders interact with employees and other organizational members while also communicating with vendors, suppliers, and other external audiences. When you, as a managerial leader, communicate with external audiences, you become the voice of the organization. On occasion, you might even be called upon to communicate with the press and other outside groups. The above diagram illustrates the three integral components of managerial leadership, with effective communication at the heart of it.

Why We Need Managerial Leadership Communication

Much research has stated what the author has found true in her own managerial leadership roles: a leader spends the majority of his or her day interacting with others. Today's organizations do not hire "hands;" they employ whole individuals who bring intellectual capital. Employees of the 21st century want to think, make a difference, and make a meaningful contribution to the organization, not just receive a paycheck. They do not seek managers who command and control, but desire their managerial leaders to listen to them, respect their ideas, and include them in problem solving and decision making.

Any organization, for profit or not, comprises individuals who are specialists in certain functions. For an organization to meet its objectives, however, these subject matter experts must communicate internally and externally in ways that their audiences can understand. If employees cannot share information in a meaningful way or discuss ideas with each other, it truly doesn't really matter how much they know. They will likely not be successful as they can't communicate that expertise with others. While all employees need communication skills, these skills are vital for anyone who desires to move into a managerial leadership role.

Google recently conducted a comprehensive study that found that "what employees valued most were even-keeled bosses who made time for one-on-one meetings, who helped people puzzle through problems by asking questions, not dictating answers, and who took an interest in employees' lives and careers."[2] Moreover, "technical expertise—the ability, say, to write computer code in one's sleep—ranked dead last among Google's "big eight" virtues—even though the study was specifically about managers at the tech company, not managers in general.[3]

Robert P. Gandossy, Hewitt Global Practice Leader for Leadership, Talent, and Employee Engagement, counsels organizational leaders to choose future managers for their communication skills as much as for their achievements. Front-line managers have the greatest influence over an employee's engagement. Managers who are engaging communicators get more from their direct reports than managers whose strong skills lie elsewhere. Managers who can communicate serve as an insurance policy for keeping the best workers focused, engaged, and productive.[4]

While I was leading our Executive MBA program, I taught the communication and leadership development modules. Too often, a student would ask that the communication and leadership modules be replaced with more finance modules. Of course, as the leader of the Executive MBA program, my role was to listen to our students and I did. After listening to their requests, my team would implement changes where we could while also stressing to these students the importance of leadership and communication. In listening to my students, I knew the reality was that, conceptually, learning economics and finance was easier than learning how to communicate and lead others. Since learning how to communicate effectively and lead others requires making behavioral changes, most individuals find it difficult to do. My students were seeking to increase intellectual intelligence and not realizing that emotional intelligence is more valuable to a managerial leader.

When managerial leaders understand that their role is to guide, coach, influence, and persuade, they will choose to surround themselves with a team of subject matter experts. They know, as managerial leaders, that their focus has switched from their having to "know everything" to having a team that "knows everything." Of course, the managerial leader should have a basic understanding of all subjects including economics, finance, and accounting so that he or she can make effective decisions. The input for those decisions, however, doesn't come from the leader, but from his or her team.

I remember one particular e-mail I received after a student had graduated from our program. He said, "Dr. Roebuck, I find that my 'people-skills' seem to be holding me back from moving into more of a leadership role. I wondered if you could recommend a book I could read." Of course, my first reaction was to laugh. But I chose to use my emotional intelligence and responded by suggesting a book that he could read. More importantly, I strongly recommended that he get a coach. The sad reality of this situation was that he had a safe environment while enrolled in the Executive MBA in which to practice and improve his leadership and communication skills, but he chose not to do so at that time, and then later realized that his lack of leadership and communication skills were holding him back. His thinking that reading a book would be enough to effect the changes he needed to make truly demonstrated his lack of understanding regarding managerial leadership. He was still trying to become a subject matter expert instead of a managerial leader.

Managerial leaders face many challenging situations, such as determining how to inspire a shared vision about goals and objectives, building trust within their units, listening with an open mind, giving feedback, and encouraging collaboration, to name a few. The focus for a managerial leader switches from his or her actually doing tasks to communicating with and through others on how to achieve those tasks. A managerial leader must exhibit effective communication. Sometimes having those communication skills can be a reason that an individual is given the opportunity to move into a managerial leadership position.

The Communication Skills of the Managerial Leader

You've probably heard the old story, or actually seen it occur in your organization. Someone who is excellent in his or her technical skills is promoted to manager. Then, once in that position, he or she demonstrates a lack of expertise in communication. Only with a willingness to be a life-long learner and a focus on enabling others can someone really fulfill the role of a managerial leader. As a managerial leader, you will need to master interpersonal, written, nonverbal, and oral communication skills.

Interpersonal Communication Skills

Many business professionals have difficulty with "soft skills," which often are the "hard skills" because they require behavioral changes. However, they are the keys to your success as a managerial leader. Even more difficult for many of us, as illustrated by my story of the Executive MBA student who just wanted to read a book to improve, is accepting the reality that we have poor soft skills and must make an effort to improve.

To build interpersonal skills, you need to focus on building a number of component skills. The major interpersonal communication skills include

- giving and receiving **FEEDBACK;**
- mastering **NONVERBAL** communication;

No longer will you find it enough to know how to analyze a balance sheet or income statement. An effective managerial leader will take that balance sheet and use it to coach his or her employees, facilitate team productivity, and lead them toward performance improvement. This leadership cannot be done simply by reading the numbers and telling people the numbers need to change. Instead, you must enable others by communicating with them in ways that encourage them, motivate them, and reinforce their value.

- employing **EMOTIONAL INTELLIGENCE;**
- choosing the right type of **LISTENING** for the situation;
- using relevant **QUESTIONS;**
- understanding **CONFLICT** and the use of different strategies;
- using **MENTORING, COACHING,** and **COUNSELING;**
- building **TRUST;**
- creating **TEAMS;**
- conducting **MEETINGS** and **INTERVIEWS.**

Because of the importance and complexity of interpersonal communication skills and day-to-day communication situations, chapters 2 and 3 are devoted to these topics.

> I am often surprised when some of my graduate students cannot distinguish between a complete sentence and a sentence fragment. My father, who taught English in high school for several years, says that he believes it is the biggest educational deficiency in college graduates and I would have to agree.

Written Communication Skills

Delta CEO Richard Anderson believes strongly in the ability to communicate and feels that it is so important that it ought to be a core capability in a business school curriculum. While Anderson stresses the importance of the ability to speak and write well, he believes that writing is not taught as well as it should be in the educational curriculum. He has stated that people really have to be able to handle the written and spoken word, and a strong foundation in grammar is essential to attaining the ability to do so. Anderson stated, "It's not just enough to be able to do a nice Power-Point presentation. You've got to have the ability to communicate."[5]

As a managerial leader, you will be involved in composing e-mails, memos, policies, procedures, proposals, reports, blogs, instant messages, letters, and tweets. These forms of written communication function as the backbone of the organization's internal and external communication. Given today's world, in which technology enables communication around the globe, written communication has become even more important.

However, former Securities and Exchange Commission chairman Arthur Levitt, who has long advocated "plain English" in business and government, says business writing is usually incomprehensible to readers. "It lacks color and nuance, and it's not terribly interesting to read," he says.[6] So the challenge for you becomes writing for your audience while making sure your writing is clear, concrete, concise, complete, correct, and courteous. Chapter 4 provides more in-depth discussion of written communication skills.

Oral Communication Skills

Managerial leaders also need to create and deliver oral presentations that captivate their audiences' interest. Effective managerial leaders need to project confidence when making informative and persuasive presentations, whether speaking to one or to 1,000.

You will find that some basics of communication apply to both written and oral communication situations, such as first determining your purpose and analyzing your audience. Effective oral and written communication takes some critical thinking before an actual communication takes place. If you think about your purpose and seek to know your audience, chances are you will be a better communicator.

The advantage of oral over written communication is that you can personalize the message and talk directly to the individual, which provides a more personal connection between a managerial leader and a colleague. Personal connections allow you, as the managerial leader, to understand others better. In addition, with oral messages, you can receive immediate feedback. Written communication does not always provide this advantage, though instant messaging and other forms of technology are now allowing for quicker feedback. You will learn more about oral communication skills in chapter 5.

As an employee, a manager, a leader, or a managerial leader, you need to understand the basic communication process, illustrated in the following diagram. As a managerial leader, you will often serve as the channel for messages.

The Communication Process

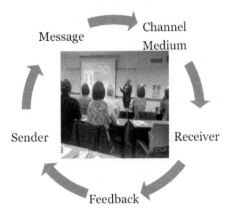

Message → Channel / Medium

Sender ← Receiver

Feedback

Reinforcing the Basic Communication Process

To increase your effectiveness as a communicator, you must be aware of the various components of the communication process. As your responsibility increases, the "how" of your communication becomes critical.

Sender

As a sender, you initiate the communication and determine the intent of the message, how to send it, and what, if any, response is required. You bear the burden in this process. You must communicate both content and feelings.

Because no two people are exactly alike, they hear messages in different ways. Some individuals want facts, while others want details. When you serve as the sender and you are communicating with your team or internally, you will need to analyze your audience and get to know each one on a personal basis so that you can tailor your message.

> Often as a managerial leader, you share messages sent by others. You may be asked to carry organizational messages to your team and other people as directed by your senior leader. When you are asked to communicate for others, you must consider whose message you are communicating.

One way I learned about my team was through a personality assessment called the WorkPlace Big Five. Before I met with a member of my team, I reviewed his or her preferences to help me tailor my communication. For example, if I had an extroverted team member, I remembered to provide positive reinforcement and give her sufficient time to talk. If I had an introverted team member, I made the meetings shorter, but gave him time to think. If I had an analytical person, we would focus on problem solving. As you get to know your team, you will know how certain people are inclined to feel and think.

You may first communicate a message to all of your team members and then follow up with a one-on-one meeting to provide a specific message to an individual. One sales strategy you might want to employ is called the *feel-felt-found.*[7] When communicating with a particular individual you might want to say, "You might be feeling this way;" "I know how you feel. I've felt that way as well;" or "I've found that if I . . ."

If you are not the original sender, your job is to first reinforce the sender's points. When communicating to your team and others, tell them what senior leadership is saying and reinforce their message. Reinforce the message by saying something like "Here's what I think this means for us." Of course, you should not disagree in public or private with your leader as it is absolutely unprofessional to do so. If you disagree, you dilute the message and send a mixed message. Your direct reports then wonder whom they are to follow—you or your manager.

As a managerial leader, you should ask yourself if you are the right one to deliver a message. Asking someone else on your team to be the person who delivers the message builds your skill in communicating through others and helps you assess the communication skills of the members of your team.

Receiver

As a receiver, you interpret messages based upon your frame of reference. This frame of reference includes your life experiences, cultural background, and the values and beliefs you hold. Because these filters may adversely affect the intent of the sender, some feedback must occur to prevent misunderstandings.

Photo courtesy flickr user Whiteafrican, CC 2.0

As a managerial leadership communicator, you will want to be direct in about 90 percent of your communications. You will provide *the bottom line up front*. To reach your audience, you will need to decide what your key points are and put them up front. You tell your reader or audience where you're going at the beginning. Using this approach is truly one of the core secrets of being a great managerial leader.

Message

The message contains ideas expressed to other individuals. The message must be transmitted in a form that a receiver can understand. Messages generally take one or more of three forms based on their purpose: to inform, to persuade, or to take action. Informative messages share information or describe something to the receivers; persuasive messages attempt to change receivers' attitudes, beliefs, or perceptions; and action-oriented messages motivate receivers to do a task.

As a managerial leadership communicator, you address the emotions or feelings of your audience. You cannot separate emotions from workplace activity. People are going to feel something about whatever is communicated and you need to learn to address the emotion. You can say something such as "I understand this may make you feel this way. Here's what I recommend." When you provide the recommendations up front, you will increase the chances that you will get feedback and that your team members will make the necessary behavioral changes.

Channel or Medium

The channel conveys the message to your receiver, either verbally, face-to-face (air provides the medium), or in another mediated fashion such as the phone, written memo, e-mail, or social media. The medium can distort the message positively or negatively, so, as the sender, you must choose the best medium for assuring effective communication. As managerial leadership communicators, we probably overuse e-mail. E-mail should not be the primary channel to communicate sensitive information with your direct reports. You still need to use the richest form of communication when possible, which is face-to-face.

Face-to-face meetings. Face-to-face meetings are the best way to impact your team and its behavior. Delivering something face-to-face in a meeting will get your team talking. Face-to-face communication still provides the best way to build trust and consensus in a team and helps others work through resistance to new ideas. Communicate through either one-on-one touch-base meetings or in a team meeting. I used to try to meet

Photo courtesy flickr user Michigan Municipal League, CC 2.0

Some of the advantages of face-to-face meetings are that you can answer questions in real time and make use of nonverbal communication. You should make this your number-one communication rule—everything you tell your team must go through face-to-face meetings. If you lead only virtual teams, your first choice should be the phone or webcam meetings because you have all mediums: verbal, vocal, visual, and nonverbal. The only downsides to face-to-face remain the time it requires and the expense of bringing team members together who are not colocated.

with each of my direct reports once a month over lunch as that seemed to make the conversation more casual. I think smart managerial leaders will also have regular lunches with subsets of their organizations. At these meetings, you can talk for approximately 10 minutes and then spend the rest of the time in Q & A. Another strategy you might want to employ would be *skip level* meetings in which you don't invite your direct reports, but go one level below. You would follow the same strategy of talking for about 10 minutes and giving them time to share and ask questions. Having *skip level* meetings will allow you to check to make sure your messages are getting to other levels of the organization.

Photo courtesy flickr user Klessblogi, CC 2.0

Videoconferencing or webcam conferencing. Although people attending the meeting may be thousands of miles apart, these types of meetings simulate live, face-to-face interaction. Videoconferences or webcam conferences give you the closest feeling to a face-to-face meeting, and technology is rapidly improving in this area. I remember the first semester that I taught an online business communication class. I only had e-mail and discussion thread interaction with my students, and I was constantly flooded with e-mails. The following semester, I started incorporating weekly webcam class sessions and my inbox became much smaller. Students could ask questions in real time and interact with me. I felt that I made more of a human connection with my students. Students began telling other faculty about my webcam sessions, and faculty started asking me how I did them. From this experience, I was reminded that people want to have human contact, and technology is available to help us to be more connected.

Phone calls and conference calls. Calls enable you to pick up important information including the tone and energy in the other person's voice. The main downside is that your participants miss the information provided from the visual aspect of communication. Another downside that I have encountered is people not listening and trying to do other work. They miss a point in the discussion because they are multitasking and the conversation has to be repeated. One way to overcome this challenge is to set some ground rules at the beginning of the call about what is acceptable and unacceptable behavior during calls.

Voice mail. Voice mail is great when used with respect. Keep your voice messages clear, concise, and action-oriented. Because you are employing a one-way channel, you will have no immediate feedback and your message may be misinterpreted.

E-mail. As stated earlier, e-mail is probably overused in today's work environment, but that will probably continue to be the case. E-mail is effective for providing details and as a record of information, which allows your readers to reference it later. The negative to e-mail is that you have no control over when and if your receiver reads or forwards the message. I would not recommend using e-mail for sensitive or negative messages.

Instant messaging. Surprisingly, instant messaging is used quite frequently within work settings. A recent study found that workers who used instant messaging on the job reported less interruption than colleagues who did not.[8] One of my MBA students even shared with me that at his work, they were now using IM to approve contracts. The difficulty with IM is that it has a different language form from formal English, and therefore the message could either be misinterpreted or incomprehensible to the receiver. Another disadvantage is that some IM systems do not provide a permanent record of the conversation.

Social media. Social media provides an outlet for telling both internal and external stakeholders about you and your organization. Sharing information about your organization through Twitter and a regularly updated blog can raise your company's profile and brand. Instant messaging and social media channels work well with the younger generations with whom you interact. You can become a thought leader in your industry and in the eyes of your stakeholders if you follow the example of Southwest Airlines. Southwest Airlines has 12 million monthly visits to its website, 1 million Twitter followers, 1.3 million Facebook followers, and 29,000 reviewers on its Travel Guide. Five employees monitor the company's social media 24/7, including hourly check-ins during normal sleeping hours, with two people typically trading off responsibilities. Southwest Airlines communication specialist Laurel Moffat recommends that organizations "listen first." Listening provides an understanding of content that's meaningful and appropriate for your audiences. Once you get active, Moffat further recommends personalizing audience experiences. One way Southwest does this is by having team members sign their names to their responses.[9] A downside to social media can be that individuals become too dependent upon it and then when they are asked to communicate face-to-face, they struggle with how to carry on a conversation. You've probably been at a meeting where individuals used their BlackBerrys or iPads to communicate back and forth underneath the conference room table. Or you might have seen that commercial where all the members of a family are communicating across the dinner table using their technology instead of talking to one another. In a meeting I had with business leaders, they commented on the fact that many younger individuals had great social networking skills but noted they were concerned about a lack of interpersonal skills. Like any tool, social media, if overused, can become a liability.

> Using multichannels will allow you to reach your audience more than once. Your team members need to hear about the mission of your team and the larger organization, operational issues, and goals numerous times and through different channels.

Frequency and Use of Multiple Channels

As a managerial leader, you have to repeat key messages over and over again. Winston Churchill once said, "If you have an important point to make, don't try to be subtle or clever. Use a pile driver. Hit the point once. Then come back and hit it again. Then hit it a third time—a tremendous whack."[10] If you want your messages to get through, you need frequent communication.

Recent reports show that job satisfaction rates in the United States are at the lowest level in more than two decades. The economic recession has caused employers to downsize, and in many places work that was done by three or four individuals is now being done by one. As a consequence, stress, anxiety, and job burnout have been made worse by poor communication or infrequent communication. According to Dr. Mary Capelli-Schellpfeffer, Medical Director of Loyola University Health System Occupational Health Services:

> Communication is critical to success. That's always true. But it's harder to do during challenging events because of all the "noise" from bad news. Shared messages can become an important vehicle for solidifying trust and a team perspective. When a supervisor stops by an employee's desk asking, "How are you doing?" the action makes an impact. The added bonus is that the supervisor is more likely to gain valuable firsthand information about what is or isn't working in the enterprise.[11]

As a managerial leader, you will often use multiple channels to ensure your message is received and understood. For example, you might have a face-to-face meeting and follow it up with e-mail. The advantage of multiple channels is that you will get feedback at each point. One manager shared how she created weekly digests of the e-mails she received. She sent the digest to her team, but first she added her comments regarding each of the messages and how it impacted them or didn't. She included links to the original e-mails and told her team that if they wanted more details, they could follow the link. She ordered the messages based upon their importance to her team. She shared that her team appreciated her filtering through the messages so that they knew which ones were important. Instead of being overwhelmed with e-mail, her team can now focus on what matters most.

Feedback

Feedback reports back to you that your receiver understood the message. When the receiver responds to the sender, the communication process starts over. Feedback makes communication a two-way process, allowing the sender to become a receiver and vice versa.

Environment

The environment in which the communication takes place can influence the probability of your success or failure. You must consider where and when to communicate to ensure you receive the results you intend. Effective managerial leadership communication depends on how successfully you take these environmental factors into account. Even when communicators consider all factors, miscommunication can still occur.

Highlighting Causes of Miscommunication

Because people come from diverse backgrounds, various parts of the United States, or different countries, they sometimes have difficulty communicating with each other. This section addresses inferences, word-meaning confusion, differing perceptions, information overload and timing, nonverbal messages, noise, filtering, defensiveness and emotions, personality differences, gender differences, generational differences, and intercultural differences.

As a managerial leadership communicator, you should be conscious of the inferences you make and be careful to label your inferences as such. Your receivers must be able to distinguish between what you know and what you think, assume, believe, or judge to be true. I was recently reviewing a proposal and the author made a statement that came across as a fact, but in reality it was an inference he had drawn based upon his beliefs and values. We all make inferences, but we need to be aware of when we do so.

Inferences

When you make an inference, you draw a conclusion based on facts. Basically, you observe something and, as a result, gain information. You then analyze the information and draw a conclusion about what you have observed. Your conclusion, or inference, may be correct or incorrect. Let's consider some examples.

1. The team members were smiling.
2. The team members were smiling; therefore, every team member was satisfied with the outcome.

The first statement contains a fact; you can easily verify it. You can see the team members smiling as they come out of the meeting. The second statement, an inference, involves drawing a conclusion based on more than what you observe, that is, you impute meaning to the facts you have observed.

In different parts of the United States, we have regionalisms. I grew up in the Midwest and later moved to Georgia. When I first stepped off the airplane in Atlanta, someone greeted me by saying, "Hey." I wondered why they were saying "Hey," which to me was a type of feed for cattle and horses. Another difference I encountered in the South occurred when my little daughter would go to the neighbor's house to see if Beth could play. Often Hillary would come back and say, "Beth's mom said Beth was ill." This happened day after day and I thought Beth must have a terminal illness. I finally learned from another mother that in Georgia "ill" referred to a misbehaving child.

Word-Meaning Confusion

When a sender and receiver give the same word different meanings or give different words the same meaning, word-meaning confusion occurs. Words have both *denotative* and *connotative* meanings: *denotative* meanings are the ones found in the dictionary, while *connotative* meanings come from the experiences individuals have and how they then assign meanings to words. For example, if you look up the word *cube* in the dictionary, you probably would find a definition of a solid with six equal, square sides. However, in some business environments, *cube* refers to an open work space in the office.

The 500 most commonly used words in the English language have 14,070 dictionary meanings. That's an average of more than 28 meanings for each word. The word *set*, for example, has 194 different meanings. Words themselves don't contain the meaning—people supply the meanings depending on past experiences. Consider the following example. A small business owner went to order some letterhead stationery. She told the sales representative she wanted a simple letterhead and the name put in the center. When she went to pick up her letterhead stationery, the supplier had done exactly as she had said and placed the name in the middle of each sheet instead of centered at the top as she had intended. A personal example also comes to mind. While I was an executive director of an institute, my office was located in a house beside the campus. I had two colleagues who were collaborating on a project with me and we agreed to meet. I told them to come to "the house." I kept looking at my watch when they had not arrived and I wondered if we had a mix-up on our dates. Then I received a telephone call from them asking where I was. I said I was at the house. They said they were at the house where I lived, and they had been sitting on my front porch for 30 minutes waiting for me! What seemed perfectly clear to me—come to "the house"—was not the message my colleagues received. I became victim to not clarifying and checking with my receivers that the message had been received as I had intended.

Jargon, which is a specialized terminology or technical language that members of a group use to communicate among themselves, can also cause problems when used with others outside of the work organization. Age, education, and cultural background can influence language use and definitions given to words. To avoid word-meaning confusion, consider the person with whom you are communicating, ask questions, and paraphrase important statements.

Differing Perceptions

Your perceptions provide your view of reality, but they depend on how you interpret what you see and hear. Perceptions are influenced by a variety of factors, including personal background, education, age, and experiences. Two categories of perception exist: sensory perception and normative perception.

- **Sensory perception.** This type of perception occurs when people selectively interpret what they see or hear on the basis of their interests, background, experience, and attitudes. Sensory perception can cause communication problems because your team members may not always perceive what you literally present to them. You must ask not only *whether* a person understands, but also *what* a person understands.
- **Normative perception.** Normative perception involves your interpretation of reality. When individuals express their opinions, normative perception occurs. As a communicator, you interpret the situation.

Miscommunication based on normative perception occurs when you attempt to communicate with others and you assume that they interpret data the same way you do. You must be careful, because we all view the world differently. To avoid miscommunication based on differing perceptions, make your message specific, clarify important points, and seek feedback.

Bottom-Line: Your Message

You can prevent such information loss by becoming concerned more with the *quality* of your communication than with its quantity. The need for clear, concise communication is essential in the face of information overload. Keep your communications short and to the point. As I have said previously, *bottom-line your message.*

Information Overload and Timing

Technology has affected the world of work in two dramatic ways. First, the office can be anywhere you choose; second, using technology, organizations can share their collective wisdom and knowledge to further their goals. But technology has also caused information overload. Technology and the global nature of work have increased the amount of communication that takes place. We no longer define business as working 8 to 5, but 24/7. Often when working internationally with various team members located in different countries, their work follows the sun and never stops so you have productivity for 24 hours. Unfortunately, you have only a limited capacity to handle and process all of this communication. Individuals tend to select out, ignore, pass over, or forget information when they have too much information. Or, they may put off further processing until the overload situation is over, which still negatively impacts communication.

Similarly, when communicating with employees, whether face-to-face or over the phone, you should check your timing. If you rush in, interrupt, and demand time, your receiver may feign listening or listen halfheartedly. This behavior could be costly to an organization if it results in miscommunication and wrong action.

Photo courtesy flickr user Pop! Tech,pho, CC 2.0

Nonverbal Messages

As part of a personal encounter, nonverbal and verbal communication happen simultaneously. When assessing nonverbal messages, be careful not to place too much importance on a single, isolated nonverbal behavior; instead, look for several nonverbal cues. If the verbal and nonverbal cues disagree, you can usually believe the nonverbal ones because they tend to be spontaneous and less controlled. Nonverbal actions provide a key to a person's true feelings and attitudes.

It is said that women, in general, are better than men at recognizing nonverbal cues. A study of Emirati women in Dubai showed that culture does not play a role in determining whom they prefer to communicate with, and that nonverbal cues and personal attributes, such as honesty, politeness, helpfulness, and so on, determine their preference to communicate with a certain individual.[12] This research suggested that differences in culture are not necessarily the main factor in influencing communication preferences.

Senders sometimes forget the importance of nonverbal messages, but as a communicator, you should pay careful attention to the nonverbal communication of the sender and listen for the message "between the lines."

> If individuals neglect getting to know their subordinates, colleagues, and associates, they may not structure their communication properly for maximum effectiveness. Such neglect does not necessarily signal an uncaring attitude, but it contributes to noise in both the sending and receiving of messages.

Noise

Noise can interfere with every aspect of the communication process. Noise may be external or internal.

External noise. External noise comes from your surroundings. Some examples of external noise include a telephone ringing, a landscaping crew mowing the grounds, or colleagues laughing in the cubicle next to yours.

Internal noise. This type of noise comes from within and could include such factors as dislike of your receiver, distraction by another problem, prejudice against a person, closed-mindedness, or lack of interest in an issue.

Filtering

When you filter information, you deliberately manipulate the information to make it appear more favorable to your receiver. As information is communicated up through the organizational levels, you often condense and synthesize it. You filter the communication through your personal interests and perceptions of what is important.

Recently an executive attended a seminar where she perceived the facilitator to be arrogant. She did not learn much because she was distracted by her perception. In the end, because her filters were too strong, she could not take advantage of the opportunity to learn.

To become aware of when you are inclined to filter, try this exercise. Pick an hour of time to *stop passing judgment* on anything and everything around you. Observe and listen to what's happening without evaluating it at all. When you look at something, don't judge, but just observe. When you listen to someone talk, don't judge what he or she is saying; instead, just listen.

You may find that you start congratulating or berating yourself on how well or poorly you're doing the exercise. Notice that you are judging yourself! The point of the exercise is to be aware of how often you judge. By becoming aware of how you prejudge and filter everything that you perceive, you can learn to switch the filters off at will. Keep in mind that we use filters even when we look at ourselves. If we have a particular quality we don't like, we may not even see that we have it. Getting rid of filters will allow you to know and accept who you truly are.[13]

When communicating with others, strive for clarity. If you are not understood, you do not need to take it personally as the receivers are not questioning your competence. For them, you have not delivered the message in a way that they can understand. So you may need to rephrase, ask questions, and clarify to make sure you are delivering your intended message.

Defensiveness and Emotions

When people feel they are being attacked or threatened, they can become defensive and verbally attack others. They do this through sarcastic remarks, becoming overly judgmental, and questioning others' motives.

Try to avoid reacting to a message when the individual is upset because he or she is not likely to be thinking clearly. To help you be aware of when you become defensive, you might consider keeping a communication journal where you reflect upon certain situations in which you acted defensively or provoked defensive behavior. As with all behavior changes, you first have to recognize defensive actions. When you have some distance from the event, reflect on ways you may have been able to handle the situation differently. In addition, you should prepare for situations where you know defensive triggers may exist. If you know that you have a stressful situation coming up, practice responses for questions or comments that might trigger defensiveness on your part.

Parents know how the tone of their voice can get results, both positive and negative. Similarly, when communicating with your subordinates, do not get parental, as a simple thing like tone of voice can provoke defensiveness in others.

Remember to pause, reflect, and then speak. We too often just speak and then think later. If you take the time to gather your thoughts, you will speak with authority and confidence. Remember what Stephen Covey states in *The 7 Habits of Highly Effective People* about stimulus and response: people have the freedom to choose. Therefore, you can choose to be proactive rather than reactive.[14]

Because everyone has them, acknowledge your hot buttons and try to avoid them. If you get into a difficult situation, sometimes you just have to call a "time out" and take a break. Then resume when both of you are calmer. You don't want to avoid the discussion—just reschedule it at a better time when you can be more proactive.

Sometimes, despite our best efforts, communication gets out of hand. You can't anticipate, prepare for, and eliminate every possible scenario. Don't be afraid to take the high road, let go of your ego, and move on. Ask yourself if it's really going to matter five years from now, and then let it go. As someone once said, we get too caught up in the individual trees and lose sight of the forest. Sometimes you have to choose which battles are really worth fighting and let some things go.

If you've provoked defensiveness in someone else, apologize and get the conversation back on track. Saying "I'm sorry, can we just start over?" can work in most situations. Recognize that sometimes you'll be wrong and leaders can admit to making mistakes. Be prepared to admit it and move forward.

Spotlight on Today's Managerial Leader

Candace Lowe Long has been in the arts and entertainment sector for 40 years as a performer, writer, composer, theatrical producer, entertainment project developer, branding and marketing consultant, and arts leader. She understands the calling and the struggles of the creative journey . . . and is known as a biblical commentator on "inspired creativity."

Highly regarded as an astute prognosticator of cultural trends, Ms. Long is pioneering a process she refers to as value reengineering, which she has been field-testing in the business sector since 2004, when she founded Creativity Training Institute. She is called on by businesses to provide creative consulting services, discover new revenue streams, help leaders identify and develop right-brain thinkers, unlock the creative/innovative spirit in their people, and provide processes whereby leaders can learn to distinguish a good idea from an inspired one.

Ms. Long has served as vice-chair of Women in Film and Television International and the Georgia Film, Video, and Music Commission. Currently, she is vice president of development for the National League of American Pen Women, the nation's oldest organization for creative women, and serves as a consultant for the Georgia Assembly of Community Arts Agencies. Most recently, she was named as an honored member of Who's Who in Executives and Professionals [2011–2013].

To help her better understand left-brain thinking, Ms. Long received the Executive MBA degree from Kennesaw State University's Coles College of Business in 2008. Her signature book is Wired For Creativity.

Navigating the Cranial Divide

Left-Brain vs. Right-Brain Thinking

My biggest communication challenge during 40+ years in business has been communicating with left-brain thinkers. You see, I am a "creative," better known as a right-brain thinker.

Creatives are different from most people and often misunderstood. Simply put, we are genetically wired to receive downloads of inspiration. Scientists call this phenomenon "bursts of neural activity." We don't just think and deduce something. Rather, we sense or physically experience it with every fiber of our beings . . . so much so that the inspiration often becomes a driving force in what we feel called to do.

The irony of this "cranial divide" has often puzzled me. While the business community cries out for creativity on the one hand, rarely do they look under the rocks where right-brained people live. We are artists, composers, writers, performers, entrepreneurs, visionaries, and others, and find it difficult to survive inside the confining walls of corporate America.

In 2007, I embarked on a very challenging Executive MBA program at Kennesaw State University's Coles College of Business to broaden my understanding of left-brain thinking. One day I dropped by a seminar on innovation and joined the conference table with some 15 men who were eager to learn what creativity is and how to get more of it into the workplace. One of my EMBA professors, a Six Sigma Black Belt, came in and asked, "Candace, what are you doing here?" I replied, "Innovation and creativity are my thing. What are *you* doing here?"

When the speaker finished, I raised my hand and asked, "I am active in two arts organizations with all right-brained thinkers. Do you ever publicize this corporate need and target the creative community?" The leader sheepishly admitted, "Frankly, we don't know how to manage you."

Aha . . . the truth was out: all too many business leaders regard creatives as a subset of humanity deemed "out there" and unmanageable. The *real* truth is that the biggest challenge most creatives have is how to manage the overabundance of ideas that we receive on a daily basis. My greatest joy would be to somehow communicate to you what creatives are and what they can bring to the workplace.

Allow me to illustrate with a vivid memory from the EMBA experience. I sat in the back row, and the two men who sat in front of me were brilliant left-brain thinkers, but had little regard for anything I had to offer. One day during finance class, I raised my hand to ask a question. One of them then said, loud enough for the class of 45 to hear, "Candace, if you are the only one who doesn't get this, can you talk with the professor later so we can get on with the material?" I was mortified, but decided to be quiet rather than display an immature knee-jerk reaction. I have learned over the years to *show* what a right-brain thinker is, not just *talk* about it.

A week or so later, this very nemesis and I were assigned to the same team to analyze a Harvard Business Review case study about a well-known microwave manufacturer concerned about declining sales. Stan (not his real name) took the lead on the analysis and honed in on what the company needed to do to lower production costs. I silently listened to the left-brain banter, waiting for the inspiration to kick in. It came, and I raised my hand. Stan looked as if to say, "Now what could *you* possibly have to offer?"

I simply said, "I believe the engineers need to study the data from women's focus groups."

Stan retorted, "Women? What do they have to do with it?"

"Women are your target market. What they think is vital to increasing sales."

"Like what?" he challenged.

""Like . . . let's say the engineers created a microwave that not only was fast, but was able to retain the nutritional value of the food."

Stan was quiet during the rest of the meeting. He approached me at the end of the exercise and said, "You know, I never would have thought of that in a million years . . . and the more I thought about it, my wife would *buy* that microwave!"

By graduation, Stan and I had developed a mutual respect for each other, a small step in communication, but a giant step in navigating the cranial divide.

Personality Differences

Because we are a combination of genes and environment, no two of us are alike. Therefore, how we get energy, gather information, make decisions, and order our lives is unique to us. We do know that our personalities are pretty much in place by the age of six and remain relatively constant across our lives. Our personalities define our preferences and tendencies for how we interact and behave around others. So our personalities are reflected in our behaviors. Our personalities may cause us to get along or clash with others. If we have similar personalities, we are likely to respond and react to situations in similar ways. On the other hand, when people do not respond or behave as you feel or think they should, you may be taking it personally by thinking they do not like you or respect your point of view. The truth is that each of us responds to others based upon our personality. Our personality is unique to us, but others might perceive it as slightly irregular or abrasive.

> The experts are still debating which has more influence on our lives, our genes or our environment. Currently, the thinking is that they are equally important to defining who we are and how we interact with others. Sometimes when people do not respond or behave as we feel or think they should, they are just responding based upon their preferred personality style.

The Myers-Briggs Type Indicator, one of the most commonly used personality profile tools, uses four dimensions to identify personality traits. Those four dimensions identify where we focus our attention, what kind of information we prefer to pay attention to, how we prefer to make decisions, and what sort of lifestyle or order we prefer. Only the third dimension, how we prefer to make decisions, has been shown to differentiate along gender lines. In a recent study of the American population, males account for 65 percent of those who make decisions using the thinking style, which uses logic and objectivity, and women account for 65 percent of those who make decisions by their personal values, convictions, and feelings.[15]

Since we must interact and get along with others, the question becomes "How do we learn to overcome personality conflicts so that we can work and live together productively?" We must ACT.

- Step 1—**Awareness.** The "A" step involves raising our **awareness**. We must look inside and hold the mirror up to ourselves. We need to learn and understand our own personality strengths and weaknesses before we can be effective coworkers and family members.
- Step 2—**Choice.** Once our awareness is raised, each of us has a **choice** to make behavioral changes in how we interact with others. In addition, we must embrace the realization that others may not think and behave as we think they should while realizing we cannot change them.
- Step 3—**Tenacity.** We have to have **tenacity** to set goals and make changes to achieve positive outcomes. A key element of being tenacious is having a support system that will encourage and motivate us to make those necessary changes. In short, getting along with others requires awareness, understanding, and effort.[16]

Francie M. Dalton, founder and president of Dalton Alliances, Inc., has classified eight behavioral personality types that can be found in the

---

Change is never easy, but if we have a willing attitude and a desire, we can do it. The outcome of our hard work will be that we lead richer and more productive lives.

workplace and provides some tips and suggestions for interacting with these individuals.[17]

Commanders. Commanders are individuals who thrive on control. They are often seen as demanding, domineering, and bossy. When they communicate, they are abrupt as they speak in crisp, direct, and hard-hitting tones without worrying about being tactful. They don't mean to come across as rude, but they are often mentally engaged in some issue and don't perceive that the softer side of human interaction is important. They are uncomfortable with talking about feelings. So, when you communicate with a commander, you should focus on the desired results or outcome without telling him or her what to do while remembering to avoid any talk of feelings.

Drifters. These individuals are easygoing, impulsive, disorganized, and have short attention spans. They often don't pay attention to the details, forget to follow up, or miss deadlines. They are often perceived as warm and friendly individuals who enjoy life and are creative. They are flexible and enjoy working on a variety of tasks. When communicating with a drifter, tell him or her how the task will help you personally and keep the communication exchange short. Let drifters know that you value their out-of-the-box thinking.

Attackers. Attackers will appear angry, hostile, cynical, and grouchy. They can be perceived as highly critical, demeaning, and condescending while viewing themselves as superior to their peers. An attacker interprets feedback as a sign of disrespect and a more indirect approach may be more effective in communicating with these individuals. One strategy to employ when interacting with an attacker is to begin by asking questions such as "What do you believe to be the most important characteristic of teamwork?" or "How do you plan to evidence these over the next review period?" You should let attackers know that you appreciate their resilience and their willingness to do the unpopular tasks that no one else wants to do.

Pleasers. The pleasers are thoughtful, pleasant, and helpful individuals with whom you find it easy to get along. They seek the approval of others, often agree to maintain harmony, and have difficulty saying "no" to requests. In fact, they will not even complain when they are treated badly or taken advantage of by others. To them, their peers are their family, and therefore, they often remember special occasions such as birthdays and anniversaries. When giving feedback to a pleaser, make sure you give more positive feedback than constructive feedback. You begin and end your conversation with praise.

Performers. Performers may come across as flamboyant, loud, jovial, and entertaining. They make people laugh and seem to find humor in all things. They desire recognition and will often volunteer and then not be able to complete the task because they have taken on too much. They build relationships with others because of their sense of humor and wit. When giving feedback, an indirect approach seems to work best. You might begin by telling a story in which an undesirable behavior is assigned to someone you worked with in another organization. Quickly the performer will get your message by discerning that you meant it for him or her.

Avoiders. These quiet and reserved individuals prefer to work alone. When working on a team, they will speak only in superficial terms or to validate what someone else has already said. Fear often prevents them from taking initiative. They shun both recognition and increased responsibility because both would require increased interaction and visibility. They focus on doing their jobs and will do them right. When interacting with avoiders, you should not threaten them but assure them that their jobs are not at risk. They prefer detailed instructions in writing and will meticulously follow your instructions.

Analyticals. An analytical is perceived to be cautious, precise, and diligent. They tend to overanalyze situations and tasks, and will often challenge new ideas. They are more comfortable with data than people. For them, understanding emotions is difficult because they thrive on logic. They can see several steps ahead and anticipate potential risks. When giving feedback, you should have examples of the behavior as, without examples, the analytical will perceive your feedback as invalid. You must show respect for the details that the analytical brings forth and express appreciation for the fact that you can rely on them for any explanations needed.

Achievers. Achievers are content, peaceful, and pleasant individuals that others enjoy being around. They are self-confident without appearing arrogant. They have an inner focus and self-discipline. They have no hidden agendas and hold themselves accountable for their results. They are interested in hearing the thoughts of others and actively seek feedback. Achievers focus on what is best for the organization. When interacting with these individuals, you should validate their objectivity and ability to interact with all behavioral styles.

The above descriptions are generalized and you may see individuals fitting into more than one category. As a managerial leadership communicator, you will need to adjust your style and use your judgment when communicating with others since, when it comes to people, you will find no simple or easy answers.

Gender Differences

Some years ago, a mass e-mail sent at Chevron led to a mass settlement by the company. The e-mail proclaimed "25 Reasons Beer Is Better than Women." The e-mail wasn't so funny to four female employees, who filed a lawsuit that cost Chevron $2.5 million. In the male culture, this message would have been intended as just offhand humor, and whoever initiated it probably didn't see anything offensive about it. Connie Glaser, author of *GenderTalk Works: 7 Steps for Cracking the Gender Code at Work*, says the differences in how men and women sometimes interpret humor can even affect how each chooses to exert power at work. While a man might casually chide a fellow coworker at the coffee machine about something he said at a meeting, a woman, Glaser says, generally wouldn't think of doing that.

> In the female culture, the relationship, the connectedness, the rapport is ultimately the most important thing. That's what really gives women their base of power and influence. In the male culture, the sense of hierarchy and status is much more important, so you see that kind of joking around to establish a kind of status among them. With females, you don't see that—you see an effort to flatten [the hierarchy] out.[18]

Communication is the source of many gender-related workplace differences. A group of women may be more likely to change the topic of conversation to include a male colleague who has just joined them as a way of making sure he feels included. But men, given the same situation, may simply acknowledge the presence of the newly arrived female, and will likely not make a special effort to bring her into the discussion. Females assign importance to give-and-take and cooperation. You can see this in meetings, where women often will hold back. When asked why they didn't speak up, they reply that they wanted to wait their turn rather than interrupt, which some of their more aggressive male counterparts didn't mind doing.[19]

Of course, the previous examples are linked to the prevailing stereotypes of men and women. You can probably immediately think of individuals who don't fit these stereotypes—men who are sensitive and women who are tough. Deborah Tannen, author of the book *You Just Don't Understand!*, stated that when men communicate they're concerned with conveying information and establishing status. When women communicate they're concerned with conveying information and building connections. Men typically attribute their successes to their own abilities. When they're not successful, they tend to attribute it to external factors. The opposite is true for women. When women experience a failure, they tend to attribute it to their own shortcomings. When they succeed, they tend to link it to external factors, such as teamwork and luck. As you know, success is teamwork, luck, *and* your own contributions, but what you communicate dramatically affects how people perceive your success. Since men's gender culture is hierarchical, their main concern is ensuring that they climb the corporate ladder. So they express, and are expected to express, their accomplishments and their strengths. Women are in an egalitarian gender culture, so they tend to downplay their own role in their success. Women see any attempt to build themselves up as disruptive to building connections.[20] I still remember my first dean mentoring me to share with others my accomplishments rather than just relying upon others to notice how hard I was working. I was more concerned about being an effective team member than moving up the academic ladder.

In an interesting research study, group members were asked to respond to *male would-be leaders* and *female would-be leaders*. The study found that group members responded to the male comments with attention, nods, and smiles. When they responded to the women, the group members would look away and frown. The group members were not aware that they were treating would-be female and male leaders differently. Field studies of small group meetings in organizations show that women leaders are targets of more displays of negative emotion than men leaders, even when they are viewed as equally competent.[21] Goman found that women undermine their authority with nonverbal communications and may not even be aware they are doing so. Women are perceived as submissive when they use too many head tilts when engaged in conversation. She further stated that women need to take up more space in meetings, sit at the table, use a firmer handshake, and smile less frequently in conversations.[22] In a research study that I conducted regarding senior women leaders, one of my interviewees spoke about men using their physicality to assert themselves. Women need to learn to be confident in verbal and nonverbal communication behaviors so that they will be perceived as powerful.

However, women are perceived as having strong interpersonal communication skills.[23] Naturally, women listen to the issues and don't just hear words; they actually listen to both the content and the way the message is delivered. A Catalyst study found that women use an inclusive style of leadership based upon open lines of communication. Women are less likely to withhold information for selfish reasons and feel that it is better to overcommunicate than not communicate and fail.[24] Figure 1.1 summarizes general differences in the ways males and females communicate, but be careful not to stereotype all men or all women as the same. Remember that even within the genders, you have differences.

Since organizations need both genders in the workplace, the beginning point of working through misunderstandings is to appreciate and respect the differences in the genders. When I was chair of the Department of Leadership and Professional Development, I first led an all-male team and we struggled. They perceived that I couldn't make a decision because I sought their thoughts and opinions. I learned that I needed to adjust my decision making style so as not to ask their opinions and thoughts relative to all decisions. For some of the more procedural tasks, I could make the decision and then report back to them. But on those decisions that I perceived would require "buy-in," I sought their input. My team learned that just because I was asking for their opinion, I was not just "wishy-washy" but that I truly appreciated having their input. So, until we took the time to understand and appreciate our differences, we initially struggled as a team. When I left that

1. Men want to think. Women want to feel.
2. Men talk to give information or report. Women talk to collect information or gain rapport.
3. Men talk about things (business, sports, food). Women talk about people.
4. Men focus on facts, reason, and logic. Women focus on feelings, senses, and meaning.
5. Men thrive on competing and achieving. Women thrive on harmony and relating.
6. Men know by analyzing and figuring out. Women know by intuiting.
7. Men are more assertive. Women are more cooperative.
8. Men seek intellectual understanding. Women are able to empathize.
9. Men are focused, specific, and logical. Women are holistic, organic, and "wide-angle."
10. Men are comfortable with order, rules, and structure. Women are comfortable with fluidity.

Figure 1.1. Communication Styles of Men and Women

Source: Simon, V. & Pedersen, H. (2005, March) Communicating with men at work: *Bridging the Gap with Male Co-Workers and Employees. Retrieved from http://www.itstime.com/mar2005.htm*

department after five years, I perceived that we had moved to functioning as a high-performing team.

Your challenge is to create a culture based upon mutual understanding and to dispel any stereotypes that exist. Both men and women can help by complementing each other and using their differences in positive ways to support each other.

Spotlight on Today's Managerial Leader

Paige Yeater is the support education manager for Blackbaud (http.black-baud.com). In her 10-year career with Blackbaud, Paige has held training and development roles in several areas of the business including professional services, sales, and customer support. In her current role as support education manager, she is responsible for managing 12 people, as well as several departmental functions, which include recruiting, new hire training, and ongoing development for over 150 people. Paige received her master's degree in business administration from the Citadel in 2007. She regularly volunteers for the Arthritis Foundation and Junior Achievement, and has also volunteered for Habitat for Humanity, the United Way's Day of Caring, and the Ronald McDonald House.

Leading Through Generational Differences

Age differences among team members manifest themselves in various ways. Generational influences on attitude and values are revealed in the following examples:

Upbringing
Gen Y individuals grew up playing sports when everyone got a trophy just for showing up; no score was kept and everyone was rewarded for just trying his or her best. Everyone was a winner. You can imagine how challenging this may be when it translates into the workforce. Gen Yers tend to want things like perfect-attendance awards. To address their need to be rewarded like this, I try to ensure that I am

regularly letting them know that I appreciate what they are doing and offer them information on how they are making an impact.

Parents of Gen Yers are more involved in their children's lives than parents of previous generations, and are often referred to as "helicopter parents." The phenomenon of helicopter parents has been written about extensively and one quick Google search can tell you more than you want to know. At one time, our HR department had a parent support line for our college recruiting program to address all the questions they received from parents asking about benefits, vacations, salary, and promotions.

Motivation

Motivation is different for each generational group. Gen Yers focus on the intrinsic as they are often more cause-based and are growing up in a world where instant gratification and information overload are commonplace. When I was growing up, most of our news came from the TV and the newspaper. Gen Yers are growing up in a world where a tsunami hits in the morning and by noon the whole world knows about it, and one can send a text message to a special number and donate to the relief efforts. This kind of instant gratification and the feeling that they are making a real difference is what Gen Yers crave; as managerial leaders, we have to figure out how to give that to them. They like recognition and rewards—status symbols are key. They don't have to be anything fancy—just something that indicates that they are being successful and collecting accolades.

Feedback

Gen Yers need specific feedback and they have a higher need/desire for frequent (and positive) feedback. They want to be recognized often and will seek your feedback if you do not offer it regularly. I have two people on my team; one is Gen Y and the other is Gen X. I will call one Sue (Gen X) and the other Sally (Gen Y). When I offer feedback to Sue, I say things like "I would like to see you focus a bit more on your attention to detail. In a couple of instances, you have missed some details, so let's work on that in the next quarter." When I have the same conversation with Sally, I say, "Sally, recently you have had some situations in which you have missed a few details (specific examples listed here). I would like us to work on your attention to detail throughout the next quarter. Some ways that I think that we can work on this are . . . at the end of the quarter we will evaluate your success." Also, if I do not provide feedback to Sally, she will actively seek it. I observed a class that Sally taught once, and almost immediately after the class she was asking me how she did, what was good, and if I liked the way she did XYZ.

Progressions and Loyalty

Recently I had two conversations (in the same day) that really made me think about this topic and brought to light one of the main differences between these two generations. The first conversation was with a Gen X person who currently reports to me. She has been in her role for about a year and as a Gen Xer, she would like to become the expert. She thinks that in about 6 to 8 months, she will be the expert and then may be ready to move on to a new challenge.

Fast forward to later in the day, when I have an interview with a prospective member of my team, who is a member of Gen Y. This individual has been in her current position for almost 6 months and is looking for a new challenge. I asked the question "Do you feel that in the 6 months that you have been in this role, you have fully mastered that skill set and are ready to move into something new?" Without hesitation, the response was "yes!"

Gen Yers want small quick moves (remember the instant gratification talked about earlier?) and like to get promoted quickly. Gen Xers, on the other hand, will work hard to earn the promotion that they want and will expect it to take some time to get there. They crave the moniker of "expert." Managers should be aware of this difference and make progression opportunities available to their employees at the appropriate times. This makes retention efforts more important and more challenging.

Technology

I believe that a great team has representation from both groups, but I have little doubt in my mind that Gen Yers bring with them a deep knowledge and inherent comfort level with technology. They are able to keep up with the newest trends and innovate in ways that Generation Xers typically don't. My son is four, and he knows how to use the computer as well as unlock, locate, and play games on my iPhone. He will grow up with this technology and expect his workplace to use the technologies that he knows. Use this to your advantage—Gen Y employees are great innovators and can help you accomplish existing tasks in newer and more efficient ways!

I remember when my mother retired from being a middle school guidance counselor; she said she didn't need to learn how to use a computer as she was retiring. That was 20 years ago; now she is quite an avid e-mailer. Just the other day, she had her birthday, and not only was she checking her e-mail for birthday greetings but Facebook as well. I find many traditionalists are like my mother and, while e-mail usage is climbing steadily in this group, it is not at the same level as in other generations.

Generational Differences

In the United States, we have up to four different generations working together. The oldest working generation is referred to as the **veterans, silent, or traditionalists,** who were born between 1922 and1945. Next we have the **baby boomers,** born between 1946 and 1964. Following the boomers are **Generation Xers,** born between 1965 and 1980. Finally, those born from 1981 to 2000 are referred to as **Generation Yers, millennials, or echo boomers.**[25] Characteristics of each generation are summarized as follows.

Veterans, silent, or traditionalists. This generation came of age during World War II, and the effects of growing up in that time period can be seen in their behavior. One of the most distinctive qualities of this generation is their concern for the plight of others. They tend to be cautious as a generation; saving money was a way of life, as was saving in general. My mother, who is of this generation, still maintains a full kitchen pantry just in case! Veterans value responsibility and tend to be team players who work within the system. They accomplish goals through hard work and sacrifice.

The best way to communicate with this generation is through face-to-face contact. Formal social events, tributes, and recognition events are much enjoyed by this generation. Direct mail, phone, and, increasingly, the Internet are great ways to communicate with this group.

Baby boomers. This group is made up of the post–World War II babies. They are also known as the generation who questioned authority. Boomers have enjoyed unprecedented employment and educational opportunities in most countries. They value creativity—while their parents were conformists, this generation searched to break the mold. They love adventure and are risk takers. Boomers tend to evaluate achievement in terms of personal fulfillment.

This generation was the first to discover that lifetime employment no longer exists, so job security is not everything to them—but job satisfaction is. With women now firmly implanted in the workforce, boomers are forced to reevaluate the role of work in their personal lives. Because boomers invented new forms of families, they also incurred new stresses. Boomers were the first generation to divorce at a higher rate than the two previous generations.

Regarding communication, boomers enjoy networking events. Direct mail, face-to-face interaction, the Internet, and e-mail are great ways to interface with this generation.

Generation X. This generation was the first to grow up in the new family systems created by the boomers, so the group is independent. The Xers also adapted the boomers' "question authority" attitude quickly—much to the dismay of their boomer parents. They are determined to be involved, responsible, and in control. Because Xers grew up watching television, they tend to have a more cynical view and they focus on the here and now. They are risk takers, but they take calculated risks and are not intimidated by authority. They are problem solvers, tend to be goal-oriented, and demand flexibility.

The best way to communicate with Xers is through e-mail. They are e-friendly and engage in a variety of online social media. They do well at social events, but do not respond well to something called a recruitment event because it doesn't sound fun. They also want to get something back from their investment, be it the actual cost or the value of their time.

I recently had an e-mail exchange with a Gen X. She was registering for one of my classes, so her first contact with me was the following e-mail.

> *Hi Deborah,*
>
> *I have registered for your upcoming August Minimester 2011 class and I would like to know which book I should purchase for this class. This will help me to do some homework. Also I am not able to see any "Start Here" folder at Home Page of Vista to work on my assignments, not sure if any action is pending on my side.*
>
> *Thanks in advance,*
>
> *Dr. Jones*

I was honestly surprised that she would call me Deborah while calling herself Dr. Jones. As a baby boomer, I felt she should call me Dr. Roebuck. She should give me the opportunity to invite her to call me Deborah. To see if she would notice that I addressed her as she addressed herself, I decided to respond back as shown below.

> *Dr. Jones:*
>
> *I have added you to my class, so you should be able to get into GeorgiaView Vista. See you on the 6th of August.*
>
> *Deborah Britt Roebuck, Ph.D. RCC*
> *Professor of Management*
> *Kennesaw State University*
> *1000 Chastain Road, MB 0404*
> *Kennesaw, GA 30144*
> *770-423-6364*
> *www.kennesaw.edu*

She responded back as follows.

> *Thanks a lot Deborah, Just wondering which book I should buy for this subject?*
>
> *Rgds,*
> *Dr. Jones*

Obviously my baby boomer expectations were different from her Gen X way of communicating.

Gen Y, millennials, or echo boomers. Gen Y is the first generation to grow up with the Internet—they do not remember a time when it didn't exist. As a result, Gen Yers tend to be technology dependent. They are often overstimulated and easily become bored. This generation understands that they will change jobs at least once every five years. As such, titles do not mean much—they believe respect should be earned based on the job, not the title. Millennials are goal-oriented and, like the silent generation, they are team players.

The Gen Yers (also known as the millennials or echo boomers) are technologically savvy, are extremely independent, and feel empowered. They will question workplace regulations and will leave one organization to go to another if they are not satisfied. It's all about technology for the Gen Yers, and they have relationships all over the world; they talk and do business 24/7 when they want to do it. Because traditional baby boomer work methods may be ineffective with these younger workers, organizations need new organizational structures and systems that result in loyalty and heightened productivity. As Don Lang, president of Talent Management, shared, "To reach the Gen Yers, managerial leaders must communicate clear outcomes and align their compensation and recognition systems as opposed to just expecting employees to work 40 hours a week." Don shared with me that employees must be given projects and tasks with clear outcomes as well as more individualized reward and recognition benefits and incentives. He also shared that organizations need to advance people based upon their competence and not continue doing it the way we've always done it in the past.[26] Figure 1.2 illustrates how the different generations interact in the workplace.

People communicate to a large degree based on their generational backgrounds. Each generation has distinct attitudes, behaviors, expectations, habits, and motivational buttons. Learning how to communicate with the different generations can eliminate many major confrontations and misunderstandings in the workplace. Consider the suggestions in Figure 1.2 to guide your communication efforts.

Tips for Communicating With Traditionalists

- Remember that traditionalists are private. Don't expect members of this generation to share their thoughts immediately.

	Veterans Silent Traditionalist	Baby boomers	Gen Xers	Gen Yers Millennials Echo boomers
Work ethic	Dedicated	Driven	Balanced	Determined Command attention
Communication style	One-on-one memos	Face time Telephone Call me anytime. E-mail	Face time Cell phones Call me only at work. E-mail	Internet—Facebook Fast-paced messaging Blogging Smartphones
Relationship to feedback	No news is good news.	Feedback is given only once a year with substantial documentation.	Sorry to interrupt, but how am I doing?	I want feedback whenever I desire it.
Motivational message	Your experience is an important asset in order for the team to succeed.	I value our work and I need you to . . .	Forget the rules; do it your way. . . .	You will be working with other bright, creative people.

Figure 1.2. Generational Views of the Workplace

Source: Business Beat, Greater Madison Chamber of Commerce, August 2006

- Focus on words.
- Use face-to-face or written communication.
- Don't waste their time, or let them feel as though their time is being wasted.

Tips for Communicating With Baby Boomers

- Use body language when communicating.
- Speak in an open, direct style but avoid language that they could perceive as designed to control them.
- Answer questions thoroughly and expect to be pressed for the details.
- Present options to demonstrate flexibility in your thinking.

Tips for Communicating With Generation X

- Use e-mail as a primary communication tool.
- Talk in short sound bites to keep their attention.
- Ask them for their feedback and provide them with regular feedback.
- Share information with them on a regular basis and strive to keep them in the loop.
- Use an informal communication style.

Tips for Communicating With Generation Y

- Use action words and challenge them.
- Do not talk down to them as they will not like it.
- Use e-mail, IM, and texting to communicate.
- Seek their feedback constantly and provide them with regular feedback.
- Use humor and create a fun learning environment.
- Encourage them to take risks and break the rules to explore new ways of learning.

These Tips Will Help You Communicate
With All the Generations

- Review and become familiar with the different generations.
- Don't judge a book by its cover—in other words, look beyond appearances.
- Be aware of what is said, but more importantly, how it's said.
- Adopt ageless thinking—one is only as old as one feels!
- Offer an information session on different generations and how to work as a team with diverse age groups.
- Consider creating a mentoring program that involves workers of various ages.
- Try adding team-building activities.
- Have collaborative planning and decision making or problem solving discussions.
- Communicate information in multiple ways.
- Be accommodating to differences in personal scheduling needs, work/life balance issues, and nontraditional lifestyles.
- Respect each other—treat everyone, from the newest to the most seasoned member, as if they have great things to offer and are motivated to do their best.
- Capitalize on each individual member's strengths.
- Be patient with each other.[27]

A major component of our Executive MBA program was virtual teaming with Romanian Executive MBA students. These teams conducted videoconferences during the spring semester. Because Romania does not follow Daylight Savings Time, the Romanian students arrived an hour late for their team's meeting. At first the U.S. students were upset, but once they learned the reason, they worked through that obstacle. Another difference that we encountered in planning the Romanians' visit to Atlanta was scheduling their time here so as not to conflict with their celebration of Easter, which is typically later than the Easter celebration in the United States.

Intercultural Differences

Individuals from different cultures bring different perceptions, value systems, and languages to the workplace. These differences make the task of communicating even more difficult. For example, holidays and vacation schedules vary from country to country. In Romania and other eastern European countries, you would not want to schedule an important meeting in August as most businesses take a three- or four-week holiday during that month. Employees in one country may be unaware that an office in another country is closed on a given day or that vacations may be taken at different times of the year.

The way a particular culture responds to deadlines and timing is often different. To be successful in business dealings, you must be aware of and sensitive to cultural differences, use appropriate language, correctly interpret nonverbal communication, and value individual and cultural differences.

Being aware and sensitive. You must be aware that an individual's background and experience can affect his or her interpretation and perception of a message. Check to see if you have any hidden biases and to see if you have formed an opinion about how people of a certain sex, religion, or race appear, think, and act based simply on their belonging to a particular group. Prejudging people as a group may make it difficult to communicate with them as individuals. Try to avoid stereotyping and the use of sexist, racist, or ethnic remarks.

Using appropriate language. Remember, the same word may mean different things to people from other countries. Some words may have different meanings in other languages. For example, the word *sensible* means *sensitive* in French and the word pronounced as *he* means *she* in Hebrew. Use feedback to clarify your message. By asking questions, you can usually determine whether or not the individual understood your message as you intended.

Interpreting nonverbal communication. Each culture interprets and displays body language differently. Certain nonverbal signs can be clues that the receiver does not understand and is trying to save face. For example, excessive nodding, inappropriate laughter, tentative yes answers, silence, and lack of initiative all point to a breakdown in communication. In Japan, nodding to the speaker does not necessarily mean agreement, but denotes an acknowledgment of the understanding of the verbal communication. Personal space requirements differ in various parts of the world. In the United States and other English-speaking cultures, an arm's length is considered an appropriate separation between two individuals engaged in conversation. Conversely, in some Latino cultures, closer contact is standard practice. When an individual has difficulty speaking English, closely observe the nonverbal communication. The body language may tell you what the words don't.

Valuing differences. As an effective managerial leadership communicator, you must learn to value, appreciate, and accept individual differences. As the workforce continues to become more culturally diverse, individuals should welcome opportunities to learn from each other. The continually changing employee population presents opportunities for personal growth and improvements in global understanding. Figure 1.3 presents some general tips for communicating across cultures.

---

1. Learn something about the country, local customs, and *cultural* sensitivities to avoid making faux pas while abroad.
2. Err on the side of formality. Be low-key in dress, manners, and behavior.
3. Don't rush greetings and introductions in an effort to get down to business quickly.
4. Expect your *meetings* and *negotiations* to be longer than anticipated. Build more time into schedules.
5. Don't show impatience or irritation. Politeness and respect matter.
6. Express yourself carefully. Accents, idioms, and business jargon may be unfamiliar.
7. *Listen* attentively to show that you care about what is being said.
8. Indicate a sincere interest in your colleagues and their concerns and issues to build *win-win solutions.*
9. Don't put global colleagues on the spot or cause loss of face by being too direct or expecting a "yes" or "no" answer.
10. Avoid public criticism or comparison with your own country.
11. Familiarize yourself with customs surrounding gift-giving and business entertaining.
12. *Build relationships* and *trust,* which is the key to successful global *partnerships.*

Figure 1.3. International Communication Tips

Source: 12 Tips for Global Business Travelers By: Sondra Sen, author of International Business Interacts, Specific cross-cultural business guides on 50 countries Retrieved from http:// www.1000advices.com/guru/cultures_communication_12tips_ss.html

---

Thinking About

What are five values you hold that direct the way you carry out your work on behalf of your organization?

Why were you chosen for your work role?

What major strengths do you bring to your work?

How do you use these strengths to further the work of your organization?

Being an Ethical Managerial Leader

As a managerial leader, you want others to perceive you as ethical in your communication, leadership, and decision making. But what are ethics and what does it take to be ethical? I believe ethical behavior starts with character.

Character

Character means knowing who you are. The American Evangelist Dwight Moody said, "Character is what you are in the dark." Theodore Roosevelt once said, "Character, in the long run, is the decisive factor in the life of an individual and of nations alike." Character means that you know your values, beliefs, strengths, skills, and personality. Good old Socrates maintained that "the unexamined life is not worth living." If you are to impact your organization, you must first examine who you are, what you have learned through life, and how those lessons have helped shape who you want to become. You must start with a clear concept of who you are and what you stand for to have the best chance of communicating and leading from an ethical perspective.

Chick-fil-A, the second largest quick-service chicken restaurant chain in the United States, has more than 1,500 locations in 39 states and in Washington, D.C., and annual sales of more than $3.5 billion.[28] Speaking about her role, Dee Ann Turner, vice president of human resources, said, "We select for character, competency, and chemistry. Character always comes first." As Dee Ann Turner has shared, character needs to be at your core, especially if you aspire to be a managerial leadership communicator. Character is something that is formed over a lifetime, and the elements of character can be discovered and developed at any time. No one can be a leader until he or she has examined his or her own strengths, weaknesses, values, and beliefs. I recently had the opportunity to meet Stephen Covey, author of *The 7 Habits of Highly Effective People* and *The 8th Habit*. Stephen stated that more organizations are recognizing the need for character. More and more people are seeing the need to look deeply into their own souls, sense how they themselves contribute to problems and figure out exactly what they can do to contribute to the solution while serving human needs. I believe you must have character to be an ethical managerial leadership communicator as ethics is character in action.

Ethics

Ethics is both a field of study and a personal code guiding thoughts and actions. Some would argue that ethics cannot be taught, but the teaching of morals and values is not a new phenomenon; rather, it has been part of our history. Plato and Aristotle in fourth-century Greece believed the role of education was to train good and virtuous citizens.

Ethics, or character in action, requires critical thinking and an understanding of the dynamics of moral development. Ethics concerns how we act and how we live our lives. Within the field of ethics there are two types: descriptive and normative ethics.

Descriptive ethics. This type of ethics reflects on facts about the moral judgment of a person or a group. For example, a manager might determine that John, an employee, appears honest because he returned a telephone to its rightful owner. It describes how and why people act the way they do.

Normative ethics. Normative ethics involves formulating and defining moral principles. This type of ethics concerns our reasoning about

Photo courtesy flickr user WalMart, CC 2.0

Rob Walton, chairman of the board for Walmart Stores, Inc., speaks to shareholders at the 2011
Walmart Shareholders Meeting in Fayetteville, Arkansas. He says being a global company isn't just about
having stores around the world; it's about being relevant to people no matter where they live. With more
than 9,000 stores in 15 countries, Walmart is not just an international company, but a global one.

how we should act. It seeks an account of how and why people should
act a certain way instead of how they do act.[29] In other words, it means
determining appropriate actions to perform.

As a managerial leadership communicator, you must realize that ethics is not just an "add-on," but an absolute necessity. Before Walmart's
CEO Lee Scott retired in 2009, he allowed the press, for the first time
ever, to hear him speak to about 7,000 Walmart employees and suppliers.
As reported in Workforce.com, "Scott shared that the company would
redouble its efforts to improve the efficiency and reduce costs in health
care, make environmentally friendly technologies affordable to customers and businesses and exert greater pressure on its supply chain to meet
higher ethical standards in the way it produces goods."[30] Lee Scott's talk
about how Walmart can be ethical, more environmentally friendly, and
health care–focused represented a huge change in the company's traditional approach. His action showed that the leadership team realized
that Walmart's scale and scope give it a unique opportunity to leverage
its relationships for the common good just as it has leveraged them in

the past for business efficiency and lower costs. By inviting the press to hear his comments, he sent a clear signal that Walmart was committed to communicating from an ethical perspective. Scott seemed to have learned that although growth and profits are at the core of any successful business, a huge market leader such as Walmart needs to do more than be successful; it needs to be an ethical leader. Current Walmart CEO Mike Duke seems to be continuing the work begun by Lee Scott. On Ethisphere's 100 Most Influential in Business Ethics list for 2010, Mike Duke was ranked number 15.[31]

Another ethical leader who has risen to the occasion is Randi Menkin, director of workforce diversity at UPS, a global company that historically promotes internally. UPS is listed number 2 in social responsibility and number 12 in the Global Top 20 of Fortune's Most Admired Organizations. Menkin shared:

> Women were leaving UPS at a disproportionately faster rate than any other employee group. What was happening to us was alarming, and then when you look at workforce trends in general—we realized that we had to compete for talent. We not only had to compete to recruit talent, but we had to do things to retain our talent, especially women. As a company we want more diversity, and if we're losing our women, then we're always playing catch-up.

Menkin formed a task force that spent a year researching, benchmarking, conducting focus groups, interviewing, and reinterviewing the departing women. The end result was the Women's Leadership Development program, a multifaceted effort designed to attract, retain, and develop female managers. This program rolled out in May of 2006 to 19 areas across the country. Menkin shared that "basically our women and, it turned out, a large percentage of our men as well didn't feel connected to the company."[32]

After a year, the results were in. Turnover was down 25 percent in the pilot districts and more than 6,000 women were touched by the program. In 2007, the program was rolled out nationally and in Canada. Menkin believes the program works for several reasons.

Paramount was the commitment of the executive leadership, including the men.

> It also melded nicely with UPS core values of diversity, promoting from within, and leadership development. It is in our fabric as a company to be involved in the community and this program actually helps facilitate our employees who want to follow their passion for community service. Employee morale was up and that helped in job performance.

UPS is not alone in realizing that their work environment might need to change. At Grant Thornton, a large accounting firm, the passage of Sarbanes-Oxley had a huge impact and caused them to rethink their way of doing work and how to deal with the high market demand for accountants.

> We started losing accountants—particularly those in their late 20s and early 30s, which are traditionally the childbearing ages—and it became apparent that we needed to look at retention and do something about it. The feeling among female accountants was that they couldn't make it work because they couldn't be successful at the firm and have a life. So they left, according to Jacqueline Akerblom, national marketing partner.

Jacqueline found it difficult to explain the need to make the firm more family-friendly, especially to the senior male accountants.

> But we convinced them that the future of their pension and the growth of the firm were tied into this. We said we needed to do something different for our female accountants and that if we did that, it would ensure the health of their pensions. That was a real awakening to some of the senior leadership. The Women at Grant Thorton program was started in 2004. The women partners, with a few men, "crystallized what they wanted and needed to do." They partnered with HR, did exit interviews and lots of research.

Basically, it came down to flexibility. The organization chose to embrace telecommuting. According to one worker, "The ability to leave the office so I can have dinner with my family and then work from home at night was huge. Not being tied to our desks was an incredible benefit."[33]

Grant Thornton is not alone in moving to a more flexible work environment. According to a 2006 Business Week article, more than 40 percent of IBM's workforce has no office; at AT&T, it's about 30 percent of all managers. Sun Microsystems, Inc, reports it has saved more than $400 million over 6 years in real estate costs by having almost half of its employees not come to an office. In fact, according to a survey by the Boston Consulting Group, nearly 85 percent of executives expect a large increase over the next 5 years in the number of unleashed workers.

Jody Thompson, who worked in Human Resources for Best Buy, felt it was time for a change in the way the company worked. So she led the company to adapting a results-only work environment (ROWE). ROWE's whole point is that physical presence does not mean productivity. The goal is to judge performance on output instead of hours. When the whole organization embraced ROWE, its productivity had increased by 35 percent.

> It's all about control—taking control of your life [Thompson says]. Work should not be a place to go; it should be what you do. The implementation of ROWE was a huge corporate and cultural change. One key difference when operating under ROWE is that you have to be clear about what is expected of you because you are managing yourself and you are responsible for the results.[34]

As ethical managerial leaders, we must be willing to challenge the status quo or the usual way of doing work. We must make changes in the workforce that will benefit all workers. Ethical managerial leaders have to realize that to stay competitive and attract and retain top talent, they may have to change how they recruit, treat, motivate, and evaluate the performance of their employees. At Alston & Bird, a law firm in Atlanta, Georgia, some partners started to realize that the way things had always been done was not working. They recognized that people wanted more flexibility but also wanted to be on the partnership track. The firm created the Alternative Career Path, a more adaptable partnership plan that does not lock an associate into a specific time period. Liz Price, a partner, has said, "The new generation wants more flexibility and personal adaptation of work. They see money as what it is. They want opportunities to live a great life."[35]

Ethical managerial leaders should realize that a leadership position is an opportunity to build relationships and to enable others to become successful. An ethical managerial leader must realize that the generations have different needs and find ways to inspire trust, define reality and purpose, align systems and processes, and unleash talent to deliver results.

Four Ethical Standards of Excellence

Ethical managerial leaders follow four standards of excellence. They include communication, collaboration, succession planning, and tenure.[36]

> Jim Collins, a noted researcher and author on leadership, advises leaders to "conduct autopsies, without blame," and cites companies such as Philip Morris whose executives talked openly about the "7-UP disaster." Even when statistical evidence does not reflect well on a division or on the financial status of the entire company, a plan of action to thwart disaster may be implemented and several lessons learned.

Ethical Communication

Every form of communication you put forth should be accurate and honest. You want your two-way communication to be

- relevant to your employee's needs,
- understandable,
- useful,
- timely,
- respectful.

You want to build a communication system that reinforces positive relationships with your employees. You may be asking, "How do I do that?" You begin by involving your employees and colleagues in creating a communication plan. When you involve others, you ensure that you will make the communication processes relevant to all individuals. However, your direct reports have to perceive that you are truly genuine when you ask them to become involved. So how can you communicate that you're genuine? By simply making sure that your words and actions are in agreement. Another action you can take that shows you are truly serious about your communication plan is to turn the creation of the plan over totally to your team or to a cross-functional team who will identify issues, brainstorm for alternatives, and create the plan. As a first step, I would recommend that the team conduct a communication audit to see what current processes are working, determine strengths and weaknesses, and identify problems. This audit can create a baseline as a beginning point from which to note and measure improvements. In addition, you can discuss your audit with other leaders to determine discrepancies in how various levels and constituencies perceive communication within your entire organization.

Part of your communication plan should include your core values, principles, and practices. If your team openly shares the values and reinforces the existence of an open, honest, two-way communication system, your team members will be encouraged to give you feedback when they think you are straying from the core values. However, when the communication plan is created, all members must buy into the plan. If your team just creates a statement of core values and doesn't really embrace and follow these values, then you might not see any change in the way team members communicate. When you put the core values, principles, and practices on paper and then have team members sign off, they are typically more committed to following them.[37]

As an ethical managerial leadership communicator, you want to ensure that you promote communication that demonstrates caring and mutual understanding that respects the unique needs and characteristics of individuals. In today's multicultural, multigenerational work world, respect is needed in all interactions. All people deserve to be respected regardless of their job, socioeconomic status, gender, or race. In addition, you should follow the ten basics of ethical communication in Figure 1.4.

1. Seek to elicit the best in communications and interactions with others.
2. Listen when others speak.
3. Speak nonjudgmentally.
4. Speak from your own experience and perspective, expressing your own thoughts, needs, and feelings.
5. Seek to understand others (rather than to be right or "more ethical than thou").
6. Avoid speaking for others, for example, by characterizing what others have said without checking your understanding, or by universalizing your opinions, beliefs, values, and conclusions.
7. Manage your own personal boundaries: share only what you are comfortable sharing.
8. Respect the personal boundaries of others.
9. Avoid interrupting and conducting side conversations.
10. Make sure that everyone has time to speak and that all members have relatively equal air time if they want it.[38]

Figure 1.4. Ten Basics of Ethical Communication

Ethical Collaboration

Ethical managerial leadership communicators need many advisors as you cannot know all the answers in today's work world; therefore, surround yourself with individuals who can provide answers. When you choose to collaborate with others, you can incorporate best practices, solve problems, and address the issues. If you use ethical collaboration, you will keep your circle of advisors more open and fluid, which then will allow you to reduce the risks, as you have assigned trustworthy experts/advisors to every situation.

Ethical Succession Planning

One of the most important aspects of your leadership will be mentoring, coaching, and grooming your team members for advancement. You will need to observe your team and give any potential leaders opportunities to build and use their leadership skills.

In his book *Good to Great: Why Some Companies Make the Leap . . . and Others Don't*, Jim Collins identifies Chrysler with many organizations that achieve greatness only to have it slip away through time. While examining the long list of organizations in his study, Collins notes that under Lee Iacocca Chrysler followed "a pattern . . . found in every unsustained comparison: a spectacular rise under a tyrannical disciplinarian, followed by an equally spectacular decline when the disciplinarian stepped away, leaving behind no enduring culture of discipline . . ." Arguably Chrysler faltered without Iacocca at the helm because he had failed to practice ethical collaboration to create a succession plan.[39]

Ethical Tenure

How long should a leader lead? Leadership expert Peter Block contends that "we search, so often in vain, to find leaders we can have faith in." Further, he notes that leadership is more often rated on the trustworthiness of the individual than on his or her particular talents, and that the mission of the ethical leader is to serve the institution and not themselves.[40] Jim Collins identifies this category of executives as level 5 leaders: leaders who are able to "channel their ego needs away from themselves and into the larger goal of building a great company."[41]

As an ethical leader, you lead at the request of your company, customers, board of directors, and stockholders. If all of these entities continue to trust you, then you should lead until you choose otherwise. Eventually, you will want to turn the organization over to a new set of watchful eyes. If a leader has jeopardized the sacred trust of employees, customers, and the public at large, he or she should step aside and let a better leader take the helm. A case in point is Congressman Anthony Weiner, who jeopardized the sacred trust of his constituents by not telling the truth. Once trust is broken, it is almost impossible to gain back. He should have told the truth in the beginning, but at least he did step aside to allow another leader to serve.

Thinking About:

My organization's effectiveness and credibility would be weakened if a leader/employee were to _____.

To encourage ethical managerial leadership communication, I should _____.

Conclusion

The workplace of today calls for managerial leadership communication, which means that managerial leaders must communicate both internally and externally to enable the achievement of goals. Because technology and organizational structure have transformed the way we work, we need to expand the traditional role of manager to include some leadership responsibilities. The future of communication depends on the continued development of an organization's most valuable resource—its people. But with people come communication challenges in written, oral, and internal situations. In the 21st century, you will deliver your messages to increasingly dispersed and diverse audiences around the world. You may even manage direct reports you never see. But as a managerial leadership communicator, you need to be careful not to let the technology take over and become the end rather than the means. Instead, use your team to grow your business and to determine the future. The written word, judgment, and common sense will never be replaced by hardware. In addition, the need for ethical managerial leadership has never been stronger. Those who lead and communicate from ethical stances will make their mark in history.

Case for Thinking and Discussing

Instructions: Read the following article and reflect upon these questions.

- What lessons from this article can you apply to your organization?
- How much social media do you incorporate in your current position? Is it effective?
- How are you doing with what you have to say?

6 Ways Sarah Palin Uses Social Media
to Stir the Beltway Status Quo

By Dom Crincoli

Dom Crincoli is a corporate communication strategist and blogger with expertise in internal communications, intranets and emerging media, human resources, and public relations. He blogs about communication strategy at *http://domcrincoli.com/*: two-way comm's blog Stirring the status quo in corporate communication and social media—a communication strategy blog.

Retrieved from *http://domcrincoli.com/6-ways-sarah-palin-uses-social-media-to-kick-beltway-butt/*

January 7, 2011

Sarah Palin's unprecedented use of social media to set the agenda in Washington is something communication strategists and leaders should study, regardless of their political persuasion.

"I tweet; that's just the way I roll," says Palin.

But she's no shrinking violet and doesn't need our permission to speak out. Some say she should have packed her political bags long ago—that she should have simply lain down in the face of withering assaults against her presidential fitness. Instead, the second most popular politician on *Facebook* and über-purveyor of *Twitter* missives continues to shake the GOP establishment to its good-old-boy core. Her star continues to rise owing in no small part to her surprising emergence as a *social media visionary* who purposefully circumnavigates the *beltway gasbags* who would silence her, opting instead for a vital connection with her ardent base of supporters as well as the entire White House press corps, who stand in queue awaiting her next tweet.

Like or loathe her—but observe the kind of influence a leader can have when she chooses communication channels that promise a direct connection, refusing to capitulate to forces of political correctness and settle for the advice of public relations mavens and party speechwriters seeking to prescribe her every word.

The New York Times Magazine records the exasperation of recently departed White House secretary Robert Gibbs as he describes the political suicide that would surely follow his inability to respond properly to Palin's tweets: "If I would have told you that I could open up a Facebook or Twitter account, and simply post quotes, and have the White House asked about those, and to have the White House press corps focused on your Facebook quote of the day—that's Sarah Palin. She tweets one thing and all of a sudden you've got a room full of people who want to know . . ."

In what she's accomplished she's thrown down the gauntlet for leaders of every stripe, be they corporate, political, or otherwise, calling them to use social media to achieve new levels of transparency and engagement with those they seek to lead. Some user guidelines we can glean from her use of social media include the following:

1. **Be confident; speak your truth.** Her description of Rahm Emanuel included "shallow/narrow-minded/political/irresponsible as they come," and she called Politico writer Jonathan Martin "full of crap." The thing is that a lot of people *agree* with her, and a kind of movement has grown around her tweets and status updates. My point is not to debate the *merits* of what she is saying, but to point out the number of followers or friends who choose to hear her opinion through Twitter and Facebook subscription feeds—*the discretionary effort* required to actually subscribe to and check these feed messages on a daily basis is the kind of *engagement* most senior leaders and communicators would kill to have.

2. **Be persistent.** Palin could have called it quits after coming under fire for some of the things she said—or more specifically, failed to say during the *Katie Couric interview* in 2008. Instead she is seeking to remake her image through direct access to her support base through social media channels. Time will determine her success in swaying the wider American public, and whether a run for the White House

is sustainable. But her public relations initiatives—her instinct to harness social media communication channels in new and creative ways—is a lesson for all communicators.

3. **Be unafraid to make a mistake.** Palin's lawyer Thomas Van Flein found out about her much-publicized tweet calling for peaceful Muslims to "*refudiate* [sic.] the ground-zero mosque" at the same time everyone else did. "This is her political instinct in action," he said. Love it or hate it, this is Palin, bringing the unvarnished truth as she sees it, unfettered, unafraid. We can obsess about her wrong use of a word (even though we understood what she was trying to say), or we can choose to admire her ability to speak out.

4. **Use social media to find change agents to help you lead.** Where did Palin find her primary speechwriter (when she uses one), researcher, and online coordinator? She found Rebecca Mansour at *Conservatives4Palin*, a blog Mansour started without pay simply to right what she perceived as biased treatment of Palin and her record. Amazing! You mean she didn't find her through a single-spaced two-page resume posted on a job board? A lesson for HR talent acquisition: *Mansour already had the fire! She was already engaged* and she didn't need anyone's permission. She was a self-starter already using social media (blogging) to find her voice and explore her passion with whomever would listen. Palin simply harnessed her near encyclopedic knowledge for the good of her campaign.

5. **Stay connected.** The ease and simplicity of communicating through micro-blogging platforms may be just right for many busy leaders who don't have the time to keep a full-blown blog but who nevertheless seek to remain in vital contact, and who are interested in gathering vital feedback from those they lead in order to make sound consensual decisions. Palin can *land a hard punch* without moving from her living room sofa in Wasilla, Alaska. Being home with her family doesn't preclude participation in the ongoing political dialogue—pretty strong argument for work-life balance too, wouldn't you say?

6. **Show your human side.** "Out for a jog in Central Park. Beautiful," tweets Palin. All work and no play made Jack . . . well, it ain't all business folks. Social media offers senior leaders a chance to show some vulnerability, even the occasional chink in one's armor.

Facebook especially has been considered to be a place where you might invite someone you met on another social media channel—like LinkedIn or Twitter—to get to know you better and form a deeper bond. But the lines continue to blur in this area and many believe most of us will opt for one social media platform for both business and personal pursuits in the future. *Mark Zuckerberg* is certainly banking on it.

There is no overarching strategy, Palin claims in the *New York Times* article, just political instinct and an ongoing commitment to participation in the political dialogue. Don't underestimate this woman and her deft use of social media to get her message across. She's not asking our permission. She's not waiting around for the beltway or media elite to provide her with a communication channel. She's created her own—she's going direct. Social media made it possible.

CHAPTER 2

Gaining Insight Into the Role of Interpersonal Communication Skills for Today's Managerial Leaders

Almost all of us feel that we are effective communicators, and, if there is a communication breakdown, "others" are the problem. We typically think that we communicate at least as well, if not better than, everyone else. However, the vast majority of people who fail at work do so for one reason: they do not relate well to other people. A recent survey of 1400 corporate executives, employees, and educators across diverse market sectors, including financial, health care, technology, and manufacturing, found that 86 percent of the respondents blamed a lack of collaboration or ineffective communication for workplace failures.[1] It seems, more often than not, the interpersonal aspect of communication stands in the way rather than someone's inability to deliver an accurate message. Ineffective interpersonal communication may lead individuals to

- Dislike each other
- Be offended by each other
- Lose confidence in each other
- Refuse to listen to each other
- Disagree with each other

These interpersonal problems generally lead to restricted communication flow, inaccurate messages, and misinterpretations of meanings. In my research study of 88 managers, the number one problem they faced daily was miscommunication, as reflected by this statement from one of the respondents: "I think the most common communication problems revolve around a failure to be in sync with each other, generally due to personal and environmental factors that make it difficult to really hear what the other person is saying." Clearly, this statement indicates that communication usually breaks down due to people issues.

It's difficult to think of any job in which communication is not vital for individual as well as organizational success. But you should not despair, because your communication style and behavior have been learned and thus you can change it if you are willing to do so. As a managerial leader, you should believe you can always grow and learn to be a better communicator, and, with that attitude, you will serve as an authentic role model for others.

I believe communication is the most important "soft skill" necessary in today's ever-changing organizational landscape. All other skills will be much easier to acquire if you focus first on developing your communication skills. Achieving success in today's workplace is closely tied to the ability of employees and managers to communicate effectively with each other and with people outside the organization.[2]

According to Colquitt, Lepine, and Wesson, authors of the textbook *Organizational Behavior*, "Much of today's work requires interdependence and involves communication."[3] So, as a managerial leader, you will find that you must interact with many individuals both within and outside of the organization to achieve your organizational objectives. Zia, Shields, White, and Wilbert have said that, as a managerial leader, you must be willing to work hard, demonstrate effort and willpower, show integrity,

Photo courtesy flickr user Argone National Lab, CC 2.0

persistence, responsibility, and decisiveness, but above all, employ effective communication skills.[4]

As a managerial leader, you will need to add members to your team. When I reflect upon my work in hiring new team members, I perceive I've made some wise choices and some not so great choices. One individual in particular comes to mind when I think of the "not so great" choices. He had outstanding credentials, which at the time I thought was the most important consideration. But I quickly came to realize that he lacked the necessary communication skills to help us move our team forward. In a study examining the emphasis given to technical qualifications versus soft skills in hiring decisions, Prabhakar, Litecky, and Arnett found that hiring decision makers placed more emphasis on the soft skills "phase" of the hiring process.[5] According to this study, technical competence is important in getting potential job candidates through the door, but demonstrating soft skills often "closes the deal."[6] I wish I had known about this study earlier in my career! This finding does support a *Wall Street Journal* survey of the 20 attributes perceived to be important for the hiring or promotion of MBA students.[7] In the survey of 20 attributes, communication and interpersonal skills were rated the highest with 89 percent of the company recruiters ranking those skills as very important. The ability to work in a team was the second highest attribute with 85 percent of the company recruiters. Given the importance of these critically important soft communication skills, this chapter will focus specifically upon giving and receiving feedback, mastering nonverbal communication, employing emotional intelligence, choosing the right type of listening, asking questions, managing conflict, and knowing when to mentor, coach, and counsel.

Spotlight on Today's Managerial Leader

Pam Napier is a retired AT&T director and is currently consulting for Cox Communications. In Pam's last position at AT&T, as Director of Customer Care Analytics, she spearheaded a team of project managers and business and systems analysts to develop and implement a comprehensive set of benchmark analytics for AT&T's wholesale and retail business units. Pam holds a BS degree in biology and chemistry from the University of Richmond, a MS degree in genetics from Virginia Commonwealth University, and an MBA degree in finance from the Terry College of Business at the University of Georgia. In her spare time, Pam enjoys spending time with her husband, Mark, and her son, Brad; showing their Airedale terrier, Abbie, in AKC conformation shows; boating on Lake Lanier; gardening; playing bridge; making jewelry; and going to the gym.

Connect for Success Initiative

An Innovative Method for Organizational Development
As BellSouth was evolving from a wire line to a broadband/wireless company, extensive changes were occurring in the areas of operations, sales, and regulatory affairs, human resources and beyond. Organizational leaders recognized communication between employees and with customers would play a central role in BellSouth's future success. So the leaders began to think about ways to enhance and improve communication as well as how they could get "buy in" to the needed communication changes. After brainstorming alternatives, they decided to seek ideas and suggestions from the employees.

Upon hearing about this opportunity, one of my teams immediately went to work and created what they called the "Connect for Success" program. Their program would include TOP Values and the STAR Feedback Model.

TOP Values: Trust, Open-Mindedness, and Participation
The **Trust** component is based on the firm reliance on the integrity, ability, or character of the person. Trust is built when the feedback is sincere, thoughtful, accurate, and delivered appropriately. Trust is gained by convincing the person to whom you are giving feedback that you have his or her interests in mind and are speaking from the heart.

The **Open-mindedness** component entails having or showing receptiveness to new and different ideas or the opinions of others. A new idea is the beginning of the creative process and must overcome many hurdles to be embraced as an organizational product or solution. The organizational culture plays a crucial role in determining whether new ideas bubble to the surface or are suppressed.

The **Participation** component is the act of taking part or sharing in something. "Connect for Success" will only work with participation from all levels. With trust and open-mindedness, participation evolves naturally.

STAR Feedback: Situation or Task, the Action, and the Result
- The *Situation or Task* is the condition the group faced, such as a problem, business opportunity, special challenge, or routine task.
- The person's or group's *Action* is what they said or did to handle the situation or task effectively.
- The *Result* is the benefit of what the person or group did.

Sincere, specific feedback should energize, encourage, and clarify what actions should be repeated. If individuals do not give sincere, specific feedback, the receiver will most likely perceive that the feedback is empty or insincere. Saying "good job" is not enough, as such statements need to be supported with details so that the receiver will know specifically what was done or why it was valuable.

In addition to being specific and sincere, timely feedback should be given when the details of the person's or group's performance is fresh in the sender's mind. Providing timely feedback should be relevant to the individual's or group's work, so that effective actions can continue.

To make sure the program would meet both the needs of the managerial leaders and employees, an employee survey was conducted. The employee feedback revealed they desired more interaction and feedback in three areas:

- Making a personal investment in the employees' growth and development
- Giving feedback that helps employees improve their performance
- Recognizing excellent performance

After the team analyzed the employee feedback and made modifications to ensure the program would include the areas employees noted, the program was implemented. The first step was to train managers who would then train others in the following actions.

1. Provide STAR feedback to each person in their group and their manager at least one time each week or on the expected frequency level.
2. Use an appropriate method of handwritten, electronic, or verbal forms for the feedback.
3. Verify completion of the feedback through a tracking tool.
4. Meet with their direct reports each month to discuss, coach, and sustain awareness for "Connect for Success."
5. Have teams discuss TOP Values and share feedback in staff meetings, as appropriate.
6. Tie the feedback to the performance evaluation. Insert "Connect for Success" as a line item in the key requirements for teamwork. Ask yourself: Are you recognizing your peers and managers for contributions?
7. Use the "Connect for Success" tools to express appreciation and thanks.

To ensure the "Connect for Success" program was working as designed, employees once again provided feedback. The second employee survey revealed employees felt more satisfied with their job and their relationships to other employees. Specifically, the employee survey results showed an average improvement in the three areas mentioned above of +4 percent on a base of 72 percent positive score.

After the "Connect for Success" program successfully launched, employees started finding additional ways to share knowledge and to connect. For example, the employees started "lunch and learn" programs.

My team and I perceived that the "Connect for Success" program was overwhelmingly successful for two reasons. First, a true need existed for this program, which became evident from the employee surveys. Second, each member of my team believed in the concept. Because of these reasons, the initial phase of this program was successful, and it is now supported by other programs that focus on providing positive feedback as well as connecting internal and external stakeholders.

A study by Todd Thornock, an accounting professor at the University of Texas McCombs School of Business, found that giving people feedback after a "short delay"—shortly after they completed a task—actually improved performance more than offering up the same feedback immediately. If they waited too long, though, the feedback again became useless.

Source: How to Give Feedback That Works By Kimberly Weisul
February 22, 2011
Retrieved from http://www.bnet.com/blog/business-research/how-to-give-feedback-that-works/791?promo=665&tag=nl.e665

Giving and Receiving Feedback

Intuitively, as a managerial leader, you know you should give your employees feedback to help them grow and improve in their roles. According to Lynda Gratton of the London Business School, "one of the most crucial organizational levers in the creation of cooperative working environments and collaborative teams, is managers who coach and mentor others"—that is, managers who provide constant feedback on employee performance.[8]

I found some interesting results in a research study I conducted with 84 managers and 427 employees . . . When I asked how often individuals received feedback from their manager, the two largest categories were several times a day and several times a week, but each category accounted for less than 20 percent as shown in Figure 2.1.

Note, however, that 35 percent of the respondents perceived that they gave feedback daily as shown in Figure 2.2. So the respondents may not receive feedback, but they perceive they provide it. Education level and number of years of full-time managerial experience did seem to impact the responses, as 60 percent of the employees who chose "Several Times a Day" had master's degrees and 50 percent of the respondents who chose "Several Times a Day" had 6 to 15 years of managerial experience. This finding might indicate that the more educated and the longer one is in a managerial role, the more he or she realizes the importance of giving feedback.

Hyler Bracey in his book entitled *Building Trust* emphasized the importance of feedback and shared how he would put five coins in his pocket.[9] His task for each day was to switch those five coins from one pocket to the other. But the key to his switching the coins was that he had to provide feedback at least five times to five different individuals during that day.

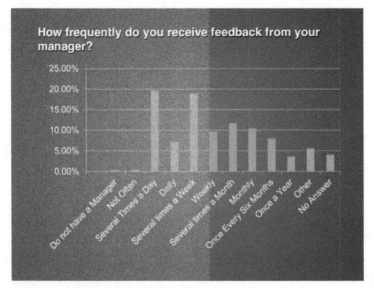

Figure 2.1. Receiving Feedback

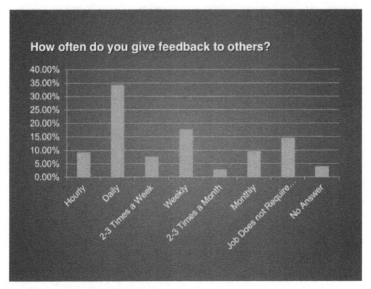

Figure 2.2. Giving Feedback

Feedback encourages individuals to capitalize on their strengths and to develop their weaknesses, which in turn produces high-performance teams and organizations. Feedback is important to managers and leaders because employees' actions and behaviors ultimately determine the corporate culture and success of an organization. Feedback shapes an employee's understanding of what is acceptable behavior within the organization.

According to Asmus, feedback can be given four ways: positively, negatively, directly, and indirectly.[10] Studies show that most negative feedback is given indirectly. Managerial leaders tend to soften the blow by using softer words and postponing critical statements. Furthermore, supervisors will tend to make suggestions for improving future performance rather than focusing on the insufficient performance of the past. However, as Figure 2.3 shows, my study found that over 40 percent of the employees and managers perceived that they did provide constructive feedback to both individuals and teams. It seems that males perceive that they provide constructive feedback a bit more than females as 48 percent of the males chose "often," while only 35 percent females chose the same category.

Marshall Goldsmith, a well-known business coach, has created a FeedForward system of giving feedback, which focuses only on future change.[11] He believes that you can't change the past, so you should not

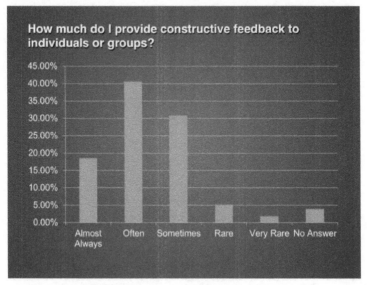

Figure 2.3. Providing Constructive Feedback

focus on it. Instead, his model asks that you promote behavioral changes for the future. In essence, learn from past mistakes so that you don't repeat them and focus upon making changes that will help you for the future.

According to Marcus Buckingham, author of *Now Discover Your Strengths,* organizations must have efficient and effective performance evaluation systems to be successful. In his opinion, a good evaluation system will have four characteristics:

- It should be based on the strengths of individual employees.
- It should be employee-driven; employees should be able to constantly monitor feedback they have received and should be motivated to keep up with this information.
- Performance reviews and feedback sessions should occur frequently, rather than just once or twice a year.
- It should highlight the strengths of individuals and the teams in which they participate. Because all employees will see each other's evaluations, personal accountability and motivation will increase. Also, you will be able to more quickly assess stock of human capital.[12]

The benefit of this type of system is that it encourages the employees to be responsible for tracking and improving their own performance. It also maintains a constant focus on performance goals while motivating employees to build their strengths.

In a counter argument to Buckingham's work, Edward E. Lawler III of the University of Southern California admits that, while Buckingham's work is clearly correct in most regards, a few clarifications must be made to the general theory for improving performance management systems. He argues that success is not solely dependent on people doing what they do best and ignoring or minimizing their weaknesses. He believes that strengths must be utilized depending on which ones are needed to reach larger goals, and work should not be tailored simply to whatever the employee is skilled at doing. Employees must be given the opportunity to improve upon their weaknesses, once these are revealed through feedback mechanisms. He does agree that feedback must be provided to motivate employees. Furthermore, he points out that, while improvement of performance management systems has been only marginally successful in rigidly hierarchical organizations, it is useful in creating organizations that are less bureaucratic and more likely to capitalize on individual talent.[13]

To prepare for the performance feedback session, as the managerial leader, you should encourage your employees to self-reflect before they receive the evaluation and feedback. Taking such action will help prepare your employees to discuss their performance. Self-reflection also gives time for the individual to think of ways to improve. I found this strategy worked for me and helped in setting employee goals for the following year. My direct reports would often come in with ideas I had not thought of, which in reality were better than the ideas I had generated. I have found that when you, as the feedback giver, and your employee, as the feedback receiver, come to the meeting prepared, you can accomplish more during your time together. You will want to make it clear to your subordinate how his or her talents and work contribute to overall organizational goals.

Experts suggest that feedback sessions should be done in person and should be done frequently enough that employees are constantly aware of exactly what is being reviewed. You might want to consider using monthly touch-base meetings. I found them to be a helpful way for me to listen to each direct report as well as to provide ongoing feedback on things each individual had done well and on opportunities for improvement. As you learned in chapter 1, the younger generations truly do crave feedback; and if you are not providing enough ongoing feedback, they will ask for it. So just go ahead and surprise them with frequent feedback!

Photo courtesy flickr user Samuel Mann, CC 2.0

Even if an employee has multiple weaknesses, praise strengths in the beginning of any discussion, so that he or she retains a sense of self-worth and importance. Then deal with the most critical negative issues to emphasize their importance. Constructive feedback should not be sandwiched between two pieces of positive feedback. If you use the sandwich technique, your improvement feedback will be perceived as not as important because your employees will tend to remember what they heard first and last in any conversation, which in this case would not be the corrective feedback. Design questions to encourage discussion, so that valuable information or explanations are not excluded. Omit individual personality traits from the discussion entirely and discuss only observable behavior. Do your best to ensure that feedback is a two-way communication—no one enjoys being criticized without an opportunity to discuss the issue.[14]

In response to the earlier challenges to giving negative feedback, Asmus, who is a former executive in a Fortune 100 company and who now offers consulting services, claims that feedback can be made more effective through giving more direct criticisms of specific behaviors. If negative feedback is stated more directly, the employee is likely to understand the reason for the feedback and is therefore given more responsibility for proposing ways to improve the behavior. Knowing that direct feedback is more effective, management scholars are able to redefine best practices, and organizations can better design feedback sessions.[15]

Regardless of the perceived and recognized value of performance feedback, providing performance feedback is no easy task and many managerial leaders aren't adequately trained to manage this integral task. In my research study when I asked the question if employees and managers had received training in how to give and receive feedback, 62 percent of the employees and managers had received no training as shown in Figure 2.4. So obviously, this is an area of concern, but also an opportunity for organizations to help grow their leaders.

According to research done by the American Management Association, the main cause of frustration during the performance evaluation process is that managers are insufficiently trained in giving feedback and do not provide quality coaching to their employees on how to perform on a higher level.[16] One MBA student recently shared:

I went through one job without ever being offered suggestions for improvement in the 14 years I worked there. In that same job, I filled out my own yearly performance evaluation and it was almost cookie cutter year after year. One year I mentioned improvement needed on my report, and it stayed on the evaluation for the next two years.

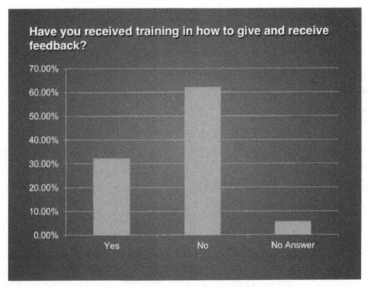

Figure 2.4. Training in Giving and Receiving Feedback

As suggested by many of my students, it seems that current training practices vary greatly, and often managerial leaders learn how to give feedback "on the fly" as aptly described by another EMBA student:

> Some general training is available [from my company]. To be honest, however, I find that I have learned most through experience. Early on, I patterned my reviews off of feedback that I had received. Essentially, I tried to deliver better, more insightful reviews than I had received.

Clearly, training and models regarding how to give and to receive feedback will help you be more effective in one of the most important aspects of your job.

Foster stated that performance feedback should be written with specific and objective language.[17] According to experts who were interviewed for Foster's article, performance feedback should

- Describe behavior, performance, and results the evaluator has observed;
- Explain, illustrate, and support the evaluator's conclusions;
- Tell employees clearly what they are doing well and describe what they need to improve.

Your delivery of feedback must be consistent, which will make the system more credible and will aid your employees by making expectations more predictable. If an employee does an exceptionally good job, you should be sure to acknowledge the outstanding contribution. Otherwise, the employee may not feel valued and may be tempted to take his or her talent elsewhere. Giving praise when it is due also encourages buy-in of your employees to the organization's overall goals. If an employee is lacking in an area, you, as the managerial leader, should take the time to discuss the weakness and to provide concrete ways to improve performance.

To help my students and business associates learn how to give feedback, I have used the BET and BEAR feedback models. My students, and others whom I have trained, have shared that they felt more confident and pre-pared to give feedback after learning about the BET and BEAR models.

BET Model

The BET model was adapted from Berry, Cadwell, and Fehrmann and focuses on positive feedback.[18] The BET model is designed to provide positive feedback and includes three steps: Behavior, Effect, and Thank you. Generally speaking, individuals do not receive enough ongoing posi-tive feedback; therefore, I would encourage you to provide more. Often individuals tell me that the only feedback they receive is when they do something wrong. But ongoing positive feedback can be a real motivator. When individuals know that their efforts are appreciated, they will typi-cally try even harder for you. Truly, as much as 75 percent of the feedback you give to others should be BET feedback.

Behavior—What the team member is doing that is valuable.

You make your comments specific and detailed. In fact, spell out exactly who did what, when, where, and why. If appropriate, you can provide a detailed but brief step-by-step replay of exactly what you observed or heard. Give recent examples of what the individual did and make your comments specific so that the comments leave no questions for the individual receiving the feedback. Too often individuals provide general-izations without the facts or examples, so employees do not understand the feedback they have received. Instead, make sure your feedback is clear, detailed, accurate, and unambiguous. You describe behavior accurately and exactly by using phrases such as "three times this month," "once a day," and "this week." Try to stay away from generalizations such as "He is a good team member" or "She works hard."

Effect—Why the Performance is Important and How it Contributes.

In describing the effect, spell out the concrete result that the behavior is having upon you or the team. You should explain how the individual's behavior/actions is/are helpful to the team.

Thank You—Let the Team Member Know
You Appreciate His or Her Work.

The third part of the BET model is to say "thank you," which is easy to do. However, I often find it something that individuals forget to do.

Sample BET Feedback

Joe, when you asked questions and sought clarification, you demonstrated to all of us your desire to meet our deadline. Thank you for role modeling behavior that can influence others.

BEAR Model

As a way to provide constructive or "do better" feedback, my colleague Stephen Brock and I created the BEAR model. We found that when we provided training on giving feedback, many individuals seemed uncomfortable providing constructive feedback. We realized that giving constructive feedback was a "bear" for many to do, so we used "BEAR" as our constructive feedback model. I would recommend that about 25 percent of your feedback should fall into the "do better" category. If you are providing regular, ongoing feedback, and the employee is making corrections, you should have less behavior to correct at the official performance review meeting.

Behavior—What the Team Member is Doing
or Not Doing that is Unacceptable.

Just like BET, you must start with observable, specific behavior. Describe the incorrect behavior in exact, observable terms, as it exists now. In addition, avoid the tendency to exaggerate behaviors that bother you by using all or nothing expressions such as "never," "always," and "every time." You will follow the same guidelines as above for the Behavior step of the BET model.

Effect—Why the Behavior is Unacceptable, How it Hurts the Team's Productivity and Relationships.

Next, you should state the concrete effect the behavior is causing. Answer this question: What happens because the individual does or does not do something? You want to describe the impact of the behavior on you, an individual or the team. I find that often people do not understand feedback for improvement until they understand the impact of their specific behavior on others. Then describe the feelings you experience as a result of the behavior and be specific in sharing how you feel. Statements that begin with "I feel that . . . or I feel like . . ." are statements of thoughts not feelings. You may find yourself struggling with this step of the process, but you cannot separate the head and the heart. Emotional intelligence requires you to be aware of not only your own feelings, but of the feelings of others.

Alternative—What you want your team member to do or do differently.

In describing the alternative, you will recommend and describe the behavior you would like to see occurring in place of the current negative behavior. Simply, ask the individual to change his or her behavior. As the giver of feedback, offer suggestions for alternative behavior and indicate how your suggestions could improve the person's or team's performance.

Give a specific number of times or a time frame in which you want to see the individual change or modify his or her behavior. You must clarify your expectations to get agreement and commitment for behavioral change.

Result—What Will Happen if the Team Member Changes (Positive Outcome) or the Consequences if the Offensive Behavior Continues.

Finally, think of other creative ways to encourage an individual to change negative behavior. Brainstorm for positive outcomes that will result from his or her making the suggested change. If your direct reports do modify or change their behaviors, you should give them an acknowledgement that you noted they were working to adapt their behavior or actions. Remember, when you affirm any change that was made, don't forget to indicate how it affected both the individuals and the team in a positive way. However, you should outline the consequences regarding what may happen if the individual does not work to change his or her behavior.

Sample BEAR Feedback

Five times in the past 3 weeks, I have noticed that you have been 15 minutes late to our Monday and Friday morning meetings. When you do not show up on time, we sit and wait for you to arrive and then our meetings last longer. I would like to see you arrive at least 5 minutes early to our next meeting. If you will come to our next meeting 5 minutes before we are scheduled to start, we will get tasks completed and be able to finish on or before our scheduled ending time.

One of my students shared with me that, because she had learned the BET and BEAR models, she was now comfortable giving feedback to her manager. She said it made the feedback session positive for both of them and resulted in the change she had requested. Another EMBA student wrote this comment:

> I have always struggled with giving feedback. I was facing a difficult situation at work where I needed to give feedback. I followed the model, wrote out what I wanted to say, and prepared for our meeting. I was so pleasantly surprised because the meeting turned out so well. I had avoided this situation for so long, and then when I presented the feedback according to the models I had learned, the session went so well. I now believe in the BET and BEAR models.

While a MBA student stated

> If I am able to master this technique in my professional career, it can make a huge difference in how my teams view their effectiveness and the sense of loyalty they would feel under my leadership.

Providing feedback the right way communicates that you respect and support the people working on your team.

If you are willing to learn the models and apply them, your effectiveness in giving feedback will grow. However, giving feedback is half of the process; you will also need to welcome receiving feedback as well.

When you receive feedback, you should view it as a "gift" that helps you keep doing what you are doing well or helps you improve in a particular area. When you receive feedback, you learn about yourself and see things that you could not see without the "gift of feedback."

By having your blind spots illuminated, you will be able to correct behaviors that may inhibit your growth. In my research study, as noted in Figure 2.5, I did find that almost 60 percent of individuals perceived that they did not become defensive when receiving feedback, thus reinforcing the belief that feedback is a gift.

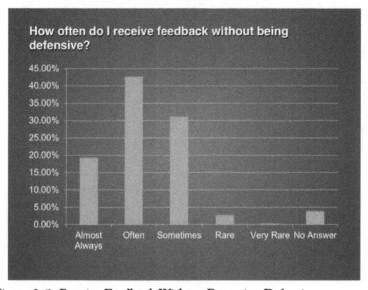

Figure 2.5. Receive Feedback Without Becoming Defensive

Mastering Nonverbal Communication

Take the following **People Skills Quiz** by author, speaker, and consultant John Boe to see how much of a working knowledge of body language you have. The correct answers are provided at the end of the chapter.[19]

John Boe, author, speaker, and consultant, www.johnboe.com

1. What is the meaning of the "palm to chest" gesture?

   A. Superior attitude
   B. Critical judgment
   C. Sincerity
   D. Confidence
   E. None of the above

2. What is the meaning of the "thumb under the chin" gesture?

Figure 2.6. People Skills Quiz

A. Deceit
B. Confidence
C. Anxiety
D. Critical judgment
E. Interest

3. What is the meaning of the "crossed arms" gesture?

A. Fear
B. Anticipation
C. Control
D. Superiority
E. None of the above

4. What is the meaning of the "thumb up" gesture?

A. Approval
B. Disapproval
C. Disinterest
D. Bored
E. None of the above

Figure 2.6. People Skills Quiz (continued)

5. What is the meaning of the "chin rub" gesture?

  A. Anticipation
  B. Decision
  C. Critical judgment
  D. Deceit
  E. Stalling of time

6. What is the meaning of the "glasses-to-mouth" gesture?

  A. Stalling for time
  B. Confidence
  C. Superiority
  D. Fearful
  E. None of the above

7. What does it mean when a person rubs his or her nose?
  A. Superiority
  B. Anticipation
  C. Dislike
  D. Anger

Figure 2.6. People Skills Quiz (continued)

8. What is the impact of nonverbal communication in a face-to-face conversation?
   A. 20%
   B. 40%
   C. 70%
   D. 85%

9. Which of the following gestures is associated with lying?
   A. Talking through fingers
   B. Eye rub
   C. Ear rub
   D. Lack of direct eye contact
   E. All of the above

Figure 2.6. People Skills Quiz (continued)

Often in training classes, I will say to the participants, "Okay, for the next 30 seconds, let's not communicate!" Of course individuals look at each other, smile, and laugh. The reality is that we can't really stop the nonverbal communication. Nonverbal defines the context and seeks to explain its effects upon our words.[20] You may think you control your communication by being deliberate, but these attempts often fail because your nonverbal behavior is still communicating. On occasion, you might even be surprised when your communication yields a different result from what you had anticipated because your nonverbal behavior may have communicated differently from your words. Some of the areas of nonverbal communication include: kinesics behavior—gestures, body movements, hand gestures, facial expressions, eye movement and posture; proxemics—human use and perception of physical space; and paralanguage—voice qualities and putting the emphasis on how something is said instead of the actual words themselves.

Kinesics

You may hear someone say "It's not what he said, but how he said it." Or you may hear someone else say "I couldn't talk if I couldn't use my hands." Gestures, eye contact, facial expressions, posture and body movements, and handshakes are all parts of our nonverbal communication. According Paul Ekman, a San Francisco psychologist who is a pioneer in studies of human countenance, you can see a smile at 300 feet, which is the length of a football field. From a distance of 150 feet, you can tell if a stranger's face is registering surprise or pleasure.[21] Often individuals receive a message nonverbally before they hear the words.

Gestures

Gestures are visible body actions that we use to communicate messages. They can be divided into four categories: emblems, illustrators, regulators, and adaptors.

- *Emblems* are intentional body movements and gestures that carry a specific verbal message. When driving down the interstate in the morning, you will not mistake individuals using an obscene gesture when they perceive you have pulled out in front of them. Of course emblems vary from culture to culture. Roger E. Axtell is the author of three best-selling books, *Do's and Taboos Around The World: A Guide To International Behavior and Gestures, Do's and Taboos of Body Language Around the World,* and *Do's and Taboos Around the World for Women in Business.*[22] You might want to invest in one of his books to raise your awareness of the various emblems and their meanings if you are visiting or conducting business in another country.
- *Illustrators* are gestures that add or clarify verbal meaning. When giving directions to someone, you might point in the direction he or she should go. In the United States, when you turn your palms up, you are showing openness and honesty.
- *Regulators* control the flow of a conversation. Some examples might be when you break eye contact to indicate the conversation is over or when you nod your head in agreement.

- *Adaptors* are habitual gestures that we use in times of discomfort. Some examples include scratching your nose, rubbing the back of your neck, or touching your hair while giving a presentation. You may not realize you are doing them, but your audience is picking up on them and noting that you are nervous during your presentation. You need to be aware of adaptors so that you do not contradict the impression you are trying to make.[23]

Eye Contact

Steward Hay, CEO of Glen Eden Wool Carpet, has stated: "Eye contact is very important. If I do not have direct eye contact I assume they (the audience) are doing something they should not be doing."[24] While George Lane III, Chairman and CEO of Lane Company, added: "Eye contact affects perceptions about the person's national and cultural norms. It also depicts whether the person is an introvert (not a lot of direct eye contact) or extrovert (fair amount of direct eye contact)."[25] Jill Bremer of Bremer Communication provided these thoughts.

> Looking at people and meeting their eyes is the first step toward striking up friendships and making positive impressions. The best advice is to make short frequent glances in social situations. Making eye contact for too long of a duration can be seen as threatening and aggressive; the subtext of interest becomes distorted. Failing to look at others causes suspicion as they wonder what signals are being masked. Honesty and the ability to look someone in the eye are very closely related. Refusing to make eye contact also sends messages of arrogance and contempt, communicating to the other person that he or she is insignificant, a non-person.[26]

The eyes are the most expressive part of your face and can have considerable effect on communication. As a leader, you should remember that the eyes control communication and keep in mind that eye behavior may be different in cultures outside the United States.

In the United States, eye contact

- Shows interest and attentiveness
- Signals a wish to participate
- Controls and persuades others[27]

In addition, the eyes can communicate power. You've probably heard the terms "icy stares," "he looks right through you," and "if looks could kill." Avoiding another person's glance in the United States is a nonverbal attempt to avoid interaction.

Many eye behaviors are associated with emotions: Downward glances may mean modesty or shame; wide eyes have been associated with innocence, wonder, or terror; fixed eyes may indicate coldness or anger; and so on.

Facial Expressions

I can still remember one of my direct reports saying to me: "Deborah, you need to get thicker skin as your feelings show all over your face." Since the face is the primary communicator of emotions, your facial expressions carry meaning that is determined by situations and relationships. Researchers have discovered that certain facial areas reveal our emotional state better than others. For example, the eyes tend to reveal happiness or sadness, and even surprise. The lower face also can reveal happiness or surprise; the smile, for example, can communicate friendliness and cooperation. The lower face, brows, and forehead can also reveal anger.[28] Face to hand movements such as holding the chin or scratching the face show concern or lack of conviction. If a person is covering his mouth while telling you something, he may be lying.

Faces reveal emotions and attitudes, but you do need to be aware that facial expressions vary from country to country, and thus the degree of facial expressiveness one exhibits varies among individuals and cultures. When you interact with others, you pay attention to the face and use the information you see within the face as the basis for the actions you take.

Posture and Body Movement

Your posture communicates different messages. For example, if your shoulders and back appear stiff, it can show tightness and quite possibly a lack of confidence. Slouching or shrugging can show a lack of motivation or lack of interest. To show interest, you can sit up straight with your back against your chair. You can turn your shoulders toward the person with whom you are speaking and lean forward a little to emphasize that you are listening. Tilting your head can also signal your interest.[29]

When you stand up and move around, such action can show dominance. When you stretch your legs to occupy more space, you show more power. You might try standing while talking on the phone, as this action will make your voice sound more urgent.[30]

Handshakes

A handshake signals openness or goodwill at the beginning of an interaction, while, at the end of a conversation, it demonstrates agreement. To show sincerity, you want to make palm-to-palm contact. While the art of handshaking does vary within cultures, in the United States, the most common rules seem to be as follows.

1. Begin with an Oral Introduction of Yourself

Before extending your entire hand, introduce yourself. Extending your hand should be part of an introduction, not a replacement for using your voice. Extending your hand without a voice greeting may make you appear nervous or overly aggressive.

2. Pump Your Hand Only Two to Three Times

A business handshake should be brief and to the point. Holding on for more than 3 or 4 seconds can make other people feel uncomfortable.

3. Shake From Your Elbow

If you shake from the shoulder, using your upper arm instead of just your forearm, you risk jolting your handshake partner. The idea is to connect, not be overbearing.

4. Do Not Use a Forceful Grip

A handshake should be a friendly or respectful gesture, not a show of physical strength. An uncomfortable handshake is never a pleasant experience for anyone.

Photo courtesy flickr user Horasis, CC 2.0

5. Avoid Offering a "Fish Hand"

You do not want to use a limp business handshake. Do return the grip, but do not get into a power struggle, even if the other person squeezes too hard.

6. One Hand Is Better Than Two

Avoid the urge to handshake with two hands. It is always better in business introductions to use only one hand for the shake. The use of two hands with strangers is seen as intrusive and too personal. In fact, a two-handed shake is called the "politician's shake," because it appears artificially friendly when used on people you barely know.

7. Shaking a Sweaty Hand

If you shake hands with someone who has sweaty palms, do not immediately wipe your hands on your clothing, handkerchief, or tissue. This action will further embarrass the other person, who is probably already aware he or she has sweaty hands. You can discreetly wipe them on something after you are out of sight.

8. Ending a Handshake

End the handshake after 3 or 4 seconds or two or three pumps. To avoid creating an awkward moment, your handshake should end before the oral introduction exchange does. Without conversation during the entire handshake, the gesture becomes too intimate and can feel more like hand holding.[31]

Warren Lamb is a management consultant, teacher, and lecturer. He is a pioneer in the field of nonverbal behavior, having created Movement Pattern Analysis, a motivational assessment tool based on movement observation.

Lamb believes the best way to determine an individual's potential to be a managerial leader is to observe what he does when he is speaking. He calls this new behavioral science "movement analysis." Some of the movements and gestures he has analyzed follow:

- **Forward and Backward Movements.** If you extend a hand straight forward during an interview or tend to lean forward, Lamb considers you to be an "operator"—good for an organization requiring an infusion of energy or dramatic change of course.
- **Vertical Movements.** If you tend to draw yourself up to your tallest during the handshake, Lamb considers you to be a "presenter." You are a master at selling yourself or the organization in which you are employed.
- **Side-to-Side Movements.** If you take a lot of space while talking by moving your arms about, you are a good informer and good listener. You are best suited for an organization seeking a better sense of direction. Lamb believes there is a relationship between positioning of the body and movements of the limbs and face. He has observed harmony between the two. On the other hand, if certain gestures are rehearsed, such as those made to impress others, the harmony disappears.

Studies by Lamb also indicate that communication comes about through our degree of body flexibility. If you begin a movement with considerable force and then decelerate, you are considered a "gentle-touch." By contrast, if you are a "pressurizer," you are firm from beginning to end.[32]

Proxemics

Anthropologist Edward T. Hall coined the term "proxemics" to describe the use of space. He identified four personal space zones: intimate zone, personal zone, social zone, and public zone.

Intimate zone is 0 to 1½ feet. I find it interesting that cocktail tables are designed to put you in the intimate zone as do elevators. The next time you get on an elevator, watch what people do because they are uncomfortable with people in their intimate zone. Typically, they will look up at the indicator of the floor or look down at the floor, their watch, or something in their arms. We only want to be in this zone with individuals we know well.

Personal zone is 1½ to 4 feet. To be in this space, you want to be well acquainted with the other person. Typically, the actual verbal communication is spoken softly.

Social zone is 4 to 12 feet. In this space zone, you are acquainted with the other person and you have a reason to speak with an individual. If you don't have a reason to speak, you will likely just say hello or may even break off eye contact with someone you do not know. This space is also known as the "business zone" because most business takes place in this zone.

Public zone is more than 12 feet. Not much interaction takes place from this distance as words must be shouted.[33]

How much space individuals need can vary by culture, and not understanding the needs of the various cultures has led to some miscommunication. For example, Latinos tend to move closer and quite possibly want to be in the intimate zone while someone from the United States will step back if his or her intimate zone is invaded. The message the Latin individual likely receives is that the American is cold and unfriendly.

The arrangement and location of your office communicates status differences and openness of communication. For example, if your desk is positioned in the center of the room, you communicate that you are in charge. I once had an individual tell me that he would lower the visitor's chair in his office as low as it would go while also raising his chair as high as he possibly could. Nonverbally, he wanted his visitors to know he was in charge.

In addition, leaders usually have offices instead of cubicles, and these offices are often located on the top floors of a building. Having an office with a door and a window indicates status. Another status symbol is the width and length of your desk. The higher you climb within an organization, the larger your wooden (not metal) desk will likely become. A larger desk puts more physical space between you and your visitors.

Where you host visitors in your office can send a strong signal. For example, if you sit behind your desk, clearly you let the visitor know you are in charge. At times, you need to show power—for example, to discipline an employee, you might choose to stay behind your desk. However, if you want to create an open environment for someone to talk, you would want to move out from behind the desk. You could simply sit in another chair beside the visitor or move to a small table where you could converse as equals. Taking these steps indicates that you want the other person to feel comfortable and that you are there to listen.

Paralanguage

Meaning is contained within the words you use, but the "how" of what you say also conveys a powerful message. For example, when you are a parent, you will often tell your child to "come here." The child typically will respond based upon the way the words are said. If the child perceives you are upset or angry, he or she will come immediately. If the child infers no threat or anger, he or she might continue to play instead of coming as you requested. The tone, vocal differentiators, and vocal identifiers convey emotions that others can judge regardless of your words.

Tone of Voice. Tone includes the loudness or softness of your voice and whether you use a raised or lowered pitch. Individuals associate meanings such as raised voice or lower pitch with fear, anxiety, or tenseness. When you speak quickly, you may be communicating urgency or a high emotional state; but if your tempo is too slow, it may give the impression of uncertainty or hesitancy.

Vocal Differentiators. This category refers to how you say something. Obviously what you say is influenced by how it is said. Examples of vocal differentiators include crying, laughing, and breaking. Breaking refers to speaking in a broken or halting manner. Clearly a phrase uttered by a crying person will mean something different than if it was said by a laughing person.

Vocal Identifiers. These refer to the small sounds we make that are not necessarily words, but have meaning. For example, ah-hah, un-huh, and huh-uh.[34]

All of these paralanguage characteristics strongly affect how meaning is extracted by the other person, and how your words may be interpreted. Paralanguage provides an additional context. So you must realize that how you say things can be even more important than what you say. As a communicator, you should be sensitive to the influence of tone, pitch, and quality of your voice on the interpretation of your message by the receiver.

Strategies for Nonverbal Communication

Try to "listen between the lines" and pay careful attention to the non-verbal communication of the sender. You should be careful not to place too much importance on a single, isolated nonverbal behavior, but instead look for several nonverbal cues while noting if the nonverbal cues changed at any point in your conversation. For example, if an individual was displaying open body language when you began the conversation and the longer the conversation went on, you saw the individual start to close him or herself off by crossing arms, crossing feet, and pulling the chin down, then you may want to back up, start over, and check for understanding. The challenge for you will be to become more observant of behavior and what the change in behavior may signal.

If the verbal and nonverbal disagree, usually you can believe the nonverbal because you can't control or stop nonverbal communication from occurring. You may say you are not embarrassed, but if your face is red, then the message your audience receives is that you are, in fact, embarrassed. One look or facial expression can convey more meaning than 1000 words.

To build trust and to show respect with others, you can use a "mirroring" strategy. When you use this strategy, you subtly match your audience's body language in the first 15 minutes of your meeting. Most people feel more comfortable and open with people in a similar position to themselves. If you notice that the other individual is crossing his or her arms, you would subtly cross your arms to match him or her. If you believe you have developed trust and rapport, you can verify it by seeing if the other person will match you. So you could uncross your arms and see if the other person will match and mirror you as you move into a more open posture. If you notice the individual subconsciously matching your body language gestures, then you have developed trust and rapport. Conversely, if you notice the individual has mismatched your body language gestures, you know trust and rapport has not been established and you need to continue matching and mirroring them. The next time you are in the break room or the hallway, observe how people are subconsciously mirroring one another.[35] You may want to add the strategy of mirroring to your tool kit.

http://www.maggieanderson.com/

Maggie Anderson, author of *Words That Work, Executive Communication*, has shared ways that you can use your nonverbal communication more effectively.[36] She says that you need to match verbal and nonverbal, think about your body, note nervous habits, practice gestures, pay attention to emotions, and control your voice.

Make Your Nonverbal Cues Match What You Say. In most situations, our verbal and nonverbal match. For example, if you are happy, you smile or have a pleasant facial expression and it shows. However, you might encounter times when you want to show a different message from what you are feeling. For example, you are nervous, but you want to show confidence. How do you do this? You begin by taking a deep breath, straightening your shoulders, raising your head up, and putting yourself in the "pose" that means confidence to you. When your posture is upright, it sends a message to your brain that you are in charge. Communications consultant Bert Decker tells participants to assume the "Miss America Pose." Decker has individuals stand against the wall and put their shoulders back against it. Then he instructs them to walk away.

He states having your shoulders back makes you stand tall, which sends the signal you are confident.[37]

Think About What Your Body Is Doing. Ask yourself these questions:

- What does your body posture convey about you?
- When you sit, what message do you send?
- Does your posture send a message of attentiveness or boredom?
- When you talk with someone, do you look at them or at your watch? Do you keep doing other things such as checking your e-mail?
- Can another person read your body language to say that you aren't interested or don't care?

You must first be aware of what your body language is communicating to others, so answering these questions is the first step. The second step might require that you ask for feedback from others you trust about the messages they perceive you send when you speak with them.

Nervous Habits Can Send Different Messages From What You Intend. The problem with nervous habits is that you may not even be aware of them. Some examples include touching your face, playing with your jewelry, jangling keys, wrinkling your nose, using filler words such as "um," or smacking your lips. Certain habits convey certain meanings and these can be a distraction for others. If your posture is slumped or you touch your face, the message you send is that you lack confidence, are not approachable, or are feeling uneasy.

Practice Making Appropriate Gestures When Making Important Points. Use gestures that enhance your message when you speak. You should reinforce your points with appropriate gestures that increase the effectiveness of your message.

Pay Attention to Your Emotions. When you don't manage your emotions, others will pay more attention to them rather than the words you speak. So, you may need to stop the conversation, take a few deep breaths, count to 10, or put a hold on the conversation until you can get control of your emotions.

Use Vocal Control. When you talk in a high pitched voice, you might sound like a cartoon character. Breathe deeply and speak from your diaphragm. It will take some practice, but learning to speak from your diaphragm will lower your natural voice. Females tend to struggle with this control more than males. Also, the volume of your voice comes from your diaphragm. If you try to talk more loudly from your throat, you may appear to be shouting. If you speak from your diaphragm, your voice will have power, and people like to listen to powerful voices.

Adjusting the pitch and volume will help with the quality of your voice. Adding emotion to your voice will capture your audience. A great trick for talking on the phone is to smile before you answer the phone. Your voice will convey the warmth of your smile to whoever is on the other end of the line.

Employing Emotional Intelligence

Intellectual intelligence (IQ) measures your cognitive and logical skills, which do not change much after you reach your teen years. Emotional intelligence (EQ) is a set of skills learned throughout life and is the ability to sense, understand, and use the power and wisdom of emotions.[38] Emotional intelligence is the capacity to understand one's own emotions and those of others.[39] Emotional intelligence engages others in ways that draw people to you.

Most authorities will say that emotional intelligence matters just as much as intellectual ability, if not more. Emotional intelligence helps you build strong relationships, succeed at work, and achieve your goals.

Emotional intelligence consists of four core abilities:

- **Self-awareness** – This ability includes recognizing your own emotions and how they affect your thoughts and behavior, knowing your strengths and weaknesses, and having self-confidence. Self-awareness begins with understanding your general tendencies for responding to different people and situations.
- **Self-management** – This core ability enables you to control impulsive feelings and behaviors, to manage your emotions in healthy ways, to take initiative, to follow through on commitments, and to adapt to changing circumstances. Self-management requires that you choose what you say and do to positively direct your behavior.

- **Social awareness** – This ability requires you to understand the emotions, needs, and concerns of other people, to be able to pick up on emotional cues, to feel comfortable socially, and to recognize the power dynamics in a group or organization.
- **Relationship management** – This ability asks you to develop and maintain good relationships, to communicate clearly, to inspire and influence others, to work well in a team, and to manage conflict.[40]

So, how do you raise your EQ skills? First, you cannot just read a book about EQ. You must apply it to your life. Just because you know you *should* do something doesn't mean you will—especially when you're feeling stressed. When you're under high levels of stress, the emotional parts of your brain override the rational parts and your best-laid plans and intentions fly out the window. To permanently change your behavior to stand up to stress, you will need to learn how to take advantage of the powerful emotional parts of the brain that remain active and accessible even in times of stress. You have to learn the skills on a deeper, emotional level—experiencing and practicing them in your everyday life.

Skill 1: Rapidly Reduce Stress

When you experience high levels of stress, your rational thinking and decision making can disappear. Runaway stress overwhelms your mind and body and gets in the way of your ability to accurately "read" a situation or to hear what someone else is saying. You are not aware of your own feelings and needs and thus cannot communicate clearly.

The first step is the ability to quickly calm yourself down when you're feeling overwhelmed. Being able to manage stress, rather than it managing you, is the key to resilience. This emotional intelligence skill helps you stay balanced, focused, and in control—no matter what challenges you face. But doing so can be difficult so you must follow these three steps:

- **Realize when you're stressed and how stress feels to you.** You may spend so much time in an unbalanced state that you've forgotten what it feels like to be calm and relaxed.

- **Identify your stress response.** Everyone reacts differently to stress. Do you tend to space out and get depressed? Become angry and agitated? Freeze with anxiety? The best way to quickly calm yourself depends on your specific stress response.
- **Discover the stress-busting techniques that work for you.** The best way to reduce stress quickly is through the senses: through sight, sound, smell, taste, and touch. But each person responds differently to sensory input, so you need to find things that are soothing to you.

Skill 2: Connect to Your Emotions

Many people are disconnected from their emotions—especially strong core emotions such as anger, sadness, fear, and joy. While you may distort, deny, or numb your feelings, you can't eliminate them. They're still there, whether you're aware of them or not. Unfortunately, without emotional awareness, you are unable to fully understand your own motivations and needs, or to communicate effectively with others. So what kind of relationship do you have with your emotions?

- **Do you experience feelings that flow**, encountering one emotion after another as your experiences change from moment to moment?
- **Are your emotions accompanied by physical sensations that you experience** in places like your stomach or chest?
- **Do you experience discrete feelings and emotions**, such as anger, sadness, fear, joy, each of which is evident in subtle facial expressions?
- **Can you experience intense feelings** that are strong enough to capture both your attention and that of others?
- **Do you pay attention to your emotions?** Do they factor into your decision making?

If any of these experiences are unfamiliar, your emotions may be turned down or turned off. To be emotionally healthy and emotionally intelligent, you must reconnect to your core emotions, accept them, and become comfortable with them.

Skill 3: Use Humor and Play to Deal With Challenges

Humor, laughter, and play are natural antidotes to life's difficulties. They lighten your burdens and help you keep things in perspective. A good hearty laugh reduces stress, elevates mood, and brings your nervous system back into balance.

Playful communication broadens your emotional intelligence and helps you:

- **Take hardships in stride**. When you view your frustrations and disappointments from new perspectives, laughter and play enable you to survive annoyances, hard times, and setbacks.
- **Smooth over differences**. Using gentle humor often helps you say things that might be otherwise difficult to express without creating a flap.
- **Simultaneously relax and energize yourselves**. Playful communication relieves fatigue and relaxes your body, which allows you to recharge and accomplish more.
- **Become more creative.** When you loosen up, you free yourself of rigid ways of thinking and being, allowing you to get creative and see things in new ways.[41]

Emotional intelligence accounts for 85 percent of what distinguishes the high achievers in top leadership positions from the low-level performers.[42]

Photo courtesy flickr user Sociate, CC 2.0

Michael Hoppe, a retired faculty member at the Center for Creative Leadership who worked with hundreds of executives and managers over his career, boiled his advice for better listening down to six steps:[1]

1. *Pay attention.* Turn off your BlackBerry. Maintain eye contact. Nod to show you understand. Otherwise the conversation is dead before it starts.

2. *Suspend judgment.* Hold your criticisms, and let others explain how they view a situation. You don't need to agree; just show some empathy.

3. *Reflect.* Periodically recap others' points to confirm your understanding. Often it turns out you missed something.

4. *Clarify.* Ask open-ended questions that encourage people to expand their ideas. For example: "What are your thoughts about how we might increase sales in this economy?"

5. *Summarize.* Briefly restate core themes raised by the person you're talking with. You're not agreeing or disagreeing; you're simply closing the loop.

6. *Share.* Once you know where that person stands, introduce your own ideas and suggestions. That's how good conversations get even better.

These steps may not turn you into a chief listening officer overnight, but you can build up your listening muscle. The more you practice the right skills, the stronger you get.

Ryan, J. (2009, September 30)
Every CEO Must Be A Chief Listening Officer
Retrieved from http://www.forbes.com/2009/12/30/chief-listening
-officer-leadership-managing-ccl_print.html

Choosing the Right Type of Listening for the Situation

When I was an executive director, I learned the hard way that my team perceived I was focusing too much on building relationships with external audiences and not spending enough time maintaining relationships with them. I have to say that was hard to hear, but I learned two important lessons that day. First, I was not too old to learn from my mistakes; and second, I needed to listen more and make that a part of each day.

Listening is actually a six-part process that includes hearing, attending, understanding, remembering, evaluating, and responding:

- **Hearing** refers to the response caused by the sound waves stimulating the sensory receptors of the ear.
- **Attending** occurs when your brain screens stimuli and permits only a select few to come into focus.
- **Understanding** allows you to analyze the meaning of the stimuli you have perceived. The symbolic stimuli are not only words but also sounds and sights that have symbolic meanings as well; the meanings attached to these symbols are a function of your past associations and of the context in which the symbols occur. For successful interpersonal communication, you must understand the intended meaning and the context assumed by the sender.
- **Remembering** is important because it means you have not only received and interpreted a message, but have added it to your mind's storage bank; but just as your attention is selective, so too is your memory—what is remembered may be quite different from what was originally seen or heard.
- **Evaluating** is the point where you weigh the evidence, sort facts from opinion and determine the presence or absence of bias or prejudice in a message.
- **Responding** requires you to complete the process through verbal and/or nonverbal feedback. When you respond, the sender can determine how much of his or her message you have received.[43]

So, if you just thought listening was hearing, you can see it is much more complicated than that, and why you need to understand all the parts of the process.

Studies have shown that we spend approximately 80 percent of our day communicating, and about 45 percent of that day is spent in listening. In my research study of employees and managers, I found that listening was the most common form of communication used by those managers and employees. In Figure 2.7, you will note how both groups—managers and employees—responded to the question, "What portion of your day do you spend in listening, speaking, reading, and writing?"

Almost 22 percent of the managers interviewed spent more than 50 percent of their day listening, while 15 percent of employees spent more than 50 percent of their day listening. While 58 percent of managers spent between 25 to 49 percent of the day in listening activities, 54 percent of employees chose the same category. Clearly, listening comprises much of an average day for both managers and employees.

While you can note that both employees and managerial leaders spend much time in listening activities, the reality is that they are probably using only about 25 to 30 percent of their listening potential. Research has shown that immediately after listening to a 10-minute oral presentation, the average person understands and remembers no more than half of what was said. One to two days later, less than one-fourth of what was said is remembered.[44]

Listening is one of the most important tasks you have as a managerial leader. Ann Mulcahy, former CEO of Xerox, was quoted as saying: "I

Time Spent by Managers and Employees in Listening, Writing, Reading and Speaking			
	Response Rate	Managers (88)	Employees (407)
Listening	<25% of workday	18	123
	25% - 49%	51	221
	=> 50%	19	63
Reading	< 25%	62	272
	25% - 49%	23	124
	=> 50%	3	11
Speaking	< 25%	24	132
	25% - 49%	58	238
	=> 50%	6	37
Writing	< 25%	61	238
	25% - 49%	24	145
	=> 50%	3	24

Figure 2.7. Time Spent in Listening, Writing, Reading, and Speaking

feel like my title should be Chief Communication Officer, because that's really what I do. . . . .Emphasizing the importance of listening to customers and employees," she said. "When I became CEO, I spent the first 90 days on planes traveling to various offices and listening to anyone who had a perspective on what was wrong with the company. I think if you spend as much time listening as talking, that's time well spent."[45]

To be an effective managerial leader, just as Mulcahy said, you must become an effective listener. The daily deadlines that cause stress and time pressure may cause you to not listen as much as you should. Then, because you are a managerial leader, you often speak rather than listen, so you are more comfortable speaking than listening. But the reality is that you will find true listening hard work. If you focus too hard on facts, you can miss the overall message. If you assume the speaker or subject to be uninteresting, you may miss out; and if you pretend to listen, you may get caught!

What also complicates the listening process is that we have different rates of listening and speaking. When you speak, you talk at about 125 to 150 words a minute, but you listen at about 400 to 500 words per minute. This difference in ability allows for ample daydreaming, which in turn leads to miscommunication.

The next time you are asked to listen to someone, see if you can answer any of these questions "yes." If so, you may need to modify your behavior to truly listen.

- Do you find yourself looking out the window, looking at your watch, playing with your smart phone, or typing on your computer while someone is talking to you?
- Do you tell someone you have lots of time to listen, but then continue to do other things while listening?
- Do you play with items on your desk while listening?
- Do you finish other people's sentences?
- Do you interrupt?
- Do you respond to e-mails or your telephone when someone is talking to you?

When you show your employees you will listen and interact with them, their morale increases. Employees typically generate more ideas and feel less discouraged when they know they can make a contribution to the organization. Effective listening makes not only a superior managerial leader, but also a healthier organization overall.

CEO Tim Clifford of Workscape, a leading provider of human resource solutions and services, believes that listening is one of the key responsibilities of a managerial leader. Tim believes that when you listen to them, your employees stay engaged. For him, the most important task a managerial leader can do is set aside dedicated time to talk with employees from different functional areas to gain an understanding of daily challenges as they happen. Tim states that an employee that deals with customer service will have a unique view of customer satisfaction and product quality that could be entirely different from a member of the sales staff or someone in product development. Tim recommends several practices that promote listening:

- Walking the office floor for a half-hour to engage employees in conversation.
- Holding periodic town hall meetings where employees are encouraged to voice questions and present ideas in an open forum.
- Holding a quarterly all-hands meeting to review the state of the company and to solicit feedback and questions on company initiatives and strategy.

As with any skill, Tim notes that becoming an effective listener requires a commitment of time and energy. This commitment often requires establishing listening as a priority relative to the numerous other objectives that are often heaped—sometimes literally—on a CEO's desk.[46]

Any time you can cause someone to "create" images in his head, it increases the question's effectiveness. By using words such as "imagine," "suppose," or "picture," the person answering the query is also somewhat removed from the present emotional situation and mentally transported elsewhere. Not only can this help diffuse some agitation that might be contributing to the problem, but it allows for a more creative solution, as well as letting you analyze body language changes.

Source: The Art of Questions
By Scott Marcus
Retrieved from http://www.scottqmarcus.com/articles/
AcrobatArticles/OpenClosedQuestions.pdf

Using Relevant Questions and Paraphrasing

As a managerial leader, you will ask questions to engage your direct reports and to keep the conversation flowing. I remember I had one direct report who worked hard to please me. Any task I would give her, she would do thoroughly and completely, but she never went beyond exactly what I was asking her to do. She would often ask: "What should I do next?" To help her grow, I started asking her what she thought would be the next step. In the beginning she was uncomfortable and afraid that she would make a mistake, but slowly her confidence grew and she would then come to me with not only what I asked her to do, but with suggestions for next steps.

Another situation I've faced is a direct report who runs into a problem and comes to you for help. Your first reaction is to provide that help, because, after all, you're the managerial leader. But is that the right thing to do for your subordinate? If you always step in, are you allowing your direct reports to grow? Are you losing out on creative ideas you might not have thought of? Are you getting trapped in an upward delegation spiral?

Instead, I would recommend that you stop, pause, and coach the subordinate to find the solution. But that requires that you ask the questions that enable your direct reports to start thinking instead of waiting for instructions. If you respond with questions, you will start to see the self-confidence of your subordinates increasing, and your subordinates will start taking ownership of results.

Questions allow you to build rapport, to identify strengths and weaknesses, and to check for progress toward tasks or goals. When you ask questions, you convey to others that you are interested and engaged in what they are saying. Questions provide deeper understanding by:

- Clarifying
- Elaborating
- Challenging
- Confronting
- Assessing
- Evaluating
- Summarizing

When you listen to the response to your question, paraphrase back to check your understanding of what was said. When you paraphrase, restate what you hear to check for content, intent, and feelings. First, check for content to ensure you understand what the individual has said. Second, dig deeper to check for intent and the reason for the statement. Finally, test for feelings and confirm your understanding of the speaker's emotions.[47] As a managerial leader, you will ask certain types of questions: open-ended, probing, closed, and reflecting. But, avoid asking defensive or leading questions.

Open-Ended Questions

Use open-ended questions to gather information and to encourage more dialogue. You are encouraging the individual to disclose thoughts, feelings, and ideas. Open-ended questions stimulate creative thinking and solutions to problems. Ask open-ended questions to ensure your understanding and to encourage individuals to elaborate. By asking open-ended questions, you are not agreeing or disagreeing with what has been said, but just seeking clarification.

When you ask questions to further the conversation, paraphrase back what you heard. Open-ended questions generally begin with who, what, when, where, or which. Some examples of open-ended questions include: What do you hope for? What do you think the problem is? and What can I do for you?

Why-questions are often perceived as implying criticism and may result in defensiveness. Another way to obtain a reason or explanation is to repeat what the person just said and end with the word *because*, so that the other person can complete the sentence.

Probing Questions

When you use a probing question, you are asking the individual to provide more details and you are looking for more of a narrative response. For example, you might say: "Tell me more about . . ." or "Give me an example of . . ."

You might want to explore more by looking for areas of agreement or disagreement. Here you want your colleague to explain his or her position in more detail. You might ask a question such as: "With whom do you find it difficult to communicate?" Also you might ask a question that asks for an emotional response so that you allow the individual to vent any feelings that might be impacting his or her performance. For example, you could simply ask: "How do you feel about that?" This question allows for an opportunity to provide information as well as an opportunity to improve relationships.

Closed-Ended Questions

Closed-ended questions encourage a yes or a no response or short responses and truly are not used much in coaching or in dialogue. While closed questions, which require specific answers, can be a good way to open and close a conversation, several closed questions in a row can make others uncomfortable.

Reflecting Questions

When you use reflecting questions, briefly restate what the other person has said (the content) or what the other person is feeling (emotions). Such responses communicate understanding and encourage open dialogue. Some examples of reflecting questions include:

"It sounds as if . . ." and "Tell me more."

Questions Not to Ask

Remember when you ask **why-questions,** in all likelihood, your direct report will become defensive or reactive. In addition, his or her self-confidence may be destroyed, and the employee may then hesitate to take risks. Questions such as the following may stop the communication flow that would allow the subordinate to clarify misunderstandings. Therefore, avoid the following types of questions:

- Why are you behind schedule?
- What's the problem with this project?
- Who isn't keeping up?
- Don't you know better than that?

You should also avoid using leading questions. This type of question seeks a specific answer but can put the person being asked the question in a negative light or can exert pressure to force agreement. Leading questions such as those below inhibit direct reports from answering candidly and stifle honest discussion:

- You wanted to do it by yourself, didn't you?
- Don't you agree that Mary is the problem here?
- Everyone else on the team thinks Rob is the problem. What about you?

So instead of asking defensive or leading questions, focus on questions that will create value in one or more of the following ways:

1. **They create clarity**: "Please explain more about this situation."
2. **They construct better working relations**: Instead of "Did you make your sales goal?" ask, "How have sales been going?"
3. **They help people think analytically and critically**: "What are the consequences of going this route?"
4. **They inspire people to reflect and see things in fresh, unpredictable ways**: "What made this work so well?"
5. **They encourage breakthrough thinking**: "What other ways can that be done?"
6. **They challenge assumptions**: "What do you think you will lose if you start sharing responsibility for the implementation process?"
7. **They create ownership of solutions**: "Based on your experience, what do you suggest we do here?"[48]

To foster a team environment that values asking questions, you will have to model the way by asking questions of the team. For example, you can track how well the team is working together by asking questions such as:

- We've been working on this project for three hours today; what did we do best as a team?
- What enabled us to be successful in coming up with an innovative strategy?
- How can we ask better questions?
- How can we apply what we are learning to other parts of our work?
- What leadership skills helped us succeed today?[49]

While going into your team or one-on-one meetings with a list of questions rather than talking points can take some thoughtful planning on your part, the payoff can be huge. By leading your team meetings with questions, you will also help eliminate ambiguity and create alignment around issues.

As you strive to lead by asking rather than telling, remember that leaders are only as successful as the people who report to them. By asking your direct reports the right questions, you help them develop their ability to solve problems, their creativity, and their resourcefulness. Not only will their greater strength in these areas reflect well on you, but it also will enable them to better help you and the whole unit when fresh challenges arise.[50]

Understanding Conflict and the Use of Different Strategies

Someone just shared some information and what she shared conflicted with your ideas or thoughts. You begin to feel pressure as your heart races. You wonder whether you should speak up and tell her what you think or if you should remain silent. You don't want her to think you are attacking her, but if you don't speak up, she may think you agree with her. So the questions running through your head include:

- How do I confront the situation?
- How do I deliver my message and create a dialogue so ideas, thoughts, and feelings can be communicated effectively?

When opinions vary and emotions run strong, you are often at your worst, but the reality is that dealing with conflict lives at the heart of managing any business.[51] People tend to avoid conflict for a variety of reasons including their family backgrounds, cultural norms, personality styles, and personal experience. Regardless of the reasons, conflict at work is inevitable and managerial leaders need to know how to handle it effectively. In fact, some studies have indicated that middle managers spend between 20 and 50 percent of their time dealing with conflict, while front-line managers report even more time spent managing conflict.[52] When you review all the changes taking place in our work environments, it would seem inevitable that conflict will increase as individuals disagree over how work should be organized, who should be involved in making decisions, and how individuals can accomplish organizational goals. Conflict over issues can lead to a stronger organization, but it must be managed appropriately.

But what is this thing called conflict? Conflict has many definitions, but the one that I like best is any situation where my concerns or desires differ from another person's thoughts. So conflict is an expression of differences, not something that is positive or negative, and it is a definite part of organizational and personal life. You will find numerous sources of conflict such as stress from limited resources, uncertainty, complex tasks, role incompatibility, misinformation, and interpersonal misunderstandings. Of all of these sources of conflict, the managing of interpersonal conflicts can be the most challenging.

Managing interpersonal conflicts can be one of the most severe tests of a managerial leader's interpersonal skills. The challenge becomes maintaining an optimal level of conflict while keeping conflicts focused on productive outcomes. Patrick Lencioni, author of the *5 Dysfunctions of a Team*, identifies conflict as the second dysfunction of a team. He states that work teams need to engage in unfiltered, passionate debate about key issues. He said if team members do not openly air their opinions, inferior decisions are the result.[53] So, when you lead others, you must give your permission for them to debate issues.

Kathy Eisenhardt and her colleagues at Stanford University have written, "The challenge is to encourage members of management . . . to argue without destroying their ability to work together."[54] They found successful work teams managed conflicts by:

- Working with more, rather than less, information and debating on the basis of facts.
- Developing multiple alternatives to enrich the level of debate.
- Sharing commonly agreed-upon goals.
- Injecting humor into the decision process.
- Maintaining a balanced power structure.
- Resolving issues without forcing consensus.

Whetten and Cameron offer these additional ideas:

- Select the most appropriate setting for the meeting.
- Set ground rules (only one person talks at a time, etc.).
- Gather information on the participants' perceptions of the problem causing the conflict.
- Maintain a neutral position.
- Have the participants agree on the problem.
- Help the participants brainstorm possible solutions.
- Ensure the participants make a plan to resolve the conflict.
- Check back about a week later to ensure the conflict has been resolved.[55]

When you, as the managerial leader, must settle interpersonal disputes, your goal should be to resolve the underlying problems while ensuring that the interpersonal relationship between you and the members of your team is not damaged. So how do you do that?

First, be authentic so that you can create a dialogue with others. You begin by speaking from the heart, which is part of emotional intelligence. When you speak from the heart, you show you desire to understand and will strive to arrive at an outcome that is a win-win for all parties. You want to think about

- What do I really want the outcome of this communication to look like?
- What are the facts?
- How do all parties feel?
- What do I ultimately want for myself and for others?
- What steps can we take to make that happen?

When you focus on the end result, you move away from the emotions you are feeling, but still speak from your perspective of the situation. For example, you could say:

What I'm hearing is that we have a difference of opinion here and I'd like to open this up to a discussion. Would that work for you?

Taking action will allow you to open up dialogue in a nonthreatening way. Do be aware that your nonverbal behavior will impact how your message is received, so remember to pay attention to what your body is communicating as well as to the tone of your voice. Once you feel you have worked through the issue, recap and work on the goals or commitments that each party has chosen to undertake.[56]

Kenneth W. Thomas and Ralph H. Kilmann have created one of the most widely known models for managing conflict.[57] In their model, two basic dimensions of behavior, assertiveness and cooperativeness, define five different modes for responding to conflict situations:

- *Competing* is assertive and uncooperative. When individuals pursue their own concerns at the other person's expense, they compete. When individuals compete, they use this power-oriented mode to win their position. When individuals compete they stand up for their rights, defend a position, or simply work to win. Competing might be used when a crisis must be addressed immediately or a top down change needs to be imposed within a certain time period.
- *Accommodating* is unassertive and cooperative and is the complete opposite of competing. When individuals accommodate, they give in and neglect their own concerns to satisfy the concerns of the other person. So when an individual uses this conflict management mode, he/she self-sacrifices to please others. When an individual accommodates, he or she obeys another person's command or gives in to another person's point of view. You might use an accommodating approach when you help an individual rebuild self-confidence, desire to maintain a positive work relationship, must resolve a problem quickly, or perceive the issues are not vital to your interests.

- *Avoiding* is unassertive and uncooperative. When individuals use this mode, they do not pursue their own concerns or those of the other individual. Basically, the individual ignores the conflict and waits for it to go away. When individuals avoid, they might diplomatically sidestep an issue, postpone an issue until a better time, or simply withdraw from a threatening situation. You may choose to use avoiding when your stake in an issue is not high, no strong interpersonal reason exists for getting involved, time is constrained, or a cooling off period is needed for people to think.

- *Collaborating* is both assertive and cooperative, which is the complete opposite of avoiding. Collaborating involves an attempt to work with others to find some solution that fully satisfies all concerns. It means digging into an issue to pinpoint the underlying needs and wants of the two individuals. Collaborating between two persons might take the form of exploring a disagreement to learn from each other's insights or trying to find a creative solution to an interpersonal problem. You choose this mode when issues are critical and managing relationships is important. Another consideration is that you actually have the time necessary to work through the issues and arrive at a solution meeting all needs.

- *Compromising* is moderate in both assertiveness and cooperativeness. The individuals want to find some expedient, mutually acceptable solution that partially satisfies both of them. It falls between competing and accommodating. Compromising gives up more than competing but less than accommodating. Likewise, it addresses an issue more directly than avoiding, but does not explore it in as much depth as collaborating. In some situations, compromising might mean splitting the difference between the two positions, exchanging concessions, or seeking a quick middle-ground solution. When you compromise, you are striving to get individuals or a team to begin a change process. So if you can achieve partial change, you can then pursue additional desired changes.

Your use of all five conflict management modes and the choice of which one to use will be dependent upon you, the other individual, and the situation. However, you should keep in mind that you do not want to rely on one particular conflict mode, as different situations call for different conflict management styles. You may find that some of the conflict modes are easier for you to use than others because you've used them before and are comfortable using them. Personality type can also influence how you use the five modes. For example, based on the Myers Briggs Type Indicator types, individuals who have preference for feeling often have difficulty using the competing mode as they naturally focus on harmony. So feeling types may avoid or accommodate because conflict creates disharmony and stress for them.

Therefore, how you choose to manage conflict is both a result of personality and the requirements of the particular situation in which you find yourself. Remember, when conflict is focused on issues and not individuals, it can foster open communication, collaboration, and creativity. In his book *Good to Great*, Jim Collins reinforced the idea that conflict is part of the perfecting and exploratory process used to confront and challenge ideas.[58]

The Six Rules for Disagreeing Agreeably

Rule #1: Give others the benefit of the doubt. Maybe the person who made that outrageous generalization isn't really insensitive. Maybe this person has had a painful experience that made him overreact.

Rule #2: After giving someone the benefit of the doubt, listen to learn and truly understand why this person holds this belief. We must let people know we've heard them and we are genuinely trying to see things from their perspective.

Rule #3: Always take responsibility for our own feelings when disagreeing with someone. Make a commitment to respond using "I" statements only. When we begin with "you" we come off as blaming and confrontational and immediately put the other person on the defensive. This reduces the chance of our point of view being heard.

Rule #4: Use a cushion. Connect or "cushion" a different opinion, starting with "I hear what you're saying" or "I appreciate your view on." Again, begin with the word "I" and not "You said . . ." or it will sound confrontational.

Rule #5: Eliminate the words "but" or "however" from our vocabulary. Once we have cushioned the other person's opinion, use "and," or pause and say nothing, following the cushion. Acknowledging the individual's point of view and following it with a "but" or "however" erases the acknowledgement.

Rule #6: State our point of view or opinion with relevant and factual evidence. Keep our emotions out of the equation by first taking time to reflect and asking yourself these questions: What do I think? Why do I think it? and What evidence do I have? Then explain: "One example is . . . ," "This shows that . . . ," and "Therefore, I think. . . . "

Source: Dale Carnegie Training E-mail June 13, 2011

Spotlight on Today's Managerial Leader

FUTREN

Nathan Kalb has over 14 years of management and operations experience. He is currently chief operating officer at Futren Corporation. In his current role, he is responsible for operations and marketing for the Georgian Club and Indian Hills Country Club, subsidiaries of Futren Corporation. Mr. Kalb also serves as an advisor for the National Alliance of Private Clubs. His responsibilities require daily interaction across multiple departments and key managers to ensure that continual operational improvement is the top priority for the company. Mr. Kalb has been a part of Futren Corporation since 2005, and has served as general manager of the Ashford Club and Indian Hills Country Club, as well as other positions within the organization. Mr. Kalb was the previous owner and operator of the North Georgia Sub Company, LLC in Forsyth County, Georgia. Nathan graduated from Florida State University with a degree in communication, and received a master's degree in business administration from Kennesaw State University. Mr. Kalb serves on the board for the Friends for the East Cobb Park, is past chair and founder of the East Cobb Chapter of Ducks Unlimited, and is currently the director of membership for the Rotary Club of East Cobb. Mr. Kalb is a volunteer with MUST ministries and Operation Mail Call. He currently resides in Marietta, Georgia, with his wife, Katie, and son, Hayes.

My Role as a Managerial Leader

I have always considered the role of a manager to be very similar to that of a coach. Like a coach, we achieve our goals through the ongoing development of our people. As in sports, bringing out the best in people mutually benefits the organization as well as the individual. Coaching is not about teaching a technical skill. It is about bringing out the very best in others, and helping them do things that they never knew they could do. It is about challenging them to be better than they think they can be, and not allowing them to let themselves down.

As COO for Futren Corporation, I am a steward of the company's assets, and our most important assets are our people. Developing people ensures that the day-to-day operational tasks take care of themselves, because the right people are in the right places, getting them done. I spend over half of my time coaching and developing the key people in our company, to ensure that they do the same for their subordinates and thus we have a depth of talent and ability for the future. I see it as my duty to advance my people to the next step in their careers, even if that means going to another company. Many people are surprised when I share that I encourage key employees to leave the company if I do not have an opportunity to promote them within our company.

We currently operate one country club property. Our golf operations department is led by the director of golf. The head golf professional runs the Pro Shop and the outside golf staff, and he reports to the director of golf. Last year, the head golf professional came to me to discuss his future. He was concerned that there was no opportunity for advancement, as our director of golf was a long-time employee who had been very successful at his job. The head pro was also extremely competent, so naturally wanted to set a path for advancement in his own career. When he sat down in my office, he simply asked me where he could go in the future. He knew that the director of golf was not going anywhere, and that we did not have another country club within the company.

My response was simple, but sincere. I told him that we hoped to acquire a second country club in the future, but that it was uncertain as to how long that would take. I told him that he would be the perfect candidate for the director of golf position at a second club. Furthermore, should he reach the point at which it was time to move to the next level, before we had another club, I would do everything possible to find him a director of golf position with another company. He seemed very surprised when I told him that. I explained that it was my job to develop him for continued advancement in his career, even if that advancement was with another company. For the rest of that year, we continued to develop him through coaching.

About a month ago, he was offered a tremendous opportunity to advance by moving to another company. As I did not have a position for him to be promoted to, I encouraged him to consider this job and that I would fully support his decision to leave our company. He ended up taking the position and I am glad that he did. Although he was a tremendous asset to our company, he needed to take the next step. Although his departure left a temporary void in our organization, we now have the opportunity to move someone into the position that is ready to take the next step, and continue coaching him for the future.

Becoming a Mentor, Coach and Counselor

As a managerial leader, you mentor, coach, and counsel. When you use coaching, mentoring, and counseling, you move the performance of your direct reports to the highest level. Organizations have long used

Coaching others to perform at their maximum potential is thus one of the most important responsibilities of every leader and should be one of the highest priorities of those in current leadership positions. Their legacy and the organization's future rest on the shoulders of those who follow them.

Source: How Do Managers Learn to Behave Like Leaders? When the Boss (does his job and) Provides Meaningful Coaching March 23, 2011 Retrieved from http://www.academyleadership .com/news.asp?page=article73

mentoring to select the next organizational leaders or high potentials while managerial leaders have used counseling to fix performance issues. Today, coaching is one of the most rapidly growing and effective strategies that you can use to help your subordinates develop.[59] Individuals who have been coached have indicated that it has increased their self-awareness, improved their ability to communicate, and developed better relationships with their coworkers. The range of improvements reported in coaching research studies has ranged from 70.9% to 93.8%.[60] In all instances, the vast majority of respondents indicated that they had changed their behavior in positive ways and that the changes had lasted across time.[61] As the popularity of coaching continues to grow, it is also being recognized as a core competency for today's managerial leaders at all levels.[62]

But what is coaching? That is a question I have posed to many individuals and found that they had different answers. Often I would learn that these individuals used mentoring and coaching interchangeably. Therefore, I felt a need for a clearer understanding of exactly what coaching was. So my faculty colleague, Stephen Brock, and I created a model to resolve the issue of "what is coaching?"

Our model is based upon the common understanding that coaching, however it is defined, is universally viewed as a helping relationship. Using that as a starting point, all helping relationships are defined along two continuums. The vertical axis focused on the help needed. For example, was help needed around a particular issue or problem or was it needed for personal development? The horizontal axis was based on the degree of intervention required from the "helper." For example, should the helper be more directive or collaborative in his or her approach to the relationship? We then identified four different types of helping relationships: mentoring, counseling, therapy, and coaching. In this model, *mentoring* is defined as a strategic approach to developing an individual (the mentee) by pairing him or her with a more experienced individual (the mentor) who will teach, counsel, sponsor, and encourage. *Counseling* is a tactical intervention typically used by a manager to correct the behavior of an employee. *Therapy* is reserved for a therapist to help an individual to understand the inner dynamics of his or her personality and to learn new ways of adjusting and dealing with life situations. We do not recommend that any managerial leader assume this role. *Coaching* is a situation in which one person works with another individual to discover, access, and leverage his or her abilities to enhance personal and professional development. Figure 2.8 presents our model.

This **Model of Helping Relationships** provides a clear distinction between each of these important relationships and allows both parties to understand the goal of their relationship.

As a managerial leader, you will play three of the four roles found in this Helping Relationships Model. As you mentor, coach, and counsel, you will serve as a sounding board and provide support for direct reports as they focus upon their personal and professional development. Your goal should be to

- create awareness of strengths and weaknesses;
- help identify ways individuals can leverage their strengths and improve or compensate for their weaknesses;
- hold individuals accountable for professional development plans.

As a mentor, coach, and counselor, you listen, ask questions, and provide feedback and encouragement. So you'll want to review those sections of this chapter when you get ready to conduct your sessions with your subordinates.

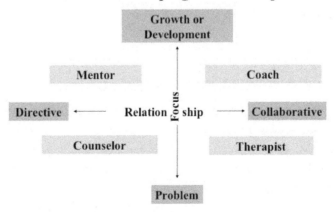

Figure 2.8. Helping Relationships Model

Another challenge you face will be to clearly communicate with your subordinates whether your role is coach, mentor, or counselor as these are three roles taking different approaches. For example when you mentor, you instruct and guide. You are much more directive than when you coach. As a mentor, you have the skills and knowledge that the mentee is seeking, so you are the sage. When you coach, you are much more collaborative and do not have to be a subject matter expert. Your role is to enable the individual to find his or her path toward development. When you coach, you help them to learn rather than teach the "how" as a mentor would do. When you counsel, you are once again more directive and focused on a particular problem. Your goal is to get the individual back on track while correcting a problem.

When you do a mentoring, coaching, or counseling session, you will want to follow four phases, which include establishing rapport, identifying session agenda, conducting the session, and concluding with action steps.

Phase One—Establishing Rapport

At your first encounter, you will want to be clear which role you are playing—mentor, coach, or counselor. You will need to determine your employee's understanding of these roles and of why the session is taking place. You will discuss the issue of confidentiality and its boundaries—that is, what you will share with others and what will not be shared. In addition you should outline how you will approach the session such as the fact that you will keep a record of the major items that are discussed and action steps.

Phase Two—Identifying Session Agenda

After you have established rapport, you may ask the individual what his or her goals are for this session. If you are conducting a counseling session, you will probably set the agenda. If you are coaching or mentoring, you will allow the individual to determine the agenda. Together you will discuss how the goals might be accomplished.

After the initial or first coaching session, ask your coachee to summarize his or her actions since the last session and tell you what he or she

Photo courtesy flickr user Clairity, CC 2.0

has done toward accomplishing the set goals. Then ask the coachee to identify the issues for that particular session.

Phase Three—Conducting the Session

During the actual session, listen, respond, and give feedback as appropriate around the issues you agree to discuss. Keep the session focused on identified concerns and goals. Many individuals find that the biggest challenge to coaching is that, as a coach, they are inclined to provide answers, which is not the goal of a coaching session. Providing answers is directive behavior and more appropriate to counseling and mentoring. When you coach, help your coachee discover the path that he or she will take. In all sessions—mentoring, coaching, and counseling—help the employee define action steps and then hold him or her accountable for following through with those steps.

Phase Four—Concluding the Session

As you come to the end of your session, you will want to summarize what you have discussed and identify any action steps to be taken. You can also ask for feedback on your performance as a coach, mentor, or counselor. Asking for feedback is a great way to make sure that the individual is clear about what role you are playing. I often tell my students that you have to be clear with direct reports and tell them exactly what role you are playing as they will generally see you only as the managerial leader. After the session, record what took place and what action steps are to be taken.

Conclusion

When A. G. Lafley stepped down as CEO of Procter & Gamble, he received widespread and well-deserved praise. During his 8-year run, Procter & Gamble's top-down, insular culture became far more collaborative and innovative. Revenues at the consumer products company doubled. How did the soft-spoken, modest Lafley make that happen? He was a superb strategist and a risk taker, but it was his commitment to one of the most overlooked and undervalued of leadership skills: communication.[63]

Just as great communication skills allow you to rise to the top, weak communication skills can take a leader down. Bob Nardelli, for example, delivered some impressive operational results during his 6-year tenure as CEO of Home Depot, but his communication style, by many accounts, was brash and autocratic. His communication skills contributed significantly to massive turnover among executives and unhappiness among shareholders, which culminated in his ouster. I even had one student who worked for Home Depot share that Nardelli had bodyguards and, if he was in the hallway, employees were not allowed to be there or had to stand back while Nardelli passed. His behavior appears to be a stark contrast to Lafley.

Lafley constantly reminded his employees of four important words: "The consumer is boss." He was a great listener, traveling the world to talk with dozens of consumers every year. He met them in their homes and joined them on trips to the grocery store to better understand what they bought and why. He made a point of getting out into the field to talk with colleagues. He knew that the best way to get good ideas was to ask for input and listen to it carefully.[64]

Research supports what I have found true in my own managerial leadership roles: that, as a leader, you spend the majority of your day interacting with others. When you become a managerial leader, the focus switches from doing things yourself to leading others to accomplish goals.

Leaders need to build and maintain relationships with all stakeholders, and that means they must give and receive feedback, master nonverbal communication, employ EQ, listen, ask questions, manage conflict, and mentor, coach, and counsel others. As Ken Blanchard has stated: "Our lives succeed or fail gradually one conversation at a time. While no single conversation is guaranteed to change the trajectory of a career, a business, a marriage, or a life, any single conversation can. The conversation is the relationship."[65] So, focus on creating open communication channels by

- Developing a positive communication climate.
- Encouraging an open door policy for direct, open communication.
- Working to eliminate communication barriers.
- Generating team or employee input and feedback.
- Conducting Q & A or town hall meetings.
- Communicating organizational decisions.
- Listening with empathy and concern while being objective.
- Asking for team members' ideas and views.
- Seeking to understand concerns and work through misunderstandings.
- Clarifying issues to facilitate greater understanding.
- Being aware of the role of nonverbal communication.
- Being visible within the organization.
- Having informal conversations with team members.

Answers to People Skills Quiz

1. (C) The palm to chest gesture indicates sincerity.
2. (D) The thumb under the chin gesture indicates critical judgment and a negative attitude. A good way to get your prospect to drop this gesture is to hand them something.
3. (E) None of the above.
4. (A) Approval.
5. (A) The chin rub gesture indicates decision. When you see this gesture, avoid the temptation to interrupt. If the gestures that follow chin stoking are positive, ask for the order.

6. (A) Stalling. When people touch their eyeglasses to their lips it signals that they're stalling or delaying a decision. If they put their glasses back on, it's a buy signal. If they put them away, you have more work to do.

7. (C) When people rub their noses, it's an indication that they don't like the subject. When you see this gesture you would be wise to probe with open-ended questions to draw out your customer's concern.

8. (C) Research indicates over 70 percent of our communication is achieved nonverbally. In addition, studies show that nonverbal communication has a much greater reliability than the spoken word. Therefore, you would be wise to rely on body language as a more accurate reflection of a person's true feelings.

9. (E) All of the above. The statue of the Three Wise Monkeys accurately depicts the three primary hand-to-face gestures associated with deceit. See no evil, hear no evil, and speak no evil.

Case for Thinking and Discussing

Instructions: Read the following article and then reflect upon the following questions.

- What lessons from this article can you apply to your organization?
- Have you ever been a witness to someone's downfall due to atrocious people skills?
- How would you rate your people skills on a scale of 1 to 10 with 10 being excellent?
- What are some challenges you have faced regarding people skills?

Can a CEO's Terrible People Skills
Affect Company Success?

By Toni Bowers Retrieved from http://www.techrepublic.com/blog/career/can-a-ceos-terrible-people-skills-affect-company-success/286

In the recent past, a number of CEOs have made headlines by being let go from their jobs due to atrocious people handling skills. How does that lack of skills translate to the bottom line?

What do these people have in common?

- Julie Roehm
- Robert Nardelli
- Steve Heyer
- Harry Stonecipher

They were all C-level executives at high-profile companies who lost their jobs due to interpersonal incompetence (aka "no people skills").

(Julie Roehm was fired from Wal-Mart; Robert Nardelli was forced out of Home Depot; Steve Heyer was let go from Coca-Cola; and Harry Stonecipher lost his job at Boeing.)

In his Forbes blog Dale Buss quotes Bob Eichinger, CEO of Lominger International, as saying such people are "promoted into their jobs for their business smarts, and they fail because of weaknesses in their people smarts."

As I think we've all learned from Donald Trump, many highly successful people rise to the top because they have some kind of genius for business. And many stay at the top in spite of a pronounced lack of interpersonal skills. As long as they're making money, the stakeholders can overlook the trickle-down problems that affect the worker bees.

Until, that is, those trickle-down problems become so severe that they start to affect profits. I shudder to think how bad things have to get for shareholders to tie in an executive's interpersonal skills with a shrinking profit margin, but I'm encouraged by the fact that sometimes the connection is indeed recognized.

CHAPTER 3

Understanding How to Communicate in Day-to-Day Situations

Each day when you arrive at work, you face multiple challenges and priorities such as returning phone calls, responding to e-mails, completing reports, and managing budgets. These tasks can overwhelm you. Sometimes you have to stop and remind yourself that the most important, and often most difficult, job is to communicate with both internal and external customers. Thomas Watson, president of IBM from 1914 to 1956, never allowed IBM to replace people as his number-one focus. The story is told that during one meeting, managers were reviewing customer problems with Mr. Watson. On the table were eight to ten piles of papers identifying the sources of problems: manufacturing, engineering, and so on. After much discussion Watson walked slowly to the front of the room and, with a flash of his hand, swept the table clean and sent papers flying. He said, "There aren't any categories of problems here. There's just one problem. Some of us are not paying enough attention to our customers." He turned and walked out.[1] This leader obviously knew the importance of communicating with others.

Research conducted by the Center for Creative Leadership shows that up to 40 percent of newly promoted managers and executives are no longer

Photo courtesy flickr user erin m, CC 2.0

in their roles within 18 months of a promotion.[2] What goes wrong? In surveys and focus groups with thousands of executives, researchers at Indiana University's Kelly School of Business identified some common reasons why new leaders can run off the rails. Some of the top derailers are

- ineffective communication skills;
- weak relationships.[3]

Nothing is more important for you than to focus each day on communicating and developing relationships. To develop relationships, you must motivate, inspire, hire, fire, coach, listen, mentor, give feedback, ask questions, manage conflict, evaluate, and encourage. Since we discussed many of those aspects of managerial leadership communication previously, the focus of this chapter will be on the more day-to-day aspects of being a managerial leader. Topics will include building trust, conducting interviews and one-on-one meetings, leading teams, and facilitating meetings.

Spotlight on Today's Managerial Leader

Rebecca Warlick has a 27-year career in developing and managing organizations involved in the development and administration of wireless Telco real estate assets. Rebecca began her career at one of the seven Regional Bell Operating Company's wireless divisions, Bell-South Mobility, Inc., where, in her 15-year tenure, she served as the director of engineering implementation and the director of real estate

development. Rebecca also served as the regional vice president and general manager of the Georgia region of Crown Castle International, where she started up and managed the Georgia region for three years. After leaving Crown Castle, Rebecca was employed by Southern Company as corporate real estate manager, where she developed a database for lease administration and lease payments that interfaced with an Oracle business platform to improve timeliness and accuracy of payments and provide a consolidated history of lease payments. Currently, Rebecca is national director of site acquisition services for one of AT&T's turf vendors, Nsoro Mastec Wireless, Inc. Rebecca enjoys organizational development and considers the company's human capital to be one of the most important assets that any company possesses.

Building Trust in a Team Environment

The foundation upon which all team performance is built is TRUST. As a manager, I have observed that when teams do not trust their peers or supervisor, they jump to conclusions about the individual's motives and intentions. They are more competitive and more protective of their own interests and goals. A person who does not trust is focused on the "I" rather than the "we." He or she hesitates to share his or her weaknesses, doubts, or concerns for fear that the team or the boss will use these things against them. He or she feels no pride in being a valuable part of a team and the team has no sense of a shared goal.

Early in my career I had a team-building exercise with a consultant whose name I no longer remember. The gentleman did, however, tell me something I have remembered for the rest of my career. He said that it is only by opening up and sharing about ourselves with others and by learning to trust others with the information that we share that a team can build trust. He further said that it is through activities experienced as a group that a team builds a basis of shared experiences that serve as the beginning of the foundation of trust.

A few years ago, I had the opportunity to establish a culture of trust in a team that had lacked this critical factor. As a new hired manager at a Fortune 500 company in the Southeast, I had a small team of five individuals. The person who hired me shared that some interpersonal problems had occurred among the team members, and that previously they had some combative moments in which HR had been involved. So it was perceived that this team needed a strong hand to bring these issues under control.

Upon joining the team, I started out by meeting with each team member individually to get his or her thoughts on the team environment, his or her role in the team, and how he or she thought the team was performing as a group. Through these conversations, I was able to begin to get a feel for the members of the team in the way they addressed areas that they saw as concerns and in how open they were about their role in any issues that had occurred. Some of the team members felt free to share some of the failings as they saw them, but only as they pertained to other people. Others dumped every possible negative thing about themselves on me as if to say, "Here is the bad and the ugly and we can only go up from here."

My next step after the meetings was to bring the team together into a group setting. My goal each week was to devote some portion of my staff meeting to helping the team members get to know each other better, open up and become more vulnerable, and begin to understand and trust their teammates.

We started with a game called Two Truths and a Lie, in which each member writes down two true things and one lie about himself or herself. The goal was to try to trick the other team members into choosing the wrong item as the lie. The team member who "fooled" the most members of the team was the winner. The beauty of this exercise was that the team learned two true things about each team member that they would not have known if we had not done this exercise. The strategy of the exercise lends itself to using things that individuals have not shared before so that the team does not immediately know whether the item is true or false.

The following week, I had the team members take a spool of thread and told them to take off a length of thread that they felt was adequate for their use. I did not share what they would be doing with the thread. Once they had all removed their thread from the spool, I told them that they would talk about themselves until they had rolled the length of thread around their index finger completely. This allowed, in most cases, more time to learn about each other while providing a fun, safe environment for sharing.

Now I felt it was time to raise individual awareness so we went offsite to do a team-building session around the Myers Briggs Personality Assessment. During this day, through interactive exercises with the facilitator, all of us learned about the various personality types, how each approached the work environment, and the different value each added to the team in terms of synergy. The team became aware that approaching someone in a somewhat brisk manner was common for an INTJ while a softer, more people-friendly approach would be more common to an ISFJ. The team began to understand that a person's work personality and communication style dictated the way he or she related to the other members of the team and, in large part, the expectations that individual had about how each team member should relate and perform. Once the team members realized that individuals had different personality types and that each person responded based upon them, they began to understand that different communication and work styles were not threatening. They also stopped taking things as personally as they had in the past.

The week following our MBTI workshop, I had each team member look at the person to his or her left and write down three things he or she admired about that person. In addition, they were also to give helpful feedback about one area on which they felt that team member could focus to improve himself or herself and the team. The team then shared the things they admired about each other in the group at large and the improvement suggestions were shared privately. As I listened to the team's conversations and feedback to each other, I noticed that the team now had a common language for talking about their differences in a more positive manner. They were starting to realize that each person brings his or her own set of strengths and weaknesses to any team. We were different, but we had a common goal, and together we could achieve that goal.

From that point forward, I started to notice that the team had begun to look forward to what activity we might be sharing that week at staff meeting. The environment was one of camaraderie and the group was beginning to function more like a team. They were jovial and joked about some of the things they had learned about each other, about some of the lies they had written, and about who had taken out the greatest length of thread and thus had had to talk the longest.

Without realizing that it had happened, they had become comfortable sharing things about themselves because the environment was fun and safe. Now they were seeking opportunities to openly share and seek each other's ideas and thoughts. Now they would admit that they might not have ALL the answers about everything to do with their jobs. The safe and trusting environment had also paved the way for them to give and receive feedback in the manner in which it was presented—to help each other and the team to grow. Since the foundation had been built for trust, I perceived the team was now ready to think as a team about their mission, vision, and goals as well as apply their strengths and differences to achieving their joint goals.

I would like to say that from here on the team had only constructive differences, but we were like any other team, so we had our moments of "storming." I would also have preferred that I not have to manage one team member out of the group, but I did what was best for the team and for that individual. The fruit of my efforts for taking time to get to know each team member was that when differences did arise, we had a common language for discussing those differences and we listened with an attitude of seeking to understand rather than confront or compete. We truly understood the power of collaboration, which led to some outstanding results.

Thinking About:

- How would you describe the level of *trust* within your department? Within the organization as a whole?
- What, specifically, are you and other leaders doing to build and sustain trust?
- How often does your department communicate to others about values and standards of conduct? Are you good at it?

Building Trust

You will spend a vast amount of each day communicating with others to build trust. When trust doesn't exist between you and your direct reports, they will look for someone else to follow, inside or outside the organization. Trust is based on integrity: being honest, keeping promises, and being fair. Leaders are judged by what they do every day. You may want to complete an exercise that James Kouzes and Barry Posner include in their book *Credibility*.[4] In the book, the authors share how they asked individuals to identify the most admired characteristics of leadership. They found that honesty was always on the top of the list! I wondered if I could get the same result so I've done that exercise with MBA and EMBA students in the United States as well as in other countries. I have also used it with corporate and executive audiences.

Regardless of the audience, I always get the result that James Kouzes and Barry Posner got—honesty tops the list. Building trust can be one of the most powerful actions you can take to grow your team. But how do you build trust and what causes you to lose it? The first step to building trust is being authentic. What you see is what you get. When you say you will do something, you do it. Your team can see that your words and actions are in alignment. Your trust erodes when others perceive that you are not **walking your talk.** Sometimes these perceptions reflect reality and sometimes they don't. So how do you change those perceptions? You must have ongoing opportunities for formal as well as informal communication. Also, you can ask for feedback and ask what you can do to support your team. It goes without saying that if you lie or keep information from your team, you will break down trust. When your employees have a positive relationship with you, they will work hard to achieve organizational goals. According to Zia et al.,[5] managerial leaders should provide greater focus on the objectivity, content, and brevity of messages, which will assist in the building of trust and respect between them and their employees. In addition, you should employ interactive communication channels with employees. These channels consist of both formal and informal meetings, such as group discussions in boardrooms, meetings over coffee, or hallway gatherings. As a managerial leader, engage your employees in an effective dialogue process to resolve their issues by selecting the most appropriate communicative channels while taking into consideration both social and cultural barriers that may exist. Alleviating these barriers improves the flow of communication, which in turn has a positive impact on the growth and profitability of an organization.

Taking these measures will result in a quick flow of information, which helps to ensure a culture of trust. With trust, you have better relationships at work, and ultimately the organization succeeds. Better communication leads to better understanding of both employees and, subsequently, customers and clients. In turn, employees and customers respond positively to these communication changes in ways that are beneficial to the whole organization.

Spotlight on a Managerial Leader

Dr. Arky Ciancutti's interest in effective teamwork grew out of his work as an emergency department physician. He helped establish the first specialist emergency departments at several hospitals. During these years, he noticed that health care delivery was sometimes compromised by ineffective communication, confusion about priorities, or overlapping efforts. His subsequent research led to an identification of the components of successful working relationships. Dr. Ciancutti has taught teamwork and leadership at the Stanford Sloan Program, Graduate School of Business, Stanford University. He is the first non-employee in IBM's history to teach the IBM Basic Beliefs (Respect for the Individual) to IBM management.

Ten Actions a Leader Can Take to Build Trust

1. **To build mistrust:** Talk with others about problems you are having with a peer without doing everything reasonably possible to solve the problem through direct communication with that peer.

   To build trust: Solve problems through direct communication at the lowest equivalent level: yourself and peers; yourself and your direct manager; yourself, your manager, and her manager.

2. **To build mistrust:** Take credit for yourself, or allow others to give you credit for an accomplishment that was not all yours.

   To build trust: Share credit generously. When in doubt, share.

3. **To build mistrust:** Make a pretended or "soft" commitment (e.g., "I'll respond later.").

   To build trust: When in doubt about taking on a commitment, air your concerns with the relevant parties. When engaged in an ongoing commitment, communicate anticipated slippage as soon as you suspect it.

4. **To build mistrust:** Manage and supervise from behind your desk only.

   To build trust: Spend "informed" time mingling, asking nonassumptive questions, making only promises you can keep, working back through existing lines of authority.

5. **To build mistrust:** Be unclear or not exactly explicit about what you need or expect. Assume that anyone would know to do or not do that.

   To build trust: Be explicit and direct. If compromise is productive, do it in communication, not in your mind alone.

6. **To build mistrust:** Withhold potentially useful information, opinions, or action until the drama heightens, thus minimizing your risk of being wrong and maximizing credit to you if you're right.

   To build trust: Be timely; be willing to be wrong.

7. **To build mistrust:** Communicate with undue abruptness when others venture new opinions or effort.

   To build trust: Acknowledge the intent and risk of innovation first, and then address the issue with your honest opinion.

8. **To build mistrust:** Withhold deserved recognition at times when you yourself are feeling underrecognized.

   To build trust: Extend yourself beyond your own short-term feeling and validate success or new effort.

9. **To build mistrust:** Hold in your mind another department's productivity or behavior as a reason for less cooperation.

   To build trust: Get in direct, tactful communication, airing your problem and seeking a win/win resolution.

10. **To build mistrust:** Make performance evaluation time the only, or primary, time for coaching input.

   Retrieved from http://www.learningcenter.net/library/counseling .shtml

---

Trust is something that must be earned and you should not take it for granted. The corporate function for building trust in organizations is communication. Companies can build a culture of trust by sharing information quickly and freely, and by building relationships with employees and their stakeholders that enable their organizations to succeed.[6]

Hyler Bracey in his book entitled *Building Trust* provides a five-step model for building trust.

T—Be transparent. Be open, readable, and vulnerable. What you see is what you get.

R—Be responsive. Give honest feedback respectfully, spontaneously, and nonjudgmentally.

U—Show understanding. Whatever I say or do comes from my heart, so that my behavior is compassionate, affirming, and understanding.

S—Be sincere. Be congruent, accountable, and keep my actions consistent with my words.

T—Be trustworthy—Be honest, honor your word, and manage by agreements.[7]

Spotlight on Today's Managerial Leader

Chris M. Festa is a consummate business professional with over 26 years experience in sales and IT management. He is currently a senior technical team lead with AT&T. In this role, he directs a group whose focus is to support corporate initiatives in the Southeast wholesale ordering arena. This role requires him to work with multiple software and hardware developers both domestically and internationally to ensure that code functionality meets the needs of the AT&T business unit, competitive local exchange carriers, and the public service commissions in the Southeast. Chris received his Master's in Business Administration, with honors, in 2006 from the Michael C. Coles College of Business, at Kennesaw State University. He is married, has two wonderful daughters, and is an active member of the EMABARK Board of Directors at the Michael C. Coles College of Business.

On Leading Teams

I came across a quote by Barbara De Angelis that epitomizes what I have learned about being a team member and leading teams: "Living with integrity means: Not settling for less than what you know you deserve in your relationships, asking for what you want and need from others, speaking your truth, even though it might create conflict or tension, behaving in ways that are in harmony with your personal values, making choices based on what you believe, and not what others believe."

For me, this passage helps define the essence of teaming, which is to be honest with yourself and with others. Only by being honest with yourself can you establish trust with others. Trust is the groundwork for all relationships and without this trust, a relationship is doomed to fail. However, the first obstacle is to understand your true self; only then can others who share your same interests, goals, and beliefs begin to trust you. In addition, trust can only be obtained when you exemplify your true self by being transparent. This allows others to know exactly who you are and how they will work and interact with you. In the book *Building Trust,* Hyler Bracey shared that transparency is the first step in establishing trust. Bracey's five-step approach recognizes the premise that as individuals we must be transparent, responsive, caring, sincere, and trustworthy. All of these traits are important; however, they are meaningless if the individual is unable to define himself or herself first.

Understanding trust enabled me to recognize the different roles that we play while engaged in a team environment. For example, on occasion, I act as a traffic cop keeping people from colliding emotionally, or even physically. At other times, I initiate discussion and dialogue. Serving in these roles enables me to grasp the importance of delegation and shared responsibilities so that the team can produce a deliverable in a specific period. When I assign and explain team roles, each team member understands how the completion of his or her assignment contributes to the achievement of the team's project. In this situation, team members become equally important because if any one task is not complete, the team fails to achieve its objective.

In the past, my previous experiences defined my views of teaming, which were that if I wanted something done right, I had to do it myself. However, after learning about myself through various assessments such as the Herman Brain Dominance Instrument and Big Five Personality Instrument, my awareness of different personality and thinking styles has allowed me to effectively understand how and why each of my team members thinks and acts in a certain way.

I capitalize on this new understanding by formatting a new belief on teaming, which focuses on building and maintaining trust while utilizing each team member's special skills. This focused understanding allows my team to apply individual and group skills to maximize our potential to succeed in any endeavor. Because we are all aware of individual and team strengths and weaknesses, we know when each of us needs to back away or step in to assist. Together we can now reach our personal and organizational goals. If you choose to raise your awareness of yourself and others, then I believe you have taken the first step to becoming an effective team leader.

Creating Positive Teams Whether Virtual or Face-to-Face

In one of the best books on teaming, *The Wisdom of Teams*, Katzenbach and Smith defined a team:

> A team is a small number of people with complementary skills who are committed to a common purpose, performance goals, and approach for which they hold themselves mutually accountable.[8]

ABCs *of Managing a Team*

Acknowledge Good Work
Be Honest
Communicate Effectively
Don't Throw Them Under the Bus
Evaluate Performance
Form Relationships
Give Credit Where Credit Is Due
Hire the Right People
Identify and Share Goals
Just Delegate
Keep the Team Updated
Listen to Feedback
Monitor Work
Never Miss the Celebration
Open Your Door
Pay on Time
Quit Assuming
Resolve Conflicts Immediately
Spell Out Expectations
Thank Them
Utilize Individual Skills
Volunteer
Work for Improvement
X Marks the Path for Reaching Specified Rewards
Yell in Private
Zip It

Written by Alyssa Gregory on May 13, 2009
Sitepoint
http://www.sitepoint.com/team-management/

So you might be wondering how a virtual team differs from a team. The primary difference is the dimension of physical space or distance between team members. As you might imagine, this distance significantly affects the way team members interact. However, the global expansion of electronic connections, particularly the new digital media, provides the link for virtual team members to interact. In all other ways, virtual teams emulate face-to-face teams.

Now that you know what a team is, what does it take for a team to be high-performing? It takes understanding of how the team fits into the overall organization and creation of a team communication protocol.

Sally Smith, CEO of Buffalo Wild Wings, follows a collaborative management style. She strives for teamwork and trust. She feels that the longer you work with a group, the more that trust comes. If you talk to anyone at the company, they know teamwork is expected. Sally joined a struggling Buffalo Wild Wings as CFO in 1994. She took the helm two years later and used her financial savvy and leadership skills to build an infrastructure that turned Buffalo Wild Wings into a thriving national brand.

She credits teamwork for increasing sales, which grew to $613 million in 2010. In 1996, sales had been at $14.6 million. Then sales rose to $127 million in 2003 the year the company went public. Stock price has soared more than 500 percent since its first month.

The number of the company's restaurants has grown from 71 in 1996 to 769 as of June 23, 2011. She expects to have 825 units by the end of 2011.

Smith recognizes her firm's 45,000 employees for doing their jobs every day. She said her recipe for success is to hire great people. Find people with passion for what they do and let them do their jobs. Be open, share your thoughts and ideas, and encourage ideas. Pick the ideas that you think can have the most impact. And share the success.

Sally is selective about who joins her team. During her first week at the company, she noted at the end of the week that the trash can was full. She went to her colleague and asked when the cleaning service would come in and take out the trash. He told her, "We're the cleaning service." Keeping that in mind, Smith looks for employees who are willing to take out the trash, which translates into being willing to jump in and do whatever it takes to get the job done.

COO Jim Schmidt praises Smith for nurturing an inspiring atmosphere. Schmidt has said that they have a culture in which people care about each other. Everyone trusts that management tries to do the right thing. He thinks that Smith has created a great vision for the company and that people buy into it. Their employees believe the company has a bright future and Sally created that vision.

Schmidt shared that Sally was his role model. When he came to the company in 2002, he had no experience in managing people. He's learned a tremendous amount from Sally about being a leader.

A Seasoned Chef Executive
By Marilyn Much
July 25, 2011
Investor's Business Daily
Leaders & Success Pages A3 and A6

How the Team Fits Into the Overall Organization

Your team must understand how it fits into the overall organization. Each team member needs to understand the context of the team's work, which includes understanding the relevance of each team member's job and how those jobs impact the effectiveness of others and the overall team effort. Too often people are asked to work on part of a task without being told how their role contributes to the desired end result, much less how their efforts are impacting the ability of others to do their work. Understanding the big picture promotes collaboration, increases commitment, and improves quality.

Team Communication Protocol

To facilitate growth and development, an effective team should create a team communication protocol. This document will provide clear guidelines for communication and for the amount of personal communication that is expected. Your team members will need to articulate their concerns in thoughtful and persistent ways and listen to each other. As team members view their world from their frame of reference or perception, they must work hard to understand the reality of their teammates. If your team can meet face-to-face to create this document, they will improve processes and build more open, trusting relationships. If the creation must take place virtually, you should at least use a webcam so that members can see the faces of their team members.

For virtual teams, the lack of physical contact may erode meaning and understanding. Therefore, the clearer and more specific the team communication protocol is, the better the team will function. For this reason, prepare thoroughly and make assumptions, expectations, roles, procedures, standards, norms, and processes explicit. If your members make assumptions based on past experience without a clear definition among teammates, you will waste time and effort.

Once your team has developed a clear agreement, members will have a common language to help them to work with a minimum of misunderstandings. A team communication protocol represents shared agreement on how to complete assigned tasks. The more thought and time you invest initially in your team communication protocol, the fewer the difficulties your team will encounter later. The common features of a team communication protocol include a purpose statement, goals, and team norms.

Purpose or mission. Your team should compose a clear, written team purpose statement so that everyone understands the expectations and responsibilities. Make your written statement concise and focused, showing how you will work.

Goals or objectives. Effective teams have agreed-upon goals that are simple, measurable, and clearly relevant to the team's task. Make your goals measurable and obtainable while spelling out the specific actions and activities needed to obtain results. Do not use general terms such as "To communicate effectively." Instead, be specific regarding how the team will communicate. For example, a specific goal might be "Team members will communicate by e-mail at least twice weekly." This statement provides a specific, realistic, and measurable goal or action called a SMART goal. Each goal includes key measurable metrics that are made available to all team members and that can be used to determine team effectiveness and improvement. Understanding and working toward these common goals together is crucial for the team's success. Figure 3.1. displays the elements of a SMART goal.

Team norms. Norms contribute to and reinforce team unity and can be anything team members feel is important for everyone to commit to do. For instance, one item might be that all team members check the team's database once a day to monitor the progress of the project. Other norms might deal with the way the team will handle information. Other agreed-upon practices might cover ways to deal with conflict. For example, a team might have a rule that if one team member has a conflict with another and it can't be resolved electronically, then they must phone or meet in person.

Establishing team norms helps clarify expectations about acceptable and unacceptable behaviors for team members. Team norms guide

S—Specific	When possible, list your goals in quantitative terms. Not all goals can be expressed in numerical terms, but vague goals and objectives have little motivating power.
M—Measurable	Provide your measurement steps and keep the steps small so that you can measure them in increments and assign specific achievement on the way to the goal.
A—Assignable	Identify who should be responsible for completing this goal.
R—Realistic	Make the goal challenging but not unreasonably difficult. If a goal appears too difficult, individuals will give up; if it is too easy, individuals may not feel motivated.
T—Time Period	Set a time frame and stick to it. A time period provides a deadline on which goal attainment will be measured.

Figure.3.1. SMART Goal

participation, communication, conflict management, meeting management, problem solving, and decision making. If your team is virtual, you may need to have more unique and detailed process norms. Team norms may include phone, audio conference, and videoconference etiquette as well as how to manage meetings. These norms may specifically address how to ensure participation from all team members and may include protocols for virtual team meetings, such as saying your name before speaking, using the mute button when you do not talk, giving people who are using a second language time to collect their thoughts, using a meeting agenda, taking and distributing minutes, and rotating time zones. Other team norms might include guidelines for

- acceptable time frames for returning phone calls and for the use of BlackBerrys and iPads;
- e-mail usage—when it should be used, when it should not be used, and how e-mail messages should be constructed, including when to flag messages as urgent and as important;
- when to use face-to-face meetings, teleconferences, or videoconferences;
- how the team will review and approve each other's work, including which team members will review work and which ones can approve deliverables;
- procedures for scheduling meetings using group scheduling systems; and
- the types of technological applications the team will use and the policies regarding upgrades.

When your team includes members from a variety of national or cultural groups, the creation and establishment of team norms become even more important as members work together to learn about each other's respective cultures, how they may differ, how to overcome these differences, and how to use them to the team's advantage. When your team comprises individuals residing in different countries, your members must realize that the quality of ideas is important and that all team members should work hard to make sure that all members have an opportunity to voice their thoughts and ideas. If your members are not completely sure they understand a message, they should be encouraged to restate the idea to make sure they interpreted the message correctly. Time differences sometimes

Building Trust in Teams

Kennesaw State University and the Helsinki School of Business and Economics, located in Helsinki, Finland, formed an educational partnership to provide students with an opportunity to experience international virtual teaming. When the students from Kennesaw State University and their Finnish teammates first began to formulate their communication protocols, the Finnish students became uncomfortable with the idea of signing the team communication protocol. In Finland, business partnerships are formed by shaking hands. The Finnish students were offended that their American teammates had asked them to sign the agreement and perceived it to be more a legal contract than a protocol for the team. They perceived that the U.S. students did not trust them. The norm for the U.S. students was to always get it in writing and have it signed. It was not until these international teams had met face-to-face that they were able to work through this cultural difference and move their team forward.

At the conclusion of the Kennesaw State–Helsinki virtual teaming experience, the international teams recommended that the following year's program begin with a videoconference to facilitate interaction.

make it difficult to pull off live discussions. Some organizations allow their team members to work at home to meet these time challenges. On days that team members need to have a night meeting, they stay home and may even take a nap during the day to be refreshed for their night meeting. My Sunday school teacher worked for Coca-Cola, where his job required him not only to travel internationally, but also to attend and lead many virtual team meetings. He often shared stories about getting up in the middle of the night to attend a virtual meeting. Most of the time, you will be able to use e-mail to address the time differences. However, be aware that it does take longer to make decisions with the lag in response time.

Occasionally, you might experience miscommunication and disagreement when working in a team environment. Therefore, instead of avoiding the situation, address the issue immediately, giving team members a chance to voice concerns, agree on a resolution, and move on.

Communication will provide the most important bond between you and your teams. Your virtual teams will rely more on effective written communication while your face-to-face teams will use more oral communication. Because of the affordability of webcams, virtual team members can see each other when they meet, which strengthens interpersonal relationships because members are able to see the nonverbal behavior as well as hear the verbal words spoken. So whether you lead a face-to-face team or a virtual team, communication and collaboration will be critical for the team's success.

Importance of Communication and Collaboration

Your team must communicate in order to share critical information, leave nothing to chance, and have personal contact. Make special efforts to create fun, celebrate progress and successes, and show the team's personality. Technology facilitates your team's ability to do these things. However, effective communication depends on much more than just developing writing strategies and technology tools. At the root of effective communication lies the importance of strong interpersonal relationships and support systems. Your team members must choose to communicate completely with each other. Communication issues are often the most voiced complaint among virtual and face-to-face team members. Virtual team members found messages difficult to interpret, especially if someone was being sarcastic or facetious. Light or constructive criticisms sometimes were judged more harshly than intended. Conflict seems to escalate when no opportunities arise to stop someone in the hallway and clear up a misunderstanding shortly after it occurs. In a virtual team, miscommunication can simmer and erupt at an unforeseen time, causing consternation and surprise.

If your team has a steady flow of communication, it will embrace collaboration and have a solid sense of interdependency, which will provide opportunities for learning, growth, and improvement. Without this sense of interdependency in responsibility and reward, blaming behaviors can occur, which will quickly erode team effectiveness. So what do you do as team leader to ensure the team's success?

Photo courtesy flickr user Savijana, CC 2.0

Professor Johan Berlett at Lund University researched how much effect a manager has on enhancing productivity of her or his team. According to the professor, "The best working climate is found at companies where the manager and the staff interact and where the manager creates good conditions for the staff to manage themselves and each other."

Source: Solutions for Leaders February 16, 2011
Message from Martha and Thad

The Roles of the Effective Team Leader

Your role as the team leader should include the following:

- **Promote understanding** of why a group of people needs to be a team. The team needs to understand its shared goals and what each team member brings to the team that is relevant and crucial to its overall successes.
- **Ensure the team has adequate knowledge** to accomplish its task. This knowledge includes information relevant to the team's goals and individual job competencies.

- **Facilitate effective interaction** in such a way as to ensure problem solving, decision making, and coordination of effort.[9]

Your first task is to make sure you have recruited the right people for the team. When you are choosing whom to hire or select for your team, you should be sure to take note of natural skills and abilities since not every person is capable of doing every job. Teams are interdependent, with team members having complementary, not identical, skills.

If training is needed regarding virtual and collaborative tools, the effective team leader provides it so that team members have the skills and resources needed to get the job done. You may also want to do some cross-training to give team members a greater awareness of how their jobs are related and interdependent.

By this point, you probably know that you have to provide accurate, detailed, and timely feedback. Receiving timely feedback is crucial to the effectiveness of the team, and you must remember to provide both BET and BEAR feedback for the whole team and each team member. The feedback should also be timely so that team members can make adjustments and corrections.

If you have instilled a culture of lifelong learning, your team will view mistakes as opportunities to improve the team's process and results. When they improve their team processes, they solve problems without asking you to fix the problems, thus creating an environment that promotes problem solving. When direct reports are allowed to create their own solutions (rather than having you impose a solution upon them), team members are more proactive and engaged. Teams also have greater ownership of solutions they discover for themselves.

Keep in mind that a willingness to participate collaboratively as a team member does not guarantee a successful outcome. People thrown into a collaborative situation, especially those without experience and training in what a team truly is, will need your guidance to be successful. As the managerial leader, you will need to promote understanding, ensure adequate knowledge, and facilitate effective interaction. If you do these things well, your team will achieve high performance.

Conducting One-on-One Meetings or Interviews

To keep the communication flowing, you'll want to schedule periodic one-on-one meetings. Effective interviewing is a conversation that is planned and has specific purposes.[10] This one-on-one meeting is driven by a list of questions versus other types of agendas. We often associate interviewing with only hiring, but you can use many forms of interviews, including counseling, employment, exit, grievance, informational, interrogational, and performance review, to name a few. So you can see interviewing is not just about hiring, but more about internal communication. Spending time one-on-one with your direct reports allows you to truly get to know your team members while building trust. For this chapter, we will focus on two specific types of interviews: performance review and employment.

Guidelines for Preparing and Conducting Interviews

Regardless of the type of interview conducted, you will follow some basic guidelines. These guidelines include preparing, setting the tone, creating an outline, listening, managing your time, and taking notes.

Prepare. This step may seem obvious, but you will want to review your notes from your last meeting and jot down any questions that you want to be sure to ask. Before scheduling the meeting, ask yourself the following questions:

- What is my purpose?
- How will I maximize our time together?
- What do I know about the other person?
- What are his or her needs and motivations?
- Where will the interview take place?

Set the tone. Let your employees know that you look forward to the anticipated meeting and assure them that what is said "stays in the room." They need to know that they have a safe environment in which to share. Let them know that you appreciate the time they are spending with you.

Create an outline. Don't underestimate the value of preparing several questions beforehand. Too often, we get too busy and then realize we forgot to ask an important question. You should remember to focus on more open-ended, probing, elaborating, and reflecting questions than closed-ended questions. Try to ask a good mix of questions—those that give insight into behavior, elicit opinion, demonstrate experience, and reveal background.

Listen. Don't forget that it should be a two-way dialogue. Interaction means that both parties have the opportunity to talk. You should not be the one doing all of the talking. A vast majority of your time should be spent listening to issues, concerns, and opportunities.

Manage your time. If you've set aside an hour for an interview, do your best to stick with that schedule. However, be prepared to cut the meeting short if needed and don't waste your time or your direct report's time by stretching the meeting out unnecessarily.

Take notes. Forget about remembering everything that transpires during a one-on-one meeting. Take notes so that you can review the meeting at a later time.

Basic Interview Organization

All interviews follow the same format. They consist of three phrases: opening, question-response, and closing.[11]

Opening. Spend approximately one to four minutes building rapport and making the individual feel comfortable. As the interviewer, select a place that is relatively free from distractions. After establishing rapport, set the ground rules, state the purpose, and share how long you anticipate the interview will last.

Question–Response Phase. The heart of the interview is the question–response portion. Make sure you have a two-way dialogue and that you have your outline and questions to ask.

Closing. For this phase, you will begin with a summary of the major points covered and any conclusions reached. The summary allows you to check for understanding and commitment to any promised actions. As the managerial leader, leave the meeting by thanking the individual for his or her time.

Photo courtesy flickr user alancleaver_2000, CC 2.

Conducting a Performance Review

Managing your direct reports' performance should be a year-long process that ends with the annual performance review. The annual performance review should truly provide no surprises if you have been doing ongoing performance management. When you do your performance appraisal, focus both on evaluation of performance and on developmental opportunities. As part of the performance appraisal, you can involve your subordinates in setting their work performance goals and developmental goals. You will

- explain that work performance goals are a way of ensuring that everyone has a clear understanding of expectations and developmental goals that provide opportunities for growth;
- ask your direct reports to identify key components of their jobs;
- have your employees break the major components of their jobs into specific tasks; and
- ask them to write a performance standard and a developmental goal for each key task.

When you must determine why an employee is not performing at his or her peak, determine if the lack of performance results from skill deficiency or from a non-skill reason. If the issue is related to skills, provide additional training. If the problem is not related to skills, probe to discover what is causing your employee to underperform.

When you conduct the actual performance review, follow these steps:

- Seek the person's own opinion of his or her performance.
- Give honest praise.
- Allow your direct report to specify areas of improvement and to set goals.
- Summarize what you discussed.
- End on an encouraging note.

Conducting an Employment Interview

When you must conduct an employment interview, follow the steps previously discussed for the performance review. You will begin by establishing rapport. One way to do this with a job candidate is to talk about some common experience such as belonging to the same professional organization. As part of the opening, explain that you will be taking notes.

After establishing rapport, start asking questions about past job performance. I would recommend that you use the behavioral-based interviewing approach, which is based upon the premise that the single best predictor of future job performance is past behavior. Use open-ended questions to encourage the job candidate to share with you his or her past experiences. You typically start with more general questions and then move into more targeted ones. You will probably have to probe to clarify understanding. You may have to give the job candidate an example of the kind of detail you want. For example, you might say something like "Bob, you can help me by sharing a specific time you had a conflict with a customer." As you probe, listen for specific names, places, dates, and details versus generalities such as "always" or "never."

Some key phrases that allow you to probe include the following:

- Tell me about a time.
- Describe a situation.
- Tell me exactly how you dealt with . . .
- It will help me if you can describe in more detail how you handled . . .[12]

When you are asking questions that require individuals to think back, give them time. If you see that they are getting nervous and uncomfortable with the silence, just assure them that they will think of an example.

When you perceive that you are getting a one-sided picture of a job candidate, whether good or bad, you can ask for contrary evidence. Asking for contrary evidence prevents you from forming erroneous assumptions or first impressions. If, for example, a job candidate has talked about how she has handled a difficult customer and all of her examples have been positive, ask for an example of a time when things didn't go as planned. Or if you think the job candidate did not handle a customer well, ask for contrary evidence for that situation as well. For example, if the individual has told you of several instances of going against normal procedure, ask him to tell you of a time he did follow procedure even though he thought he had a better idea.[13]

After you have asked the questions you desire, allow the individual being interviewed to ask questions of you. You may want to take notes on the questions the individual asks you. Then when he or she has no more questions, close the interview and thank the candidate. You will summarize the next *action* step and what will be happening next. Finally, review your notes and evaluate the candidate's suitability for your position.

You want to make sure you hire the right person who has the right skills and a positive attitude and who will fit with your organization's culture. Conducting internal interviews such as performance appraisals and periodic one-on-one meetings are important tools for maintaining and improving employee work performance.

Spotlight on Today's Managerial Leader

Kathryn O'Neil is a former senior consultant, talent management, at RockTenn in Norcross, Georgia. After a career of over 25 years in human resources development in various industry settings, including newspaper publishing, homebuilding, banking, and manufacturing, she has become an Assistant Professor of Business Communication at Sam Houston State University in Huntsville, Texas. Katie has designed and delivered training in sales, management and supervision, customer service, and technical topics. She is an expert meeting facilitator as well as a certified Six Sigma Green Belt. She earned her PhD from Georgia State University in 2003 and holds a BA in journalism and MA in communication.

Creating Effective Flipcharts

When leading a face-to-face meeting or providing a training session, you may want to involve your audience. Engagement is critical so that you can get buy-in for any changes or improvements you make in your organization. You want to get your participants to share their ideas, thoughts, and feelings. Using a flipchart allows you to facilitate this sharing. In addition, a flipchart gives you an opportunity to clarify, simplify, and reinforce your key learning points. The following paragraphs provide some tips on how to create an effective flipchart, how to use it during your meeting, how to post each one as you complete it, and how to use all the flipcharts to summarize and close your meeting.

Creating Flipcharts

The following are some simple tips to follow when you create flipcharts.

- Use water-based markers. They will not bleed through to the next page, wall, or tabletop and typically they have no unpleasant odor.
- Use dark colors (black, blue, green, or brown) for text. Use bright or light colors—orange, pink, yellow, or red—for highlighting only as they are more difficult to read.
- Alternate colors from line to line. Using this strategy helps to separate ideas when capturing the comments from others.
- Use three main colors for each page as using too many colors may be distracting to the audience.
- White out small mistakes instead of recreating the whole page.
- Keep letters one to two inches high. Smaller letters, as you might imagine, are difficult to read. If you use large letters, you will not put too much information on the page, which might overwhelm your audience.
- Keep drawings and charts simple. If your drawings, charts, or graphs are too complex, your audience might get confused.
- Skip a page to write on every other page. Sometimes the paper is thin so the audience members can see through to the next page. Skipping a page stops that from happening.
- Use tape tabs or fold down a corner to help you find your place or to show a page that you have hidden on purpose.
- Use pencil notes. Your audience can't see your notes if you write them lightly in pencil on the chart, and you will not have to refer to a separate note pad or to your facilitator's guide for details.

Using Flipcharts

- Hug your chart. Stand close to one side of the chart with one arm behind and above the stand. This technique prevents you from completely turning your back to your audience and also prevents you from talking to your flipchart.

- Print. Cursive writing is faster, but your audience will find it harder to read.
- Write exactly what people say. If someone's idea or thought is too long, ask him or her to reword it to something shorter.
- Get permission to abbreviate.
- Use arrows, circles, and underlines. Using these techniques allows you to reinforce ideas while encouraging your audience to participate.
- Use pencil notes. Make notes that cue you what to do next.
- When you turn a page, grasp the paper and keep it close to the chart. You do this as you roll your page to turn it.
- Touch, turn, and tell. Touch the word or line, turn to face your audience, and tell them what you want to say. When you refer to prepared flipcharts, use this technique to allow your participants to follow your review of the chart. It also prevents you from talking to your chart.

Posting Flipcharts

- Pretear pieces of masking tape. You can put these on the back or the side edge of your flipchart stand. Rip with confidence. Grasp the page at the bottom and holding either top corner above the perforation, tear the chart from right to left or left to right.
- Post only the charts you need to refer to later. Posting too many charts will result in a cluttered atmosphere.
- Rearrange and prioritize. Periodically, you may want to rearrange your posted charts to reflect your priorities. In addition, you should remove any that are no longer applicable to your topic.
- Avoid making comments about tearing. If you accidentally tear a page, just ignore it or make a joke about it.

Summarizing and Closing With Flipcharts

- Briefly review topics using posted charts. Flip back to previous charts or review posted charts.

- Circle and underline key ideas on previous charts.
- Wrap up the meeting by linking ideas to the next steps to be taken.

According to a recent study by the management consulting firm McKinsey, across industries, frontline managers spend 30 to 60 percent of their time on administrative work and meetings and 10 to 50 percent on nonmanagerial tasks (traveling, participating in training, taking breaks, conducting special projects, or undertaking direct customer service or sales themselves).

Source: Six Keys to Unlocking the Potential of Frontline Managers
By Gwen Clarke, Profiles International, 2011

Leading Effective Meetings

As a managerial leader, you probably attend and lead numerous meetings each day. If you involve your employees in a meeting, you will probably have more employee commitment, better decisions, and quicker completion of projects. However, you must weigh the advantages of meetings against the disadvantages. Meetings do take a great deal of time and cost money. They can be ineffective if you run the meeting poorly, invite too many or the wrong people, don't start and end on time, and don't manage the interaction between the attendees.

An effective meeting can achieve its objectives in a short time to the satisfaction of all the participants. However, sometimes a meeting is called when it is not needed. Before you call a meeting, ask yourself these questions:

- Have we done our homework?
- Have we prepared for the meeting?
- Have the discussion ideas been fully developed?
- Can a meeting speed up my work?
- Do I need input from others?
- Will enough information be presented to make a decision?
- Can a decision be made immediately after receiving the information?

Types of Meetings

The reasons for having meetings can be best understood by examining the different types of meetings. When you call a meeting, you may develop ideas, elicit information, make plans, or make decisions.

To develop ideas. Such meetings take place when you need to expand present activities of the participants. Do not allow this meeting to turn into a "bull session." Specify the areas to be discussed and the constraints on the discussions.

To elicit information. Hold this type of meeting if individuals need to know information and need to interact about it. Participants should write a summary of their information before they meet and submit it to the meeting leader.

To make plans. Hold this type of meeting after you have developed your ideas and elicited information. Here, you and the participants combine ideas and information to create functional programs for implementation. During such a meeting, discuss resources needed for plans, people, timetables needed for plans, and alternatives.

To make decisions. Hold this meeting when you need approval of your plans from a higher authority. All the above meetings should have already been held, as this meeting will be reserved for presenting proposals, answering specific questions relevant to the proposal, and moving to a decision.

Photo courtesy flickr user erin m, CC 2.0

Problem Solving Methods

When you lead a meeting, you will decide how the group will discuss each issue. You can choose from three commonly used problem solving methods: **reflective thinking, nominal group,** and **brainstorming approaches.**

Reflective thinking model. This method starts with defining the problem. Often what you believe to be the problem is in reality just a symptom of something else. Therefore, the problem must be accurately defined. After the group has defined the problem, they can analyze and discuss it. The group determines a standard or set of criteria to measure the problem and develops possible solutions. They must evaluate each solution and pick the best one. After the team chooses the solution, they must decide how to implement it. An important final step involves evaluating the implementation and getting feedback from the individuals involved.

Nominal group model. When individuals use this method, they begin by listing ideas independently, without talking to other members. Then, as a group, the participants go round robin to compile a list, recording at least one item from each person's list until they have included all items. As a group, they revise this list of ideas—rewording, combining, and avoiding duplicates. Next, each person independently orders the master list. The last step requires that the group collate these orderings. This method allows all individuals to participate in the decision, because each team member must first generate a written list.

Brainstorming model. To conduct an effective brainstorming session, you must divide the session into two distinct stages. **Stage one** allows participants simply to record their ideas without evaluations or reactions. Listing ideas helps individuals to feel more comfortable sharing. A team recorder lists every item as stated on a flip chart. **Stage two** allows the group to review, list, and group related items, and to strike irrelevancies. From the more organized list, the group can work on reaching a decision.

As chair, you will ultimately decide how to resolve the issues the team has discussed. You can choose from a decision by a single individual, a decision by a minority, a decision by majority, or a decision by consensus. The value of a given decision making mechanism depends upon the situation, the participants, and the task. Take care not to base your choices on a method, ideology, or habit. After reaching the decision, finalize how to implement the decision. Then formulate a specific list stating action items, who will perform them, and deadlines for completion.

Decision Making Mechanisms

Once the group has explored the problem, they must make a decision. As previously stated, you will choose from four decision making mechanisms.

Decision by a single individual. You, as chair, make the final decision, with the group serving as a sounding board. This strategy works best when the individual has the competence to make a decision or time is critical.

Decision by a minority. Often one or two people who are more vocal can make the decision for the group although they are a small minority. Often these more vocal members think others agree because they have remained silent. So the minority represents the majority because those individuals did not speak. This method may be inefficient if the minority members are not competent. Additionally, the other members may not support the decision.

Decision by majority. The most popular decision making mechanism is majority rule. After a thorough discussion of the issue, the chair calls for a vote. A shortcoming of this mechanism is that the losers may not support the decision and may feel left out.

Decision by consensus. This mechanism is one of the most effective. When using the consensus method, the team may reach a final decision that may not have been anyone's first choice. However, each person willingly agrees to support and implement the decision after exploring all other alternatives. Consensus decision making requires time to explore the advantages and disadvantages of the alternatives, but it eventually provides a decision agreeable to all. The team reaches this type of decision by agreement, not by voting.

Task Duties When You Serve as Chair

When you serve as chair, you have multiple roles to play. You must manage both the task duties and the people duties. Before your meeting begins, you must do some work. As chair, you must develop an agenda, select the participants, and decide where and when to hold the meeting.

Developing an agenda. Every meeting should have an agenda. (See Figure 3.2.) Agendas formalize the activities to take place during the time allotted to accomplish the objectives. Too often, individuals do not distribute a complete agenda to allow individuals to prepare for the meeting. The complete agenda should guide the discussion and provide the meeting with a sense of direction. Deliver your written agenda at least 24 hours before the meeting, if possible, so that participants have enough

---

TO: Gladiators
FROM: Robert
DATE January 30, 2011
SUBJECT: Meeting to discuss and develop our team charter.
PLACE & TIME OF MEETING: Wimba Team 1 Classroom 7:00 p.m.–9:00 p.m.

Prior to meeting: Review team project guidelines.
Bring to meeting: Bring copy of team communication protocol.

For discussion:

8:30–8:45 p.m.	Review upcoming team project.
8:45–9:00 p.m.	Review upcoming individual oral presentation.
9:00–9:15 p.m.	Review team communication protocol.

For decision:

9:15–9:45 p.m.	Add the necessary changes to team communication protocol.
9:45–10:00 p.m.	Prepare a secondary rough draft of team communication protocol.

For announcement:

10:00–10:05 p.m.	Announce the next biweekly leader.
10:05–10:15 p.m.	Remind attendees to complete the leadership evaluation.

Figure 3.2. Sample Agenda

time to prepare. If possible, include the names of people in charge, also called the PPR (primary person responsible), of certain aspects of the meeting. Participants can volunteer information to those people before the meeting. You can include references to source materials or reports, so that participants can read them before the meeting or bring them to the meeting.

Experts agree that meetings should not run over two hours. Include start and stop times on your agenda and budget tentative times for agenda items. Include only those items consistent with the tasks you are trying to accomplish. Solicit agenda items from other people in advance. Label agenda items with headings such as *For discussion, For your information, For announcement, For decision,* or any other relevant heading. Be careful not to use the heading *Any other business.* This heading invites participants to waste time and get off track.

Selecting participants. The most important decision you will make about a meeting involves whom *not* to invite. Having too many people at a meeting causes confusion, congestion, and discontentment. Refer to Figure 3.3 for the recommended number of participants for your meeting type. Invite only those people who need to attend.

When *developing ideas,* you include individuals who have the technical knowledge to determine the feasibility or practicality of your ideas. You may want to invite people from other departments (a limited number, of course) who can tell you about the soundness of your ideas.

Meeting type	Maximum number of participants
Problem solving	5
Decision making	10
Problem identification or brainstorming	10
Training seminar	15
Informational	30
Review or presentational	30
Motivational	No limit

Source: 3M's Meeting Network "Mastering Meetings."

Figure 3.3. Meeting Type and Number of Participants

When *eliciting information,* ask individuals for information to cover at the meeting. Ask them this question: "Does this information need to be given out in person or can I communicate it through e-mail or a written memo?" If they feel it must be presented orally, then include it in your agenda.

In a *planning meeting,* be sure to invite those people who will carry out the plans. Supervisors and top employees can tell you the problem areas of a plan before you go into action, saving you time, money, and embarrassment.

In *decision making meetings,* remember that the real decision making power lies in the hands of a select few. Invite only those individuals who have the power to give the green light. Gauge the level of authority needed to decide and stop. The president of your organization probably will not be interested in a decision affecting only your department. But your president would want to know about a major reorganization of your division. If you do not know whom to invite, ask your managerial leader.

Deciding where and when to hold a meeting. Where and when you should hold a meeting are almost as important as what will happen during the meeting. Observe these basic rules for selecting and arranging the location and choosing the time.

Selecting and arranging the location. The meeting location and its setup contribute significantly to an effective meeting. When you choose proper facilities, they go unnoticed, but if the facilities appear inadequate, they detract from your meeting.

Allow more space than necessary for the number of people who will attend. You never know who might decide to attend, and you want your participants to be comfortable.

Choose a convenient location. An onsite meeting room is attractive; however, interruptions frequently occur. If possible, try to eliminate phones in the meeting room and ask participants to turn off cell phones and smartphones.

If you plan to use visuals, make sure the room will accommodate audiovisual equipment. Control the lighting to adjust for slides or other types of visuals. When you set up the room, be guided by the communication needs for the type of meeting. You usually want those talking with each other to maintain eye contact. Therefore, in meetings where individuals must discuss items together, have them face one another. If the meeting involves formal presentations, you can have the participants face the front of the room. Research on the nonverbal dimension of meetings suggests that seating shapes the dynamics of the interpersonal communication at the meeting. Your goal as meeting leader should be to create easy interpersonal contact among all the participants of the meeting.

Seating formations impact visibility, contact, interaction, networking, and bonding between participants as well as safety, access, and special effects. Seating arrangements affect participants' listening, viewing, and learning as well as their comfort level. The next time you sit in a straight row, look at and talk with the second person to your right or left. Someone has to lean back just to make eye contact. Lengthen the row and you increase the difficulty of seeing everyone on it.

To control interaction you can seat people who tend to talk to each other on either side of you. People who tend to sit at the corners of the table often symbolically reflect their marginal attitude about the topic or the group. Some organizations now conduct stand-up meetings with a 20-minute time limit for peer review of proposed projects. To emphasize that you do not want long-winded presentations, consider an occasional stand-up meeting.

Choosing the day and time. When choosing the meeting date, make sure you give any individuals who will be presenting adequate time to prepare. Check with them to determine their schedules and get their input as to when they feel they can be ready to present.

Certain times of the day should be off-limits for meetings. Avoid any meetings before 9:00 a.m., because most individuals need the first hour of the day to get their workday organized. On the other side, avoid scheduling meetings after 4:30 p.m., because people will be more interested in the time than in accomplishing the objectives. Having a meeting just before lunch can also prove dangerous, as you may compete with growling stomachs.

Consider vacations, holidays, and other time factors in setting up meetings. Be sure to have the necessary people present so as not to waste anyone's time. Avoid a late afternoon meeting before a holiday or a weekend. If you must have a meeting before work or during lunch, consider providing food; your attendance will be greater.

Preparing the leader's introduction for the meeting. As the leader, you should help your participants focus by beginning the meeting with an explanation of the meeting's purpose and the expected outcomes. Use the following model shown in Figure 3.4 to help you prepare this opening.

Leader's Meeting Introduction

1. Explain the purpose of the meeting by concisely stating the problems, objectives, expected outcomes, and procedures.
   - The basic problem/issue on the table today is

     _____.
   - The general objectives today are _____.
   - The procedure or format we'll use is _____.
2. Provide the information base to promote informed listening and discussion. Most of you are aware of the history of this problem/issue, and understand our need to resolve/address it. Briefly, we

   _____.

   - The present status is critical for us. Right now the problem or issue is _____.
   - I think most of us would agree on the following three or four basic causes of the problem (or points related to this issue).

     _____   _____

     _____   _____

   - Note the boundaries and constraints of the discussion. Should we put limits or parameters on our discussion? Let's focus mainly on _____ _____. And let us agree we will not talk about _____, because _____ _____. Another constraint on our discussion will be the criteria for an effective solution. For our problem or issue, an effective solution would be _____ _____ _____.

   - Announce the specific responsibilities or duties of participants. Who is responsible for the mechanics of the meeting?

                    [name]   has agreed
           to _____.
   - Review the agenda and note any revisions.

Source: Dr. Thomas Hajduk,
Teaching Professor
McDonough School of Business
Georgetown University

Figure 3.4. Leader's Meeting Introduction

People Duties of the Chair

Once you have completed the task duties for your meeting, put your people skills into action. Traditionally, leaders have had to lead and facilitate interaction. Now, many experts recommend using a *facilitator* to accommodate the people issues. This individual helps keep the meeting on track and is concerned only with keeping things running smoothly.

Whether you use a facilitator or decide to handle all aspects of the meeting yourself, you must encourage, support, and listen to your participants. Remember that by supporting others' right to speak, you do not show agreement. Instead, you show your respect for them, accept them, and allow them to express their opinions. For example, you could say, "That idea shows much thought. What do the rest of you think?" Or "Let's consider what Kathy has just recommended." Ask open-ended questions and encourage all to provide input to make your meeting more effective. Do not let yourself or anyone else dominate the meeting. To control yourself, avoid interrupting, don't talk for more than a couple of minutes, keep asking other people to contribute, allow someone else to present background information, and hold your opinions until the end. To control others—especially those with high status or authority who tend to talk too much and interrupt more often—avoid a direct confrontation in front of the group. Instead, try talking to the person outside of the meeting. If that does not work, try nonverbal signs, such as giving attention and providing visible signs of approval to other people trying to speak. As a next step, try a tactful but firm interruption, such as, "Excuse me, Nancy, but we need to keep our remarks brief so that everyone has a chance to talk."

You may have to place the disrupter at your side, rather than across from you, and call on him or her minimally. You can try giving the disrupter a job to do—keeping the minutes or chairing a subcommittee. Often these people need some kind of status or recognition. You can channel their energy for the welfare of the group.

To encourage participation and stimulate discussion, sit opposites across from each other. People generally do not communicate with people sitting next to them as much as they do with the people sitting across from them. If you need to encourage a particular individual to speak and participate, seat that individual directly across from you.

When leading your meeting, try to avoid hostile conflict. When individuals conflict over ideas, they avoid the "groupthink trap" of just going along. Nevertheless, conflict of personality can be destructive to the group. If the latter kind of conflict arises, summarize or paraphrase the different viewpoints and emphasize the places where people agree. Try to keep the discussion centered on ideas, not on attacking people. Instead of asking other participants to choose sides, try to work toward a solution allowing all sides to win and maintain their pride.

Suppose that, as the leader, you have closely followed your agenda, and the time has just about run out. To bring the meeting to closure, indicate your intention to end the meeting on time. Briefly review the problem, summarize the progress made, emphasize major agreements, inform the team of developments, and thank the group for participating. You may need to send the participants a summary sheet of what you accomplished or what necessary follow-up activities are required and who is doing them. In effect, as the leader you must monitor yourself and the progress of the members. Effective, thorough follow-up contributes to the continuation of the progress the group meeting began.

To analyze your success as leader, ask yourself the following questions—better yet, ask the participants these questions as well.

- Did I meet my goals?
- Did everyone participate?
- Did the participants seem comfortable?
- Could I have done anything better?
- Did I plan for the meeting?
- Did people know the purpose of the meeting?
- Did I start and end according to my agenda?
- Did I stick to my agenda?
- Did I choose an appropriate meeting room for the participants and audiovisual needs?
- Did I project my voice so all participants could hear?
- Did I involve everyone in the discussion?
- What should I do differently next time?

- What worked that we should continue to do?
- What follow-up needs to take place?[14]

People responsibilities during meetings. During most meetings and conferences these days, it is common to see laptops being used. Many programs may use audio sounds. If you are using a program such as this, the sound should be turned down or off during meetings, or in other situations where it could cause a distraction. As a general rule, you should give full attention in a meeting. No program should be open that isn't relevant to the meeting. If you need to listen to the audio to use the program, try headphones. Headphones that can fit in just one ear might be your best bet. That way you can attend to the meeting while using the program.

Summary of Meeting Notes

On some occasions, you will keep a record of your meeting. Minutes of a meeting serve as a written record of what took place. They serve as a permanent, official record of those who attended the meeting, significant discussions taking place during the meeting, any decisions made, and follow-up actions to be taken. It may be best to ask for someone to serve as the recorder because leading and recording at the same time can be challenging. Within 24 hours, the recorder should distribute copies of the minutes to all individuals who attended the meeting.

Minutes vary in the degree of formality required. An informal meeting may require only a simple, concise record; a more formal meeting requires a detailed account of actions taken and the exact wording of motions and resolutions.

If the leader of the meeting asked you to be responsible for preparing the minutes, become familiar with the agenda items before the meeting and review minutes of previous meetings.

Formats differ depending on the organization. But Figure 3.5 provides one example of an alternative format.

TO: *gselden@kennesaw.edu, Thall@kennesaw.edu*
FROM: Deborah Roebuck < *droebuck@.kennesaw.edu*
SUBJECT: Boss/Subordinate Relationships
DATE: November 12, 20XX

I appreciate your attending our November 10 meeting on "Managing Your Boss." I hope you found it not only interesting but helpful. Nancy and Juanne gave tremendous presentations that provided pertinent information. We now have some important information not only to use in our department, but with our associates.

Nancy discussed the importance of a boss—he or she can both improve your career and improve your performance. On the other side, though, a boss could also bring your career to a screeching halt if you do not perform to his or her expectations. While playing the "game," you need to understand office politics. We should note the perceptions of those around us. If we understand these perceptions, we will encounter few barriers to a successful working relationship with our boss. Finally, Nancy talked about how to improve your relationship with your boss. Attitude plays a large role in this. In other words, we should not criticize the boss behind his or her back, but try to understand the situation from the boss's perspective if a disagreement arises.

Juanne provided a wealth of information. She gave some characteristics of outstanding leaders as well as characteristics of incompetent leaders. She stressed the need for the boss to share information. When a boss does share information, he or she gains the trust and respect of his or her subordinates. In addition, information sharing gives followers responsibility, which they definitely enjoy. Juanne ended her portion of the meeting by discussing performance appraisals. She encouraged individuals to separate the performance review from a reward or punishment. She also noted that the expectations for performance should be jointly determined by both the boss and the subordinate.

Nancy and Juanne provided oustanding presentations that complemented each other. Nancy presented how a subordinate should act toward a superior, and Juanne reversed the situation and illustrated how a superior should act toward a subordinate. No matter where you work, you will always have to relate to a boss or a subordinate. By following Nancy's and Juanne's advice, we can overcome many of the potential communication obstacles found in the workplace.

Thank you again for attending the meeting. Hope you enjoy your weekend!

Figure 3.5. Written Summary of Meeting Results

Online Meetings

You may find that an online meeting will allow you to connect with people in multiple locations or enable you to reach large audiences. My husband primarily works from home, but he is in meetings several times a day with people all over the United States. A group of individuals in distant locations can see each other and exchange ideas without the fatigue and disruption caused by travel. As equipment costs decline, many companies have begun using electronic meetings as a way to replace face-to-face meetings.

Conducting successful meetings over the phone or online will require you to put in extra planning. Just like face-to-face meetings, you should send your agenda out in advance, but you must include login information at least one day in advance so that your meeting participants can test for any software downloads needed. Another tip is to ask participants to log in at least 15 minutes prior to the start to test connectivity. Conduct a roll call and verify that the technology is working; provide a method to reach your office offline if a participant encounters problems getting connected.[15]

Because virtual meetings offer less visual contact and less nonverbal communication than in-person meetings, you will need to make sure everyone stays engaged and has the opportunity to participate. Paying attention during online meetings takes greater effort, so individuals will have to stay committed and focused on the meeting.[16]

Conclusion

In this chapter, you have learned about the importance of trust, how to build teams, the role of interviews and touch-base meetings, and duties involved in facilitating meetings. As a managerial leader, take the following actions as you lead others:

- Admit it when you make a mistake as doing so will demonstrate your honesty and build trust with your team.
- Empower your team and give them the freedom to explore new ideas and to be creative; to do this you will have to build a culture that encourages mistakes and that respects each member of the team.

- Promote open dialogue and discussion of issues as some of the best ideas come at the end of discussions rather than at the beginning.
- Remember to find value in each member of your team.
- Schedule frequent touch-base meetings with each member of your team.
- Ensure that you prepare, set the tone, listen, and take notes during your interviews.
- Complete all task and people duties to ensure a productive meeting.

Sandra Shirley, President of First Global Financial Services, Limited, has stated the following:

In my opinion, the role of the CEO today is to facilitate staff innovation and team building for better service delivery. In today's corporate environment, we employ professionals with a view that they will enable us to draw on the knowledge base and expertise available and make prudent decisions. Formerly, only a few people knew where their organization was going and how each person contributed to the whole. Today, everyone must understand the overall strategy of the organization so that they can find meaning in their work and be self-actualized.

I also believe that a good CEO is someone who can pull people together and build a team. There is a movement toward coaching in institutions and mentoring for excellence, which is a new approach to management. Very often, people simply want to be appreciated. A word of encouragement and a feeling that management is compassionate, rather than purely extractive, is critical.

Source: What is the Role of Today's CEO?
Team Leader or Team Builder
April 8, 2010
Retrieved from http://www.businesssuiteonline.com/2010/04/08/
what-is-the-role-of-today%E2%80%99s-ceo-%E2%80%9Cteam
-leaders-or-team-builder%E2%80%9D/

Cases for Thinking and Discussing

Instructions: Read the following article and then reflect upon the following questions.

- What action plans can you take to improve your meetings?
- How many meetings do you attend or lead that feel productive? How many feel like a waste? Track the proportions.
- What is the mindset that lies underneath the terrible meetings? What are the assumptions about what meetings should be like that seem to be feeding the lack of productivity?
- What assumption would you need to have to believe that your meetings should be some of the most helpful and productive hours in your day? What would it be like to hold that assumption?
- What action plans can you take from these cases to improve your meetings?
- What lessons from these articles can you apply to your organization?

Case 1

Dr. Jennifer Garvey Berger, a partner in Cultivating Leadership (www.cultivatingleadership.co.nz), supports leaders internationally through coaching and leadership development programs. She writes about these ideas (her latest book is *Changing on the Job: Developing Leaders for a Complex World*) and also teaches coaches and consultants in advanced workshops around the world. Jennifer has a master's degree and a doctorate from Harvard University. Formerly an associate professor at George Mason University, Jennifer learned about deep change in 2006 when she moved to New Zealand with her husband, two kids, and the family dog. Jennifer loves that her life is a blend of watching the sun set over the Tasman Sea and having conversations with interesting people all around the world.

Leaders Should Run Great Meetings: A 3-Point Plan

April 25, 2011
By Jennifer Garvey Berger
http://www.becomealeader.org/articles/
how-leaders-run-great-meetings

Think back to the best meeting you ever had. This could have been a regularly scheduled thing or a one-off get-together for coffee with an interesting colleague. (Some of you may have to think way back.)

What made the meeting so good? You felt like you had something powerful to contribute? You felt like your fellow participants were also pushing their thinking and were adding things you hadn't known about before? Maybe you left the meeting with new ideas, new possibilities for moving forward, and a new sense that you were all engaged in the same project in your different ways.

Now think back to a less productive meeting. This is the kind in which time creeps by, your colleagues say either boring or obvious things (or both), you wonder whether you can type e-mails under the table in front of you so that you'll at least get something worthwhile done.

Which of those experiences is more common for you?

If you're like most of my clients, the terrible meeting experience is more typical. In fact, there are a variety of calls for ending meetings altogether, for going virtual or in other ways cutting out the dead wood that they have become in order to make way for the actual productive time in our work lives—those times when we are blissfully not in a meeting.

I have a different take on this. I have been to enough fantastic meetings to believe that we don't want to cut out meetings altogether—they're too important for us to be able to think and create together to solve some of the really huge challenges of the modern work world. But we do want to cut out nearly all of those unproductive meetings. If you've already done this at your workplace, that's fantastic! (Maybe you could send me an e-mail to let me know how you made that possible.)

Here's my bottom line on this. **At every regularly held meeting, not only should everyone in the room learn something, but something new should also be created—a new idea, plan, product, or solution.** At every regularly held meeting, most people should agree afterward that is wasn't a waste of time. If you cannot say this, your meetings need a makeover.

The first thing to change is your mindset. **One of the most amazing parts of this whole meeting issue to me is the ease with which we accept that meetings will be a waste of time.** Imagine just shrugging your shoulders and knowing that most of the money you just deposited in the bank wouldn't find its way into your account. Or that gas stations would routinely offer you pumps that spilled more gas than they managed to get into your car—while charging you for all of it. We get angry when people cheat us in some way, and yet we rarely feel cheated by spending 25 percent to 70 percent of our work days on useless activities.

Instead, imagine the following: what would it mean if you really believed that everyone else in the meeting was making sense of things in a different way? How would that change the questions you asked, the agenda you set, the expectations you had of your colleagues? Meetings can be places where culture is carried and lived out and spread, where silos can be dismantled, where new ideas can be born.

For the next week, try to go into all your meetings with the belief that they can and should be productive and helpful spaces for your work to thrive. Once you believe such things are possible, you can set out to create the conditions that make them happen—not just occasionally, but each time you go to a meeting.

Case 2

Andy Smith is an emotional intelligence coach, appreciative inquiry facilitator, and NLP trainer. He specializes in the practical application of leading-edge approaches to the personal development of leaders and key professionals. Andy is the author of *Achieve Your Goals: Strategies to Transform Your Life* (Dorling Kindersley, 2006) and *The Trainer's Pack of NLP Exercises* (Coaching Leaders, 2010).

Andy's work ranges from executive coaching (using the Hay Group's Emotional Competence Inventory 360° assessment as a starting point) to the design and delivery of coaching skills training for managers and coaches. He has developed a number of coaching models that incorporate appreciative and solution-focused tools in practical and jargon-free formats.

Website: www.coachingleaders.co.uk

Tips for Running Better Meetings—From NLP and Elsewhere

Monday, June 13, 2011 at 4:36PM

Do you ever find yourself in meetings that drag on, don't achieve as much as they should, in which people seem to be bored and disengaged?

When I was an employee, I took part in a lot of unproductive meetings. Sad to say, I probably chaired a few as well. Later I discovered NLP, emotional intelligence, and appreciative inquiry, and realized that there are certain things you can do to make your meetings run better, get things done, and that people actually feel are worthwhile attending.

A doctor mate of mine used to do a stress management presentation for overworked general practitioners. One of the slides was captioned "Meetings: the practical alternative to work." So if you want your meetings to work better, try these easy-to-implement tips.

Things are always easier to remember with acronyms, so get ready to remember . . . MODEM, RASTA, and, err, RRUBS.

Here's how to run emotionally intelligent meetings:

Remember: outcome, sensory acuity, flexibility

Preparation

1. Must we meet? Is the meeting necessary?

Meetings fit well with someone on "Managers' schedule," by which the day is divided into one-hour intervals.

"Makers" (programmers, technicians, etc.) need longer chunks of time to be productive. For them, a 10:30 meeting means switching work modes, and breaks up the morning into chunks too small to do anything hard in.

(*Managers vs. makers' schedule* distinction from Paul Graham at paulgraham.com)

Information updates can be handled by e-mail or phone. **Anything with an emotional impact needs a face-to-face meeting.**

2. Outcome: Establish where you want to get to by the end of the meeting.

"This is what I want to happen by the end of this meeting."

Evidence frame: What will you see/hear/feel as a result? What will be measurably different?

Having an outcome for the meeting switches your focus from yourself to your desired outcome. This can make a huge difference if you have previously been unconfident in meetings.

3. Decide what you will do for each contingency.

Explore what could happen and establish "if-then" options for what you will do if it does.

4. Establish who needs to be there, and agree on the agenda.

Only have attendees who actually need to be at the meeting. Discover their outcomes and get agreement on the agenda.

5. Meeting place.

Make the environment conducive to the outcome you want—no interruptions.

Have the seating arrangements in a circle so that everyone can see each other's eyes.

To really make sure that people concentrate and don't waste time, have the meeting standing up.

Opening the Meeting

6. Rapport.

As people come in, greet them and establish rapport.

7. Sensory acuity.

Check out their body language: you are looking for alert, responsive people. If someone appears to be in the grip of a strong, negative emotion, this could disrupt their concentration or even the whole meeting if you don't deal with it.

You can ask them about it; they might, for example, have left their car on double yellow lines.

Throughout the meeting, use peripheral vision to regularly check what is happening.

8. State and agree on the outcome and evidence procedure.

"This is where we want to get to by the end of the meeting, and we will know when we've gotten there because . . ."

9. Time frame.

Make sure everyone knows the time the meeting has to end. Ensure that everyone has time to say what they need to say.

10. Achievements: Start with successes.

With team meetings, use the appreciative frame. A good way to get people into a better (and therefore more capable and creative) state is to ask, "What successes and achievements have we had since we last met?" This will make the rest of the meeting flow more easily and make the whole thing more productive.

This should be in the spirit of an invitation to contribute, rather than picking on individuals: "You! What have you achieved?"

During the Meeting

11. Right level of detail.

Discuss ideas, objectives, and responsibilities rather than every little detail of how someone is going to achieve them. If this needs to be discussed, it can be done outside the meeting.

Remember, the more you drill down into detail, the less interesting it gets for people not directly involved in that topic, and the more opportunities you have for people to disagree.

12. Relevancy challenge: How to keep the meeting on track.

Make the agenda and desired outcome explicit and put it up where people can see it.

If any participant goes off on a tangent, you can respectfully challenge by saying, "Excuse me, how is this relevant to the agenda/outcome we agreed on?"

Pretty soon, just a nod or gesture to the agenda should be enough to bring people back on track.

13. Unproductive participants: How to deal with them.

a) Disengaged participants

If the person appears to have switched off, you need to establish what's going on.

Are they worried about something outside the meeting? Consider allowing them to deal with it (see step 7).

Are they thinking they shouldn't be there? Ideally you would find this out beforehand. Consider letting them leave if they don't need to be there for the rest of the meeting, and their responsibilities and actions have already been established.

If this happens regularly, with more than one person, take it as evidence that your meetings are too long.

b) Objectors and nitpickers

If the person is constantly raising objections (a mismatcher or polarity responder), give them the job of devil's advocate. Ask them to make notes of any flaws or objections they notice, and allocate them some time at the end of the meeting to report back on these.

14. Backtrack frame to handle disagreement.

If there's major disagreement or objection at any stage, interrupt and summarize what has been agreed up to now, starting from the beginning of the meeting and continuing up to the last point of agreement. Match the tonality of the objector, leading them toward a calmer state.

This has the effect of a rewind and is an opportunity to start over on the controversial area.

Closing the Meeting

15. Summarize.

Summarize what has been agreed on, who is going to carry out each action, and the completion date.

You could also do a mini-summary at the end of each stage.

Confirm the date for the next meeting and thank the participants.

CHAPTER 4

Developing Written Communication Skills

As a managerial leader, you will spend your day engaged in various communication activities; however, many experts believe that written communication will constitute a majority of each day. Charles Cofie, managing director and CEO of Unilever Ghana, Ltd., believes your primary means of communicating with management is in writing. Although effective oral skills are important, he believes you should learn to think, write, and then speak, in that order.[1] He emphasizes that your letters, e-mail messages, reports, and memos may be the only way you deliver an impression of yourself and your organization. In today's international business world, you may never meet business associates face-to-face and may be limited to interacting only through your written words. According to PlainLanguage.gov, writing skills especially matter on the Internet because people tend to read about 18 percent of what's on the page.[2]

Photo courtesy Flickr user slosada, CC 2.0

Therefore, you want to make sure that the letters, memos, e-mails, blogs, and reports that you write get read and represent you in a positive way.

A survey from the College Board's National Commission on Writing revealed that one-third of United States workers don't meet the writing requirements of their jobs. Individuals who completed the survey stated that clear, concise, and accurate writing is more important than ever, especially in this age of electronic communication, which has made every employee a writer.[3] A survey of human resource directors from large U.S. companies revealed the following responses about the importance of writing:

- One-third of employees in fast-growing service sectors have some writing responsibility. Two-thirds of salaried employees in large American companies have some writing responsibility.
- The ability to present yourself persuasively and articulately on paper is a big part of individual opportunity in the United States.
- Most of the new jobs in the years ahead will emphasize writing. Individuals who want to work in service firms, banking, finance, insurance, and real estate will need to know how to communicate clearly and concisely.
- Writing is a "marker" attribute of high-wage work.[4]

Joseph Tucci, president and CEO of EMC Corporation and chairman of the Business Roundtable's Education and the Workforce Task Force, says, "With the fast pace of today's electronic communication, one might think that the value of fundamental writing skills has diminished in the workplace. Actually, the need to write clearly and quickly has never been more important than in today's highly competitive, technology-driven global economy."[5]

Article after article cites poor writing as a problem in the workplace. Why do these articles repeatedly charge that employees as well as managers have poor writing skills? Could it be that individuals suffer because they do not understand the basic techniques of writing? I believe that if individuals have a better understanding of the process of writing, they will find the writing task easier. The writing process I recommend consists of these steps: determining your purpose, analyzing your audience, organizing your thoughts, establishing a logical order, constructing your draft, and editing your writing using the 7 Cs.

Determining Your Purpose

Writing professionals Braun and Butler believe you should spend at least one-third of your time planning and organizing before you begin to write.[6] So the first step in the planning process should be to ask yourself these questions:

1. What do I want to accomplish in this written communication?
2. How do I want to achieve it?

Once you have determined the specific goal of your communication, then you can decide what to say and how to say it. To communicate effectively, your writing must have a clear purpose. Besides maintaining goodwill and creating a favorable impression of you and your organization, you want to accomplish a particular goal.

The following table presents general objectives of business writing with specific examples.

General objectives	Examples of specific objectives
Seek ideas or facts	Request information on a proposed HR change
Obtain action	Get a customer to buy your service
Send ideas or facts	Provide a copy of a report on a new process; respond to a request
Direct action	Persuade a potential client to consider you as a coach
Instruct	Give instructions on how to prepare a presentation
Persuade	Convince a consumer to switch to your company
Promote goodwill	Send congratulations on a new promotion

Before writing, answer the following questions:

- Does my purpose seem realistic?
- Have I chosen the right time to deliver this message?
- Am I the right person to deliver the message?
- Will the receiver find the purpose acceptable?

If you cannot answer yes to each question, consider again why you are writing.

Remember Who Your Audience Is and Write Appropriately

A secondary teacher wanted to invite school board members, the district superintendent, the executive leadership team, and local juvenile judges to attend a GED ceremony. She sent me the e-mail invitation to review. In the subject line, she had written

"U R Invited to attd a GED Ceremony, Fri. at 2."

I was appalled at this not only from a former English teacher's viewpoint, but also simply from a professional appearance viewpoint. I was concerned about how our community would perceive our teaching staff. I had to put on my mentor hat and help her understand why we needed to send a more professional e-mail to her intended audience. When examples like this cross my desk, I come to realize why our students don't write well!

Source: Janet Wyatt, J.D.

Chief Legal Officer

Brighton School District SD27J

18551 E. 160th Ave.

Brighton, CO 80601

Analyzing Your Audience

Your purpose becomes even clearer when you try to see the situation from your reader's point of view. What does your reader want or need to know? Answering this question can help you clarify your thinking. Some additional questions to ask yourself include the following:

- How much do I know about the receiver?
- How much experience and knowledge does the receiver have about my reason for writing—that is, about my product or service, the new process, the issue under discussion?
- What is the cultural background of the receiver?
- What kind of relationship do I have with the reader?
- Should I be formal or informal in my communication?
- What position will the reader take on my issue?
- Do I need to be detailed and thorough or short and direct?
- Will the receiver's response be positive, negative, or indifferent toward the response I need?

You must consider the reader's background, reading level, interests, feelings, and knowledge of the subject matter. Knowing your audience helps you know not only what to say, but also what not to say. I have found throughout my career that, when I have had to communicate with my supervisor, it served me well to stop and think about his or her preferences. For example, I had one manager who liked everything to be short, direct, and to the point. So I knew to send an e-mail with three bullet points. For another supervisor, who liked more details, I would often draft a two- or three-page report that I sent him in advance. One of the biggest mistakes individuals make is thinking that they can write the same way for every audience. You can certainly do that, but the question becomes whether or not you will achieve your objective. The better you know and understand your audience, the more effective you will be.

Organizing and Establishing a Logical Order for Direct Versus Indirect Writing

You must consider the audience's reaction to what you will be sharing with them. Figure 4.1 presents some typical reactions audiences may face when receiving a communication from you and indicates the message strategy that would likely be more effective.

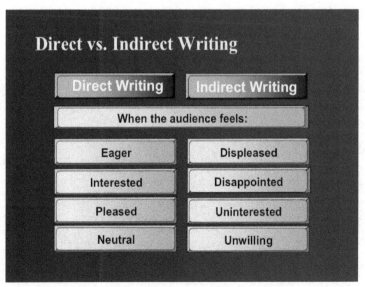

Figure 4.1. Audience Reactions and Appropriate Writing Strategies

To establish the correct strategy for your audience, you need to put yourself in the reader's place and decide whether your message will be favorably received or resisted. If you think your information will be favorably received, you can usually take the direct approach, called bottom-lining. On the other hand, if you think the reader will be unhappy or will need persuasion, you will use an indirect approach. Figure 4.2 summarizes the writing strategies for appropriate audience reaction.

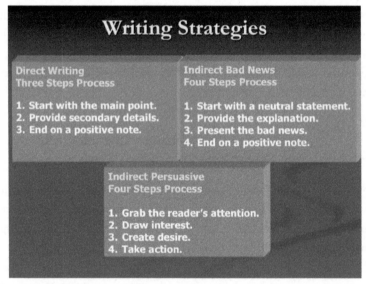

Figure 4.2. Direct and Indirect

Photo courtesy Flickr user U.S. Army Africa, CC 2.0

Direct Writing

When you write directly, much like newspaper writing, you arrange your ideas with the most important news first. Many readers never read beyond the first few lines of most documents; therefore, you must make those lines count. Follow the advice of Chris Barr, one of Yahoo!'s managing editors, and front-load the most important information in the first paragraph. He states that you've only got 5 to 10 seconds to hook the reader, so don't bury the lead.[7]

Many times writers use a subject line to save the reader's time by establishing the positive news and the nature of the document. Whether you use a subject line or not, you should make sure your first paragraph contains a specific main idea that gets straight to the point. The second paragraph will then provide secondary details, while the third paragraph will end your communication with a positive close.

Indirect Bad News Writing

The indirect approach gives you the chance to let your employees, clients, or customers buy into ideas they agree with or a problem they need to solve before you present your solution. This approach allows you to soften your readers' resistance, arouse their interest, and increase the likelihood of their seeing you as fair-minded. You spell out your support first and finish with your generalization or conclusion.

When using the bad news indirect strategy, begin your opening paragraph with a neutral statement that acknowledges the situation politely in a way that leads to agreement. The following examples provide some approaches to opening bad news documents:

- **Appreciation:** Thank your reader for the information.
- **Compliment:** Compliment your reader on something positive.
- **Good news:** Begin with good news if you can grant any part of the request or make an offer you think will please your reader.
- **Neutral courtesy:** Keep the opening paragraph noncommittal.

In your second paragraph explain in a positive manner and give the reason for not being able to grant the request. Be short and specific, but do not use the words *company policy*. The reader probably won't feel sympathetic to that excuse. Carefully lay out the logic of your side of the issue so that your reader can understand your actions and rationale and reach the disappointing conclusion. Sometimes you do not even have to specifically state the bad news; a simple statement of fact will make the refusal clear.

However, if you must state the bad news, in your third paragraph write so that the reader understands that you are refusing and do not be vague in your denial. The reader should not need further communication with you to understand the refusal clearly. Ideally, the bad news should flow logically from the reasons. If you explained your reasons well, your reader can probably infer a refusal even before reading it. When you do actually state your refusal, deemphasize the bad news. Avoid putting it at the beginning or end of a paragraph. Additionally, to help soften unpleasant ideas, use positive words and avoid using words that stir negative feelings. If you can offer an alternative or make a counterproposal, do so. You might be able to offer an alternative product or service, suggest a substitute, or make a compromise.

Your final closing paragraph should provide a positive, goodwill ending. Close your document with a positive statement and tone to preserve the established goodwill of the readers. You want your readers to feel favorably disposed toward you and to feel you care about them. Whatever you write, do not bring up the bad news again. In any negative message, move carefully and constantly keep goodwill in your plan. Get the reader on your side by establishing some common ground and by using a positive tone.

I can still remember that first credit card rejection I received. I was just out of college and I was so excited to be able to apply for my own credit card. I tore open the envelope and read the first sentence, which stated, "I regret to inform you that . . ." I was crushed and immediately threw the letter in the trash can. Then I wanted to find out why I was rejected, so I got that letter out of the trash, but I could not find an explanation. I found only a sentence stating that according to policy 6457, my application had been denied and if I had questions, I could call the office. Using this approach is not a way to win customers and clients.

When you must give bad news, show concern for your reader. Choose positive, courteous words, but don't use qualifiers or euphemisms to avoid accepting responsibility. You want to be considerate, yet not too subtle or you may mislead your readers into believing their requests will be granted. Even when you offer criticism, deliver it in a positive way.

On occasion, you may use the direct approach to present bad news, such as when communicating bad news to your manager. If you are presenting the results of a project, your boss may want you to get directly to whether the results are positive or negative.

Indirect Persuasive Writing

In addition to bad news situations, you will use an indirect approach in situations that require you to persuade others to take some specific action or to support a particular idea. Persuasive writing requires you to show benefits to the reader. In other words, you tell readers what is in it for them to accept your idea or proposal. As a persuasive writer, you must be viewed as credible. Readers must respect your ideas if they are to decide to buy in to your request or change their behavior. Your credibility as a writer hinges on these questions:

- Do you appear trustworthy?
- Do you have expertise and knowledge?
- Do you appear dynamic and excited about your proposal?
- Will your reader identify with your message?

The indirect approach works best for persuasion because you want to explain before presenting the main point. To write persuasively, follow the AIDA approach: attention, interest, desire, and action. The AIDA approach is credited to American advertising and sales pioneer E. St. Elmo Lewis (1898).

Attention. When you open with an attention-getting statement, you capture your readers' attention. You want your readers to keep reading, so you try to hook them with your first sentence. The term *hook* comes from the advertising and public relations fields, where presenters have only a few seconds to make a point. Your first sentence should be your best so that your reader will want to keep reading. Some strategies you can use to hook your audience include

- starting with a startling fact such as "Did you know that the average employee spends 35 percent of his or her time in meetings?";
- making use of a quote from a respected authority;
- offering something of value to the readers so they will continue to read;[8]
- referring to an event;
- telling a story; and
- stating a problem and sharing how you can solve it.

Interest. Once you have captured your readers' attention, you must maintain that interest. Introduce your major selling point by stating a benefit, filling a need, or showing a distinct advantage. Your idea should have a specific appeal, so determine what your appeal will be and then explain how it will satisfy your readers' needs.

Desire. At this stage, you build up the readers' desire to act. You want to move your readers from "I'd like to have that" to "I really need that." The desire you create will make the readers feel a need for what you have to offer. You can choose to use an emotional appeal, a logical appeal, or both.

If you sell your idea to your customers or clients, you will likely use an **emotional appeal** aiming at the heart or ego. Try to stir up various types of feelings within your readers with an emotional appeal.

You will often use the **logical appeal** for internal transactions. Often decision makers make choices based on cost versus benefits. When employing this appeal, use logic emphasizing high benefits for relatively low cost.

The following examples present different ways to appeal to your readers:

- Experiencing a sense of satisfaction
- Saving time, money, effort, or merchandise

- Creating and maintaining goodwill
- Adding prestige, exclusiveness, or distinction
- Increasing attractiveness
- Gaining safety or security

Typically, you deemphasize the cost of the product, service, or idea, unless price happens to be your major selling point. You want your readers to value what you offer and believe that the benefits outweigh the costs.

Action. The last paragraph presents the main message and moves your readers to take some action. You want to make taking that action easy, specific, clear, and immediate. You do not want to give them the opportunity to defer, but gently move them toward action. You may offer incentives or special reasons that will show them the value of not waiting but of taking that action now. The closing allows you to stress any timely connection and to reaffirm your hook.

Constructing Your Draft

Becoming an effective business writer does not happen in just one day, so it might take several drafts! E. B. White in *The Elements of Style* states, "Few writers are so expert that they can produce what they are after on the first try."[9] Effective business writers will tell you that practice is the key. When you feel more confident, you may encounter occasions when you can get it right the first time, but for most writers, getting it right takes time. Improving your writing requires rewriting, rewriting, and rewriting. In the drafting stage, do not worry about perfection. As Mario Puzo, American author and screen writer, has said, "It's all in the rewrite." Review the following writing tips included in Figure 4.3.

Here are some constructive tips to overcome writer's block.

- Start in the middle where you usually have plenty to say. Write your introduction last, so you will know what to emphasize to your readers up front.
- Write anything down, no matter how rough, and consider it a written brainstorming session. You can always polish it later.
- Circle what you don't like and keep going. You can rewrite anything, which is easier than starting over from scratch.
- Think out loud. Explain your ideas to others. You'll be surprised at how easily the words flow in conversation. Listen carefully for feedback that might give you a new perspective.
- Write a message to someone explaining the topic you're trying to write about and use this as your first draft.
- Decide on a reward to give yourself if you write a page.
- Break your material down into pieces.
- Write the easiest section first.
- Ask for a second opinion.
- Read more—good readers make good writers.

Figure 4.3. Writer's Block

Editing and Polishing

Once you have completed your draft, you must edit the document, applying the principles of effective business writing. I spend at least a third of my time on editing and revising. Occasionally, I can express my ideas correctly the first time, conveying my message as I would speak it. But editing and polishing my work enhances my credibility, and it will enhance yours as well. Use the seven *C*s—completeness, clearness, concreteness, correctness, conciseness, courtesy, and character—to make sure your message says exactly what you intend it to say.

Completeness

To write a complete document, you need *all* the facts surrounding the situation. Gather all the information before you start to write. To check for completeness, ask yourself the following questions:

- Who?
- What?
- Why?
- How?
- Where?
- When?

Your answers to these simple questions will help you identify what you need to say in your message.

Clearness

Clear writing is a direct reflection on you and your organization. Whether writing an article for your website, a business letter to a key prospect, or an informational message for a blog, you need to know what to say and how to say it clearly to capture and hold your reader's attention.

When you fully understand your purpose for writing, you can write a clear document. Delta Airlines CEO Richard Anderson says, "I don't think PowerPoint helps people think as clearly as they should because you don't have to put a complete thought in place."[10] I believe he makes a valid point, because clear writing should grow out of a clear, complete thought. When you write clearly, you use familiar words, avoid "technical talk," and make documents readable.

Familiar words. Familiar words help your reader understand your document. People like to read things they can comprehend quickly and easily, and using conversational words allows them to do so. When I am working with organizations, I often ask them why they would use a $5 word when a 50 cent word will accomplish the objective. If your goal is for your audience to understand, use simpler, more familiar words. When you write clearly, your writing leaves no doubts in your reader's mind. Test your sentences by asking yourself, "Would I say it this way in conversation?" If the answer is "no," rewrite your sentence. Readers find short, simple words easier to understand than longer, complicated words.

Don't say	Say
In an active manner	Actively
Render assistance to	Assist
We shall endeavor to	Endeavor
Terminate	Fire
Prior to	Before
Subsequent to	After
Transmit	Send
Utilize	Use
Cognizant	Aware
Necessitate	Require

Your goal should be to achieve clarity of understanding and not just to impress someone. I was once told the story of a manager who did not think of his audience or recognize the need to write for readers' clear understanding. He sent the following message to his employees: "Management has become cognizant of the unnecessary vegetation surrounding the periphery of the facility." If he just wanted his employees to get rid of the weeds, he should have just said so! Figure 4.4 presents some commonly used phrases and their perceived meanings.

Technical jargon. Technical jargon, a verbal shortcut, allows specialists to talk together. For example, doctors, lawyers, accountants, and

It is in process.	It is so wrapped in red tape that the situation is almost hopeless.
We will look into it.	By the time the wheel makes a full turn, we assume you will have forgotten about it.
We will advise you in due course.	If we figure it out, we will let you know.
We are aware of it.	We had hoped that the fool who started it would have forgotten about it by this time.
It is under consideration.	Never heard of it.
It is under active consideration.	We are looking in the files for it.
We are making a survey.	We need more time to think of an answer.
Let us get together on this.	I am assuming you are as confused as I am.
Please note and initial.	Let us spread the responsibility for this.

Figure 4.4. What Does That Familiar Phrase Really Mean?

computer experts use special words specific to their occupations. When individuals use jargon, they make the assumption that specialists in their discipline share a similar level of knowledge. Therefore, jargon can save time and achieve understanding. At one point, my husband, my brother-in-law, and my sister all worked for the same information technology company. When we would go out to dinner, they would talk in language unknown to me. The problem occurred because they were specialists using jargon known to them, but I did not share the same background knowledge. The longer specialists work within their chosen fields, the more inclined they become to use jargon with everyone else. When writing in business, avoid jargon unless you know the reader will understand it. The list in Figure 4.5 provides some commonly used technical jargon phrases.

Readability. Long words and sentences make your documents difficult to read. Hard-to-read documents add to the cost of doing business because it takes a reader longer to read and comprehend documents written in a bureaucratic style than those written in plain style. Bureaucratic writing buries meaning under run-on sentences, big words, and long paragraphs. The U.S. Navy determined it could save $27 million to $57

actionable	circular file	in bed	out of the loop
axe	core competency	in the black	ping
back burner	down and dirty	in the loop	pushback
bait and switch	downsize	in the red	put to bed
ballpark	get your ducks in a row	level the playing field	rubber check
bang for the buck	gofer	leverage	silver bullet
behind the eight ball	golden handcuffs	lost in the sauce	skill set
best practice	face time	low-ball	stakeholders
bean counter	fall guy	low-hanging fruit	take away
bearish	food chain	micromanage	talk turkey
brain dump	free lunch	mom and pop organization	timeframe
bullish	game changer	org chart	traction
buzz	headcount	not invented here	value-added
change agent	hired guns	out of pocket	zero sum game

Figure 4.5. Examples of Business Technical Jargon

million a year if officers wrote memos in a plain style with shorter words and sentences.[11]

You can write any idea, no matter how simple, in such a complicated way that your reader will not understand it. To write well, you do not draw attention to style. The *Flesch Reading Ease and Flesch-Kincaid Grade Level* are two commonly used indices to measure readability and are found within most word processing programs. The *Flesch Reading Ease* rates the text on a 100-point scale. If your document has a high score, the reader will find your document easier to understand. For most standard documents, you should aim for a score of approximately 60 to 70. The *Flesch-Kincaid Grade Level* rates text of a document on a U.S. grade-school level similar to the *Gunning Fog Index*. For example, a score of 8 means that an eighth-grade student should be able to read and understand your document.

The following tips provide suggestions for clearer writing. Many of the ideas directly influence readability.

- Keep sentences short. Aim for an average sentence length of 20 words or fewer.
- Vary your words, sentence length, and sentence construction to sustain interest.
- Use familiar, simple words.
- Avoid unnecessary words. Read what you wrote and cross out unneeded words.
- Use action verbs; avoid passive voice writing. An example of passive voice writing would be "The speaker was given 10 minutes for her speech." To make this sentence active, you would say, "The group gave the speaker 10 minutes for her speech."
- Write the way you talk, with a conversational tone.
- Use concrete terms your reader can picture.
- Write for your reader.
- Connect your sentences and paragraphs for unity, coherence, and transition. Coherence seems to serve the same purpose as a GPS system in a car. It guides the reader along so that he or she knows where the writer is going. The skillful use of key words makes for unity and coherence.
- Use white space to give your reader a break.

- Write to express ideas, not to impress the reader.
- Position the most important information at the beginning or end of sentences and paragraphs.
- Emphasize important words and ideas by setting them apart in short sentences.
- Be careful of overusing capital letters. Research has shown readers find lowercase letters easier to read.[12]

Concreteness

You write concretely when you paint a clear and definite picture in the reader's mind. Skillful business writers avoid vague words and words that create disagreeable mental pictures.

Creating clear mental pictures. Write using specific, concrete language and avoid generalities. Compare the two examples that follow:

- Abstract: Nancy is a good team member.
- Concrete: Nancy has not missed a single team meeting. She has submitted all of her assignments ahead of deadline. She listens to the opinions of other team members, but she will speak up when needed.

In the second example, you have examples of specific things that Nancy has done. Unclear references in your writing can confuse your reader. What do the vague pronouns *that* or *they* mean? What *thing, object,* or *matter* do you mean? Be as precise as you can and use pronouns or general nouns only when constant repetition of the main words or key words becomes awkward. Even then, try to use more precise substitute words like *product, campaign,* or *process* instead of a vague pronoun, such as *it.* Vague, general words may have different meanings to you and your receiver. What does it mean when you say you read a "good" book? What was *good* about the book? We don't know until you get specific and paint a picture in the mind of your reader. Some vague words to avoid are shown in Figure 4.6 on page 200.

Avoiding disagreeable mental pictures. Because you want to get a result, you need a positive attitude. You strive to create desire for, not opposition to, your writing. Avoid using words that antagonize your

Vague Words

a few	low	nice
quick	small	high
more	several	soon
large	most	short
slow	many	a small
number	very	a lot

Figure 4.6. Examples of Vague Words

reader. Therefore, don't say, *"You failed to pay,"* *"You are wrong,"* or *"You cannot return."* Some other words you should use with caution include *careless, for instance, weak, foolish, but,* or *misguided.* The word "but" is an "eraser" word that undoes all the good work in the previous thought, as in "You're a terrific manager, but we have a few suggestions."

Correctness

Henry Ford has been credited with saying, "Paying attention to the simple little things that most men disregard as unimportant makes a few men rich." More individuals should listen to Henry Ford! Too many people feel the little things do not count, and they do! The fourth *C* in effective communication involves the avoidance of grammatical mistakes and passive writing.

Grammatical mistakes. Readers can often understand written communication in spite of grammatical errors; however, correct grammar improves your credibility as a writer. Even when you have great ideas, the use of incorrect grammar will cause many readers to discount your ideas because the grammar detracts from them. In a survey of Fortune 1000 executives, 80 percent said they've decided not to interview job candidates solely because of poor grammar, spelling, or punctuation in résumés or cover letters. Of those same executives, 99 percent also said poor writing and grammar hurt an employee's chances for promotion.[13]

To help you overcome costly errors, make sure you use the spell and grammar checkers on your word processing package. However, you

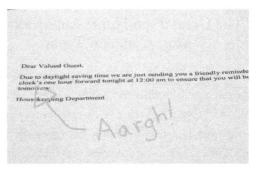

Dear Valued Guest,

Due to daylight saving time we are just sending you a friendly reminder clock's one hour forward tonight at 12:00 am to ensure that you will be tomorrow.

Housekeeping Department

Aargh!

Photo courtesy Flickr user Mr. T in DC, CC 2.0

should remember that word processing tools and computer programs can identify potential grammatical mistakes, but the writer must know how, when, and what rules of grammar to apply to the situation. As the author, you make the final decision whether to accept the recommendation of the grammar aid.

Your grammar checker can tell you

- your average sentence length (words per sentence);
- how hard your words are to read (characters per word);
- the percentage of your sentences that use passive writing; and
- the overall readability score of your writing (readability index).

Three grammatical mistakes business writers consistently make involve dangling modifiers, lack of parallel structure, and subject-verb agreement. Examples of each follow.

Dangling modifiers. Modifying words or phrases should be placed as close as possible to the words or phrases they modify. Adjective participial phrases often cause problems when they open the sentence. Such open participial phrases can be taken to modify the noun, but when the noun does not appear in the sentence, the phrase does not make sense.

- **Incorrect:** Loudly protesting, the child was taken from the man.

    (The first word has been left out so the introductory phrase does not complement what follows.)

The Great Typo Hunt: America's
10 Most Common Typos

Jeff Deck and Benjamin D. Herson traveled across the United States for two and a half months to find and correct typos in public signage. Deck and Herson tell the tale of that journey in their new book The Great Typo Hunt: Two Friends Changing the World, One Correction at a Time. They unearthed over 400 spelling and grammar errors during their adventures, and certain kinds of typos kept popping up along the way. Here are the top 10 most common typos in America today:

1. The unnecessary apostrophe
   - Example: Restrooms'
2. The missing apostrophe
   - Example: Please do not open without managers approval.
3. The wrong its or it's
   - Example: The dog and it's housekeeping staff reside here.
4. The wrong your or you're
   - Example: Everyone thinks your an idiot.
5. The misplaced apostrophe
   - Example: Mens' boxed ties
6. Words spelled similarly
   - Example: For sandwiches, pastries, cakes, or desert call 123-4567
7. Misspelled words
   - Examples: Cappachino, capuccino, or cappucino
8. More misspelled words
   - Examples: Restaurant and restuarant
9. Double-letters
   - Example: Fed Ex shiping and dinning room entrance
10. Agreement
    - Example: To make a apple crisp pie.

Source: The Great Typo Hunt: America's 10 Most Common Typos
September 8, 2010
http://www.huffingtonpost.com/2010/09/08/great-typo
-hunt_n_708087.html#s135736&title=Agreement_ErrorsErrors

- **Correct:** The man protested loudly when his child was taken from him.

    (Now the reader knows the man was protesting, not the child.)

A second problem occurs when a phrase or word in a sentence is too far from the idea it modifies.

- **Incorrect:** A dependable vehicle, the family decided to buy the Jeep.

    ("A dependable vehicle" should be placed closer to "Jeep.")
- **Correct:** The family decided to buy a Jeep, a dependable vehicle.

    (Now the modifying phrase is placed next to the idea it modifies.)

Lack of parallel structure. A device for facilitating cohesion in text components of a sentence is the use of coordinate structures having the same grammatical form. Parallel structure requires the writer to compose lists, series of words, phrases, or clauses in the same grammatical form. Use all verbs or participles or infinitives, not one of each. For example

- I like *speaking* more than *writing.*

    (A gerund is paired with a gerund.)
- I like *to speak* more than *to write.*

    (An infinitive is paired with an infinitive.)
- The main results of the company's restructuring included decreased span of control, more teleworking, and flex time opportunities.

    (All three items in the series are noun phrases.)

When word structures are parallel in form and length, readers comprehend the written word more swiftly. Correlative ideas are formed with correlative conjunctions such as either-or, neither-nor, not only-but also, both-and, whether-or, and as-as. The structure after the second part of the pair should be exactly parallel in form to the first structure. Parallel grammatical structure gives balance and flow to your writing. Examples of parallel structure follow:

- He made up his mind either to accept the proposal or to stop trying. (To accept follows *either*; therefore, an infinitive, *to stop trying*, should follow *or*.)

- He loves both writing and making presentations. (An *ing* word [gerund] follows *both*; therefore, an *ing* word [gerund] should also follow *and*.)

For proper use of an idiom, place the correlative conjunction immediately before the parallel terms:

- **Incorrect:** Rob has *both* experienced the sweet taste of success and the bitterness of defeat.

  (A correlative conjunction is misplaced.)
- **Correct:** Rob has experienced *both* the sweet taste of success and the bitterness of defeat.

  (Both, the correlative conjunction, is placed before *sweet taste of success* and *the bitterness of defeat.*)
- **Incorrect:** Miaka completes her tasks with patience, hard work, and takes pride in her work.

  (The series of *tasks* consists of a noun, a noun phrase, and a participial phrase all acting as objects of the preposition *with*.)
- **Correct:** Miaka completes her tasks *with* patience, hard work, and pride.

  (All three items in the series are nouns serving as objects of the preposition *with*.)
- **Incorrect:** To do well at work, you should have excellent team skills, demonstrating outstanding oral and written communication skills, and be hard-working.

  (The series mixes compound verbs with a verbal form.)
- **Correct:** To do well at work, you should demonstrate excellent team skills, show skills in oral and written communication, and work hard.

  (All three items are compound verb forms.)

Subject-verb agreement. A singular subject takes a singular verb while a plural subject takes a plural verb. The subject and the verb must also agree as to person: a first-person subject takes a first-person verb.

- **Incorrect:** Delta serve customers worldwide.
- **Correct:** Delta *serves* customers worldwide.

Rule: Even though company names or titles may appear to be plural, they are singular and require singular verbs.

- **Incorrect:** Becky and her boss works at Perimeter Mall.
- **Correct:** Becky and her boss *work* at Perimeter Mall.

Rule: When one subject joins another by the conjunction *and*, the subject is plural and needs a plural verb.

- **Incorrect:** Neither the manager nor the employee know the answer to the question.
- **Correct:** Neither the manager nor the employee *knows* the answer to the question.

Rule: When two subjects are joined by "or" or "nor," the verb should agree with the closer subject.

- **Incorrect:** Everybody in the office have a two-week vacation.
- **Correct:** Everybody in the office *has* a two-week vacation.

Rule: Some indefinite pronouns are always singular; others are plural. Refer to the following list for guidance.

Always singular	Always plural
anyone, anybody, anything	both
each, either, every, everyone	few
everybody, everything	many
neither, nobody, nothing, someone	several
somebody, something	

Passive writing. In passive writing, the doer of the action is often buried as an object of a preposition. To write effectively for business, use active writing where the doer of the action is the subject of the sentence. Usually you put the *subject* or *doer* up front, and then the verb tells what happens. Note the following example: The manager (the subject or doer) approved (the action) the request. This sentence clearly states who does what.

> Using the passive voice makes you sound like a bystander. Instead of "Our effort was led by me," write, "I led our effort." Remember, you are the initiator.
>
> By John Baldoni, June 23, 2011
> Retrieved from http://www.bnet.com/blog/leadership/
> write-a-cover-letter-that-gets

Generally, writers want to write actively; therefore, they use the active voice because this approach decreases wordiness and makes it easier to determine who did the action. Writing actively involves using action verbs. When you use action verbs, your writing becomes more dynamic and exciting. To write actively, eliminate the weakest verb form, *is,* from your writing. You can do this by using your word processing package's search-and-replace feature. Every time your word processing feature finds one of these forms, ask yourself where the action really resides. Try to think of an action verb to replace the weaker verb form. You can also use your electronic thesaurus to help you think of other action verbs. Sometimes when you write, you overuse the same verb. Using the thesaurus allows you to use different words. An example of passive writing versus active writing follows:

- **Passive:** The report was completed by Kathy.
- **Active:** Kathy completed the report.
- **Passive:** These guidelines have been changed by the manager.
- **Active:** The manager changed these guidelines.

Passive writing can be your enemy because it requires more words and makes your writing less forceful. When you write passively, your writing becomes vague, denies responsibility, and creates an artificial distance between you and your reader. It makes your writing sound clumsy and increases wordiness. According to many software editorial aids, if your letters, memos, or reports contain more than 25 percent passive writing, your writing style appears dry, wordy, and uninteresting. Your goal should be to have no more than 10 percent passive writing in any document.

Use simple action verbs to cut down on inefficient words and to add more impact to your documents. The following examples illustrate how you can eliminate wordiness while making your document more active:

Take into consideration	Consider
Make an announcement	Announce
Send an invitation	Invite
Bring to a conclusion	Conclude
Make your selection	Select

Incorporate the following tips to change your passive writing to active writing:

1. Turn the sentence around.
   - **Passive:** After the total amount has been determined, the discount percentage will be calculated.
   - **Active:** We will calculate the discount percentage after determining the total amount.
2. Change the verb.
   - **Passive:** A list of clients can be found in Attachment A.
   - **Active:** Attachment A lists our clients.
3. Rethink the sentence.
   - **Passive:** A meeting should be set up so that the problem can be dealt with.
   - **Active:** We should get together to solve this problem.

Sometimes you want to use the passive voice to soften the message. You should use the passive when you need to do the following:

1. Deemphasize the doer of the action.
   - **Active:** You must analyze all data before you make a decision.
   - **Passive:** All data must be analyzed before a decision is made.
2. Stress the receiver of the action.
   - **Active:** The manager accepted the application.
   - **Passive:** The application was accepted.
3. Avoid personal, blunt accusations.
   - **Active:** You didn't include your check for payment.
   - **Passive:** The check for payment was not included.

4. Present bad news.
- **Active:** You will not receive any bonus money.
- **Passive:** The bonus money will not be distributed.

5. Make a smooth transition from one sentence to the next.
- **Active:** To simplify maintenance requirements, we started using a different kind of software package.
- **Passive:** A different kind of software package was installed to simplify maintenance requirements.

Conciseness

When you write concisely, you say what you want to say in the fewest possible words. Avoid filler phrases such as

- replying to your inquiry, we would say
- we have your inquiry, and in reply will say
- referring to your inquiry
- in reply to your letter

These openings just take up space and add nothing of value to your document. Do not rehash an earlier document from your reader, who already knows what was said. Plunge right into the subject of the message, unless you must deliver unpleasant news.

Writers can often omit the word *that* without distorting the meaning of a sentence. In fact, to improve the conciseness of a sentence, some writing authorities recommend the word *that* be deleted in most situations in which it functions as a subordinating conjunction.

Deciding whether to delete *that* from a sentence is largely a writer's option. However, when writers physically delete *that*, it is still part of the sentence, much like the understood *you* subject in sentences such as "Do not overload the copier!" That is, in most instances, a dependent clause still exists, even if *that* is not physically in the sentence. *That* is the understood subject.

In general, writers can eliminate the wordy *that* in the following situations:

1. When *that* is used to introduce a subordinate clause functioning as the object of a verb
   - With: Joe says *that* he is poor.
   - Without: Joe says he is poor.
2. When *that* is used to introduce a subordinate clause stating a fact, wish, reason, or cause
   - With: Jack hopes *that* he will win the promotion.
   - Without: Jack hopes he will win the promotion.
3. When *that* is used to introduce a subordinate clause modifying an adverb or adverbial expression
   - With: She will work anytime that she can.
   - Without: She will work anytime she can.
4. When *that* is used to introduce a subordinate clause that is joined to an adjective or noun subjective complement
   - With: Bonnie is positive that she is right.
   - Without: Bonnie is positive she is right.
5. When the subject of a relative clause is different from the referent of the phrase preceding the clause
   - With: Carl has the report that I was reading.
   - Without: Carl has the report I was reading.
6. When a sentence contains more than one *that*
   - With: I told Marshall that the guidelines that he prepared meet with my approval.
   - Improved: I told Marshall that the guidelines he prepared meet with my approval.
   - Without: I told Marshall the guidelines he prepared meet with my approval.

A concise writer avoids wordy expressions, trite phrases, and useless repetition. The following sections present these ideas.

Wordy expressions. Wordy expressions create dead weight in a sentence. Many wordy sentences begin with a form of the infinitive "to be," which expresses passive voice, such as *there are, it is,* or *there is.* You can say the same thing without these slow-starting phrases; they stand for nothing! When you use them to begin a sentence, they often mask the true subject of the sentence and they add extra words. Eliminate them whenever possible. Use the *global search-and-replace* on your word processor to identify and eliminate these weak beginnings.

Don't say	Say
There are three fine restaurants in Canton.	Canton has three fine restaurants.
It is important for all employees to read the handbook.	All employees should read the handbook.

Use the following examples to make your writing more concise:

Why say this	When you can say this?
at all times	always
at the present time	now
costs the sum of	costs
due to the fact that	because
enclosed herewith for your	enclosed
first of all	first
in the amount of	for
in the month of June	in June
we would ask that you	please
in the neighborhood of	approximately

Useless repetition. Writers sometimes repeat ideas for emphasis and to make an impression in the reader's mind. For example, persuasive advertisements repeat information to help customers remember their products and services. Yet sometimes writers use useless repetition of the same idea, which just creates a longer document.

Here are some examples of useless repetition:

Attempting to qualify a term that can't be qualified

absolutely free	finish up
absolutely complete	reduce down
true facts	past experience
human volunteer	continue on
exactly identical	cancel out

Needlessly qualifying a term

second in sequence	during the year of 1987
audible to the ear	first began
for a period of one month	stockbroker by occupation
rectangular in shape	frown on her face
for the month of July	for the purpose

Redundant couplets

thought and consideration	immediately and at once
permanent and lasting	full and complete
opinion and belief	if and when
anxious and eager	hope and trust

Trite phrases. Trite phrases are phrases that have been used for so long they have lost their meaning and really contribute nothing to a document. If you use them in your documents, you sound stuffy and stereotyped. You can eliminate some trite phrases completely, and use more current replacements for others. Review the following examples:

Instead of	Try
Per your request	As you requested
Under separate cover	By UPS (or whatever)
Enclosed please find	Enclosed
This writer	I
The undersigned	I or me
Pursuant to your request	As you requested
Copy of said report	Copy of the report
Kindly advise	Please tell us
Permit me to say	(Simply say it!)
We wish to say	(Simply say it!)
At your earliest convenience	(Give a time frame.)

The following examples show some commonly used expressions and how the receiver might react:

Saying	Reaction
I wish to state	Why wish? Just say it!
We beg to state	Get off your knees!
Kindly place your order	Must I be kind?
We would like to thank you for	Just do it!

Courtesy

When your writing contains courtesy, it expresses an attitude of friendliness and goodwill. You have probably visited a business establishment where people made you feel they cared about you. You will return to that store, theater, or restaurant because of that customer service. To establish positive relationships, you must employ courtesy when writing. Expressing courtesy means using a "you-attitude" and positive words.

You-attitude. Courtesy includes using a *you-attitude*, rather than a *me-attitude*, which means putting yourself in the reader's place. See Figure 4.7 for some hints for developing a *you-attitude*.

- Do not allow your personal feelings and attitudes to interfere with your message.
- Use a style you would enjoy reading.
- Prepare a blueprint of your finished product before you start writing.
- Carefully select the right nouns and verbs to set the tone of your writing.
- Be prepared to rewrite, as rewriting results in better writing.
- Use logic and evidence to convince your reader.

Figure 4.7. Helpful Hints for Developing a You-Attitude

A business document written with this attitude shows empathy and understanding of the situation and stresses the reader's point of view or interest. The message talks about the receiver's convenience rather than the company's convenience. When you write messages using a *you-attitude*, your documents are courteous and sincere.

I once worked with a family-owned business that did not perceive that their communication with customers was getting the results they desired. When we reviewed some of those communications, we found that the messages spoke primarily with a *we-attitude* instead of a *you-attitude*. When they changed the focus to the customer and used more *you's* than *we's*, they noticed a positive difference.

Positive words. A final component of courtesy focuses on the positive, not the negative. You want to create a pleasant climate and produce goodwill for your organization. You do so by using words such as *please,* *thank you, and appreciate.* As much as possible, avoid using the following negative words:

delay	can't	impossible	inconvenience	will not	do not
trouble	blame	sorry	fault	unable	error
disagree	damaged	failure	prejudiced	complaint	little value
unfortunate	wrong	mistake	difficult	failed	refuse
never	regret	neglect	no	prohibit	hesitate

The following examples show how to turn around negative sentences:

Negative: Please do not hesitate to call me when you have a problem.

Positive: Please call me when you have a problem.

Negative: You neglected to give the color of the paper you desired.

Positive: Please send us the color of paper you need and we will promptly fill your order.

Negative: Don't wait until the last minute to submit your performance review.

Positive: Get your performance review done early.

Character

The final *C*, character or personality, combines all principles of effective business writing. Character lifts your document above the drab and commonplace. Your business document should be your original creation. Never try to copy the writing style of someone else; it just will not work.

Your document contains character when it holds no stereotyped words or worn-out clichés and when it breathes the spirit of consideration for your reader. You gain character when you use concrete language, and when courtesy shines through the words, sentences, and paragraphs. Character shows clearly what the writer thinks about the needs, wants, and interests of the reader. As you can see, character encompasses all the other six *C*s.

The Paramedic Method

Richard Lanham is widely known for his textbooks on revising prose to improve style and clarify thought. He is also a notable scholar of the history of rhetoric. He has developed what he calls the "paramedic method."[14] This method allows you to edit your writing to make sure you have included all the elements of effective business writing. His simple method includes the following steps:

1. Circle all the prepositions. Then determine which prepositional phrases add extra words you can leave out.
2. Circle the *is* forms. Replace forms of *is* with stronger action verbs.
3. Ask yourself these questions: "Where's the action?" "Who's kicking whom?" "Did I write using active or passive writing?"
4. If your document contains passive writing, change to active writing. Put your "kicking" action into a simple active verb.
5. Start fast—no slow windups that use delayers or extra words.

Here's an example of how the paramedic method works:

- **Original Sentence:** After we have carefully reviewed your present proposal, we are of the opinion that we are not in the position at this time to accept your offer.
- **Revision:** We cannot accept your offer now.

Proofreading

I have heard writing experts state you should spend your writing time in the following ways: 25 percent planning, 25 percent writing, 45 percent

Photo courtesy Flickr user Undertaw851, CC 2.0

revising and editing, and 5 percent proofreading. Too often individuals forget to proofread their work or say they just do not have the time. As we know in quality management, 99 percent may not be enough. If you compose a 99 percent error-free document, the offending 1 percent could still destroy your document's value, waste your time, and seriously damage your credibility. When you sign your name at the bottom of a letter, initial your memo, or send out an e-mail message, you demonstrate you have read and approved your work. You indicate that you want it to represent not only you, but also your organization. If you send out sloppy work, it hurts not only you, but also your company.

Sending a document with mistakes communicates that you do not care enough to take the time to proofread your work. Do you really want to send that message? If not, use the following tips to eliminate errors.

Tips for Proofreaders

Most routine documents require light proofreading. Print out a rough draft copy of your document. Your document will look different on paper from how it looks on your computer screen. When you see the hard copy, you may decide to change the format or spacing if, for example, your page breaks do not occur where you planned them.

People forgive spelling errors the least because of the resources we have available to prevent them. Dictionaries, reference materials, and computerized grammar and spelling checker programs help identify spelling errors.

For extremely important or complex documents, utilize a partner system. A partner system allows you to receive help and also to give help. Have your partner read the final draft while you follow along on the receiver's copy. Read the message at least twice—once for word meanings and once for grammar and mechanics. For an extremely long document, read it a third time to verify consistency in formatting. When proofreading, reduce your reading speed and concentrate on individual words rather than ideas.

If you do not have a partner, try reading the material backwards so that you won't get caught up in the sense of the document and overlook errors. Look for errors your spelling checker won't catch, such as *to* for *too*, or transposition of numbers.

Note the type sizes and styles you have used. Make sure you have consistently used the same formatting throughout your document. If you have used any figures, illustrations, or graphics, make sure you have properly located and identified them.

Check for errors in spacing between words and sentences. Leave one space between words and one space at the end of sentences. Make sure you do not have any paragraphs with only one line or part of a line left at the top or bottom of your page—called *orphans* and *widows*. You must have at least two lines to start or finish a paragraph at the top or bottom of a page.

Before you send your document, look at it closely to make sure it meets several important requirements. Ask yourself:

- Have I positioned it properly on the page?
- Did I spell all names correctly and accurately reflect numbers?
- Will it make a favorable impression on the recipient?

When you can answer "yes" to these questions, send it.

Spotlight on Today's Managerial Leader

Paul McElvy is a CPA with over 17 years of experience in financial reporting, taxation, and information systems. He is currently first vice president for External Credit Risk Reporting at SunTrust Banks, Inc. In his current role he is responsible for various external reporting deliverables such as investor relations presentations, SEC filings, and Federal Reserve reporting. His responsibilities require daily interaction across multiple departments and senior level management to help tell the SunTrust story. Paul received his master's degree in business administration from

Kennesaw State University in 2006. He is a father of three beautiful daughters and is an active member at East Cobb Presbyterian Church.

Importance of Clarity, Tone, and Accuracy

Throughout my career I have had the opportunity to work at a couple of large corporations and a few small businesses along the way. Meetings, e-mails, and phone calls represent the bulk of day-to-day interactions with other coworkers. Face-to-face meetings take up about 50 percent of my calendar in any given week, sometimes leaving little time to get the "real work" done. One place where I worked actually had a meeting to discuss whether or not we were having too many meetings! They can be a real time drain. However, face-to-face meetings and conference calls are necessary to gain consensus on action items or departmental direction requiring contact both inside and outside of your department. It is here, in my experience, that e-mail becomes a more powerful and efficient communication tool. How effective you are in your e-mail communication can have a big influence on how you are perceived both inside and outside of your department. Dale Carnegie said, "There are four ways, and only four ways, in which we have contact with the world. We are evaluated and classified by these four contacts: what we do, how we look, what we say, and how we say it." While I am not perfect when it comes to my communication skills, I give extra attention to three areas in my e-mail responses: clarity, tone, and spelling.

I frequently engage with senior vice presidents in my company through face-to-face meetings, phone calls, and e-mails. Often, I am required to obtain data for various presentations and external reports. For example, when corresponding with our director of investor relations I give extra attention to what I say or write knowing that what I communicate can have an impact on the external investment community. Recently he asked me in an e-mail to provide some "color" on how well our earning assets were growing over a five-quarter trend and contrast that with our portfolio de-risking strategy. I knew that what I needed to provide would require significant research and solid backup. In my response I could have given him deep insight into my level of research, supplied a great deal of data to support his request, and provided 10 to 12 different talking points for his presentation. However, I knew that he would not have time to digest that level of research and, no doubt, trusted me to provide the brevity needed for his presentation. As a result, I boiled down my research to four main points that would quickly tell the story that he was looking to include in his presentation.

I have three quick recommendations for giving clarity to your e-mails. First, delete redundancies. Saying it one time is enough. If you keep repeating the same thought or concept the reader may jump ahead or call you to explain what you mean. Second, add missing context. Your reader may not know that hot dog buns are required on sunny days in Chicago in order for the company to make the $50 million sales target. Finally, focus on your strongest argument. You may have multiple reasons to get the hot dog buns shipped to Chicago but try to pick the strongest reason to get those hot dog buns shipped and on the road. A long-winded and rambling e-mail reputation can result in a checked career.

I probably should not have to mention this next topic about constructing a proper e-mail response, but I have seen too many people damage their reputations with the tone of their e-mails. You probably have your own story about an improper e-mail a coworker sent out prompting the response of "what in the heck was that guy thinking?!?." Admittedly those kinds of e-mails create all kinds of office gossip and stories for the next few days of how "so-and-so" really messed that one up. Tone is really something usually associated with your voice. Given that the reader of your e-mail cannot interpret your e-mail inflection or even body language, you are left with the burden to ensure the proper tone is relayed in your e-mail communications by virtue of the words you choose and how you choose to use them. I had a coworker who was once responsible for finding out some information about a proposed departmental change as to how our old file servers were going to be decommissioned and when our new ones were going to come online. My manager saw an opportunity to give this guy a chance to increase his exposure outside of the department since he was new to the company. My manager also told him that he would need to contact someone in the IT department who had a solid reputation in the company and had been a real ally to our department. Here was his first opportunity to make an impression outside of our group and e-mail was his method of choice to find out what the plan was for our new file servers. So once he sent his inquiry, how do you think it went? Do you think he took the time to explain that he was new, that he was appreciative of this person's time, or that he understood this was a big undertaking on everyone's part? Quite the opposite—my coworker made a demand of this person's time, never said he was new to the group, and never said thanks to the IT group for all of their hard work. Once our IT counterpart replied to this "train wreck" of an e-mail, he decided to bring a few other "higher-ups" into the e-mail reply, thoroughly making a fool of my coworker. Now, did the IT guy handle his reply in the most professional of manners? No, but my coworker really brought it on himself and he is still labeled to this day as someone who comes across as pompous and arrogant. The lesson to learn is to take your time, re-read your e-mails "out loud" before clicking Send, and work on your tone skills constantly so you don't squander the opportunity to come over as courteous, thoughtful, and appreciative as a person!

Finally, in this day of electronic communications, you should not have misspelled words and poor grammar as they can be reputation killers as well. If you use Microsoft Outlook, never turn off the automatic spell checker. I have an employee who is the worst speller and frequently sends me sentences that make no sense (see the comment above about reading your e-mails out loud). As you can imagine, he also can be seen with his shirt untucked and with a messy desk area. I will give an anecdotal statistic here: 0 percent of the e-mails I have ever received from a senior vice president or above have ever included a misspelled word. That is not to say that their grammar is always perfect but misspelled words should never be found in a business setting. Recently I received an e-mail from my employee where he said, "perfect, thank you for the explination." I had to laugh out loud at the spelling of "explanation." Little details like this show me that he is prone to missing details in his work deliverables and makes me pay closer attention to the data he gives me. Can you say performance review improvement opportunity? Here's another example of the importance of reading out loud the content of your e-mails. I was given the following sentence the other day, requiring me to go back and ask my employee what he meant. He wrote, "How hard is it to pull data? *Then where like we will start working on it.*" Uuugh! Other examples include the wrong use of there/their, spelling probably as "prolly," and other silly mistakes. If you are prone to making these kinds of mistakes, please know that misspelled words and poorly phrased sentences are absolutely destructive to your growth potential. These kinds of mistakes may not make it into a performance review, but they can serve as negative reputation markers. The good news is that this can be easily fixed if you just pay attention to what you write.

I hope that these three areas I have explained will jog your memory about other examples you may have seen over your career. These qualities of clarity, tone, and accuracy are absolutely critical in any business communication setting whether it is e-mail, telephone, or interpersonal communication.

Specific Types of Written Documents

Regardless of the type of document you write, you should plan, write, and edit according to the guidelines already given. But different types of documents require specific guidance.

E-mail

E-mail eliminates telephone tag, speeds up decision making, shortens the communication cycle time, and flattens corporate hierarchy. It allows organizations, employees, and clients to communicate on a global basis at virtually any time and any place. According to numerous studies, e-mail is the primary channel for written communication in most organizations. E-mail can be used for various types of messages and not just simple, direct ones. E-mail messages require senders to use the same concepts of effective business writing used in traditional documents; therefore, you should continue to plan, compose carefully, and revise as needed. Begin by determining whether e-mail will be the appropriate medium for your message.

Do You Use Dear as Your E-mail Salutation?

On her blog, the author Amy Tan has reflected on the different salutations she has received in her inbox. "'Dear Amy Tan' is from eBay or PayPal, telling me I have either paid for something or should pay for it. 'Hey Amy' is only from someone I know well enough to hug," she wrote. "No salutation is from my husband, my assistant, my friends I am in touch with everyday."

Many e-mails we receive do not even start with a salutation but immediately move into the message. Familiarity breeds lack of "hello," "hey," and "dear."

Etiquette experts state that the salutation sets the tone for message. They believe if you drop a greeting and use only a name, you can come across as cold, while using "hey" can seem too familiar. Lynn Gaertner-Johnston, who runs the Syntax Training business writing school in Seattle, tells her clients they can forgo dear in e-mail but must use it in business letters. "We don't use 'dear' because someone is dear to us," she says, "but because we understand the standards of business writing and recognize the standards of intelligent business people."

The Emily Post Institute has stated you can, in general, drop "dear" but advises you should use it in particularly formal e-mails. "I don't think it's as important as it used to be," says author and institute spokeswoman Anna Post, the great-great-granddaughter of etiquette guru Emily Post. "You can still certainly use it. If you don't know someone well, or for a new client, I would absolutely use 'dear.'"

Source: Hey Folks: Here's a Digital Requiem
For a Dearly Departed Salutation
Author: Dionne Searcey
January 6, 2011
http://online.wsj.com/article/SB10001424052
7487041115045760600044212664436.html

E-mail messages are slightly more polite than telephone conversations simply because you have taken the time to type them and because they are somewhat less intrusive. Of course, the format you use when producing an e-mail message is a contributing factor to the message's politeness. Just because readers see e-mail messages as informal, you are not exempt from using appropriate business writing techniques when constructing them. Some rules to keep in mind include the following:

- Continue to use a salutation even though the recipient's name is prominently displayed at the top of the page.
- Use a colon, not a comma, after the salutation when sending a business-related message just as you would with a business letterhead.
- Use upper- and lowercase letters just as you would in a letter or memo while using the appropriate punctuation to close each sentence.
- Use appropriate paragraphing.
- Use clear, concise language and avoid using jargon or slang.
- Sign your e-mail with your complete name and title.

The subject line tells the recipient the purpose of the message and can be the most important part of your message as it can be the factor that determines if an individual will open your e-mail or not. People who get a lot of e-mail, especially people who do not know you, will use it to decide what to do with your message. A message with a blank subject line or a general subject like "Question" will likely receive a low priority. If you are forwarding an e-mail or replying, change the subject if necessary to make it more accurate. Mark messages as urgent or routine in the subject line, but use "urgent" cautiously.

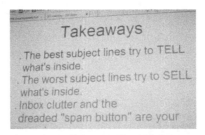

Photo courtesy Flickr user MikeSchinkel, CC 2.0

I once worked with clients in an organization who did not believe their employees were reading the memos and e-mails sent from their managers. When we reviewed the documents, we found that the writers were using the same subject line repeatedly. We talked with employees and discovered that they thought they were receiving duplicates of the same message. This story presents another example of the importance of paying attention to the details and making your subject lines specific.

In most e-mail situations, you will use the direct approach and present the main point first. If you are making a proposal, you can summarize the situation and then present your recommendation. If you perceive you will need a longer document to explain the situation, you should probably just add an attachment. Use the 7 Cs to assure your document is clear, concise, and courteous while telling your receiver what you expect.

Spotlight on a Managerial Leader

Dr. Rick Brinkman has been a keynote speaker and trainer for over 30 years, known for his unique presentation style of educating through entertainment. He is the co-author of the international bestselling McGraw-Hill book Dealing With People You Can't Stand: How to Bring Out the Best in People at Their Worst, *which has been*

translated into 20 languages. He is frequently used by media as a communication expert and has been featured as a communication expert in the Wall St. Journal, O Magazine, CNN, CNBC, *and* The New York Times. *Visit Rick's website to watch his video entitled E-mail, will you go with the Devil or the Angel? http://rickbrinkman.com/blog/category/communication/email/*

E-mail Tips

When composing your e-mail messages, consider the following:

- Use a clear subject line that relates to the content of the e-mail.
- Include only one subject for each e-mail. If you have three items of business to discuss with someone, generate three different e-mails. Each e-mail should discuss only one item and the subject that relates to it. A descriptive subject line assists in sorting your inbox and makes later retrieval easier.
- After you sort by subject, read everyone's e-mail on that subject, and then create only one e-mail to answer every-one. If you reply to each individual e-mail and everyone else does the same, you will, as a workgroup, generate an e-mail blizzard. If you quote different people, you will need to take the time to make sure you put the person's name next to the quote so everyone knows who said what.
- Use symbols to indicate what is required from the reader. This immediately orients the recipient to the e-mail and saves time because she knows what is required of her. The symbol should be included in the subject line as well as the body of the e-mail. When the symbol is included in the subject line it should be last; otherwise, it will mess up the alphabetical sorting of e-mail by subject. Here are some suggested symbols: FYI (For Your Information), ACT (Action Required), OPN (Your Opinion), DCN (Decision Needed), DDLN (Deadline), APPT (Appt Confirmation), DATE (Date

change), QUES (Question), UPDT (Update), INFO (Info
Needed), THKS (Thank you), FUN (Just for fun).

- Choose to forgo "post–e-mail" pleasantries. They make the
assumption that people say "thanks," "you're welcome,"
etc. so they eliminate such wording to decrease the volume
of e-mail messages.

- Specify when to cc everyone and when to only respond
to the sender. Think of it like a virtual meeting; if you are
discussing something and everyone needs to hear your
opinion, then you should cc everyone. If a sender is asking
for something from a group of people, you only need to
reply to the sender.

Memos

The memo simplifies communication within organizations. These informal messages request information, reinforce agreements, clarify previous
messages, or deliver short reports about daily organizational problems.
E-mail memos have largely taken the place of traditional paper memos as
organizations embrace paperless correspondence. Memos have one distinct advantage over e-mail, which is a formal message format. Memos
are typically sent to individuals and groups within an organization, while
letters usually are sent to those outside the organization. With a memo,
some niceties of letter writing are omitted for the sake of conciseness. The
memo format helps simplify and speed up internal communication by
ensuring consistency. Typically, the memo uses a standardized heading
with four basic elements: *to, from, date,* and *subject.*

Note that in some organizations, the four basic elements may appear
in a different order. However, the key for any organization is to develop
and use a consistent format. As the writer (From), you show your title or
position unless the reader knows this information. Usually, Miss, Mrs., or
Ms. does not appear before the receiver's name (To) in a memo, although
you can include them if you prefer. However, Mr. is never used before a
man's name. To show that you, the writer, proofread your memo, place
your initials beside your name (either written in paper correspondence

or by using a script font if the memo will be sent electronically). Because you normally do not sign a memo, the complimentary close is omitted.

Single-space the body of your memo and double-space between paragraphs. You may block or indent your paragraphs, but most writers use block paragraphs to save time. Side margins should be approximately one inch. Do not center the memo vertically; instead, place the memo heading one inch from the top of the page.

If a memo requires a second page, use a second-page heading. List the receiver's name, the date, and the page number. Center or block this information, depending on whether you indented or blocked your paragraphs. Be consistent throughout your document.

As in all business writing situations, the appearance of a memo paints a picture of you and your organization. A neat, attractive document will get read!

Letters

While memos are used internally, write letters to communicate with external stakeholders. To avoid sending letters with an unattractive or disorganized appearance, you must plan your layout. The placement of the letter on the page determines a pleasing appearance. If you balance your letter on the page, your document appears more attractive. You can achieve a picture-frame effect by surrounding your message with ample margins. If you vary the top and side margins based on the message length, you can produce a letter with eye appeal.

If you compare business correspondence from a variety of companies, you will notice obvious differences. Although diversity occurs in stylistic features, writers agree on the standard or required parts of a letter. A letter should contain seven basic parts: letterhead, date, inside address, complimentary closing, salutation, body, and signature block.

A letter can also contain optional parts. The optional parts include subject lines, attention line, reference initials, enclosures, copies, and postscripts.

You have two punctuation styles to choose from in punctuating the salutation and the close of a letter. With open punctuation, no punctuation follows the salutation or the close. Mixed punctuation requires a colon following the salutation and a comma following the complimentary close. See the following examples.

- **Open:**   **Dear Mrs. Williams**   **Sincerely**
- **Mixed:**   **Dear Mrs. Williams:**   **Sincerely,**

You will find four widely-used letter styles: full block, semiblock, modified block, and simplified.

Full block style. In full block style, every line begins at the left margin including the date, close, and signature block. Because you focus on the left margin, you make few adjustments on the computer, thus saving time. See the example of a full block letter in Figure 4.8.

Semiblock style. The two differences in this style from the full block style are the indention of paragraphs within the body of the letter and that the date, closing, and signature begin to the right of center. Paragraphs are indented five spaces.

Modified block style. In modified block style, the date begins at the center of the page. Align the close and the signature block with the date. All other parts stay the same as in full block style. Figure 4.9 illustrates modified block style with mixed punctuation.

Simplified style. In the simplified style developed by the Administrative Management Society, you do not use a salutation or a close. A subject line replaces the salutation and the writer just signs his or her name above the signature block.

Most of the business letters you send or receive will represent one of these four placement styles, although writers sometimes devise special formats to get their readers' attention. They may use devices such as unusual margins, color, or boxes to enclose important information. Remember, your letter should look like a picture in a frame. On multiple-page letters, leave a margin of at least an inch, and preferably a little more, at the bottom of the first page. When using memo and letter templates found within word processing software, be careful as they do not always follow the correct strategies and formats.

Reports

Organizations cannot function without information, and much of that information is transmitted in reports. Individuals use reports to communicate with internal as well as external stakeholders in the organization. Reports serve as a vital link among many different audiences. Reports

Show Me Farm
2230 Henry Scott Road
Ball Ground, GA 30107

June 3, 20XX

Mr. Rich Blackinton
1356 Hendon Road
Woodstock, GA 30188

Dear Mr. Blackinton: (Salutation with mixed punctuation)

Subject: Letter Format (if used, always following salutation)

This illustration covers practically all the points explained in the preceding directions concerning format and style of letters. The following paragraphs emphasize vital facts. Remember, your letters represent you; therefore, take pride in them, for you play an important role in your organization.

This letter illustrates several points in the handling of correspondence. Note the pleasing appearance of this letter. The satisfactory effect comes from attention to details such as even margins and effective paragraphing. Both add not only to the appearance, but also to the ease of reading. If the recipient finds your letter easy to read, you will likely get a prompt response.

The reputation of your company depends largely on the impression you make on your customers, clients, and associates. Sometimes your only contact with an individual is by letter. Therefore, you should write every letter with utmost care.

Before you sign a letter, proofread it and check the spelling carefully for mechanical and typographical errors. Check, too, to make sure it says everything desired. You want your letter to make a favorable impression for you and for your company.

Regards, (Complimentary closing with mixed punctuation)

Deborah Roebuck

Deborah Roebuck, Ph.D. (Signature Line)
Enclosure
Copy

Figure 4.8 Full Block Style

Callao Community Bank
1279 Main Street
Callao, MO 66366

June 3, 20XX

Mrs. Mary Britt
Highway 3
Callao, MO 66366

Dear Mrs. Britt (Open punctuation)

This letter illustrates the modified block style. Remember, when you write a short letter, you can move the date line down as this will provide more white space at the top of your letter.

Be sure to single-space the inside address in block form. With the modified style, you have the option of indenting or not indenting the first line of each paragraph five spaces.

Unless otherwise instructed, address letters to individuals rather than to companies, corporations, or partnerships.

Sincerely (Open punctuation)

Joe Henry

Joe Henry, Branch Manager

Enclosure
Copies: 1

Figure 4.9. Modified Block Style Letter

monitor progress, provide information, guide decision making, help implement organizational changes, and document work. Reports can be classified as *short* or *long. Short reports,* sometimes referred to as *informal reports,* are typically used in the day-to-day operations of the organization, while *long reports* or *formal reports* require some type of data analysis and recommendations.

Keep the following guidelines in mind as you write your reports:

- Keep your reader in mind when you write. Ask yourself these questions: What does the reader know? What does the reader need to know? Outline the points to be covered, and then start writing.
- State the purpose clearly and concisely.
- Make the report objective and not personal. Managers want reports to present all sides of an issue.
- Be exact with details and support your facts.
- List the facts in sequence and use headings to ease reading.
- Use attachments for extra information not needed within the body.
- Keep paragraphs short. Remember, you want your reader to read the report.
- Use bullets, boldface, and underscores to emphasize important information.
- Make your report inviting to read by positioning the information attractively. Don't crowd too much information on one page.
- Conclude with a brief summary of key points and offer recommendations.

The format of reports varies widely according to the nature of the information reflected and the preferences of the organization.

An executive summary should "boil down" a report to its barest essentials, without making the overview meaningless. Top executives should be able to glean enough information and understanding to feel confident making a decision.

Source: Business Communication
16th Edition
Carol M. Lehman
Debbie D. Dufrene
South-Western Cengage Learning, Page 381

Executive Summaries

Executive summaries can range from one to four pages depending upon the length of the report, proposal, or business plan. Typically, your executive summary should be approximately 1/10 of the length of your report, proposal, or business plan.[15] The executive summary highlights the major sections and findings of a longer document. The summary should grab your audience's attention with a strong hook in the first sentence and then tell them why they should continue reading the executive summary. Investors, lenders, executives, managers, and CEOs are extremely busy. So before handing them a lengthy report, business plan, or proposal, you tell and sell them on the reasons why they should read your document. "The most important reason to include an executive summary is that in many cases, it is the only thing the reader will read," says Pablo Bonjour, founder and CEO of Katy, Texas-based SMG Business Plans, a company that offers entrepreneurs assistance in writing business plans. According to Bonjour, investors will read the executive summary to decide if they will even bother reading the rest of the business plan. It's rare for an investor or lender to read an entire business plan, at least in the initial stages of analysis and consideration for funding, so having a strong executive summary is key.[16]

Typically, your reader wants a quick overview of what you have written in the report. Therefore, make sure it answers the following questions:

- What are the conclusions and recommendations?
- What are the implications for the managerial leader or his or her organization?
- What is the subject, when was it written, and who wrote it?
- What does it contribute and what's it in for the audience to read the entire report?

After the attention-getting start you should consider these categories as a logical approach to the rest of your summary:

- A company description summary
- The problem
- Your solution
- Why now

> "An executive reads for certain keywords, and for the price," says Stacia Kelly, president of Catklaw, a Woodbridge, Virginia–based writing boutique. "If he likes it, he'll hand it to an assistant and ask them to read the whole thing."
>
> Source: Crafting a Powerful Executive Summary
> By John Clayton
> Retrieved from http://hbswk.hbs.edu/archive/3660.html

Clearly, an executive summary demands your best thinking, planning, and organizing so that it gets read.

Blogs

A blog typically is written by one person who makes frequent, not daily, updates. Usually blogs are in chronological order from the most recent post (or entry) at the top of the main page to the older entries toward the bottom. Today's blogging tools allow you to post new material within minutes and to respond quickly when needed. Many CEOs use blogs to communicate with their internal and external audiences. Blogs also aid project management, team communication, company news, customer support, public relations and media relations, recruiting, policy and issue discussion, crisis communication, market research, brainstorming, employee engagement, and viral marketing.[17]

Some guidelines for writing a blog follow:

- Write with the reader in mind.
- Make it valuable and worthwhile.
- Proofread for typos and glaring grammatical errors.
- Keep it short and simple.
- Keep it lively; make it snappy and snazzy.
- Link often.
- Use keywords often.
- Write clearly (in short sentences with only one concept per sentence).
- Write as you talk.
- Use a clear headline, and don't be afraid to make bold statements.[18]

The Ultimate Blogger's Writing Guide

1. **Put the reader first**. If you write to impress, you will distract the reader from the content. Impactful writing is like a store window being clean and clear so that you have an unobstructed view of the contents within.

2. **Organize your thoughts**. You don't need a detailed outline for most writing. But you do need to know what you want to say before you say it. Simply jot down the important points you want to make and arrange them in the order you want to make them. Eliminate any ideas that are not directly related to these points.

3. **Use short paragraphs**. Look at any newspaper and notice how short the paragraphs are. That's done to make reading easier since our brains take in information better when ideas are broken into small chunks. In ordinary writing, each paragraph develops one idea and includes many sentences. But in blogging, the style is less formal and paragraphs may be as short as a single sentence or even a single word.

4. **Use short sentences**. You should keep sentences short for the same reason you keep paragraphs short: They're easier to read and understand. Each sentence should have one simple thought. More than that creates complexity and invites confusion.

5. **Use simple words**. Since your purpose is to communicate and not impress, simple words work better than big ones. Write "get" instead of "procure." Write "use" rather than "utilize."

6. **Be specific**. Don't write, "Many doctors recommend Brand X." Write, "97% of doctors recommend Brand X." Don't write, "The Big Widget is offered in many colors." Write, "The Big Widget comes in red, green, blue, and white." Get to the point. Say what you mean. Use specific nouns.

7. **Write in a conversational style**. If you write as if you're wearing a top hat and spats, you distance yourself from the reader and muddle the message.

8. **Be clear.** This is probably the most important rule of all. Without clarity, your writing fails on every level. You achieve clarity

when you accurately communicate the meaning in your head to the head of your reader. This can be difficult. Look at your writing with an objective eye. Consider what might be misunderstood and rewrite it. Find what is irrelevant and delete it. Notice what is missing and insert it.

Source: The Ultimate Blogger Writing Guide By Dean Rieck
Retrieved from http://www.copyblogger.com/
blogging-writing-guide/

In Figure 4.10, you will find an example of a well-written blog entry.

FOR THE LIFE OF YOUR BUSINESS

Leadership: What to Say When You Can't Fix the Problem

By: Charlene Diaz, April 28, 2011

A garden center owner sold a ficus tree to a lawyer who wanted to put it in the window of her street-front law office. We could make a lot of lawyer jokes about the reason the leaves fell off the tree after the lawyer put it in the window, but ficus trees are finicky about where they like to sit, and every time you move one, the leaves may fall off.

The attorney asked to exchange the tree. The owner explained. The woman demanded. The owner gave her a new tree. The lawyer put it in the window. The leaves fell off and the attorney sued the garden center.

Getting your message across effectively without losing the client is tricky, Patricia L. Harms and Deborah Britt Roebuck report in the December 2010 issue of *Business Communication Quarterly.* *They describe* a way to give feedback using a model that provides for a positive return. They advocate that "feedback aligns workplace behavior with the overall goals of a team or an organization." While Harms

Figure 4.10. Example of a Blog

and Roebuck focus on providing performance feedback to employees, their models could be used to give good or bad news to customers, vendors, or other business associates.

For good news, Harms and Roebuck suggest using the BET method:

B Behavior

E Effect

T Thank you

With the BET model, you focus on what happened, its effect, and saying thank you.

For bad news—which is the harder news to deliver—Harms and Roebuck suggest the BEAR method:

B Behavior

E Effect

A Alternative

R Result

In this model, once the behavior and its effect are identified, Harms and Roebuck suggest finding an alternative behavior or solution that would correct, or make up for, the effect. The result can be reported as either what might happen if the alternative isn't applied (negative outcome or consequences) or what might happen if the alternative is applied (a more positive outcome or consequences).

The BEAR model provides one or two places to focus positive energy that could result in a better outcome.

Using the BEAR method, the garden shop owner might have said the following:

Ficus trees are finicky and don't like to be moved (Behavior). They tend to lose their leaves whenever they are moved to new locations (Effect).

The alternative needs to be a solution that both parties like. The garden center owner needs the attorney to leave the ficus tree alone for three weeks. The attorney is a customer who needs to be heard. So, the garden center owner could have said, "You need to leave the tree alone for three weeks. If it still has no leaves after three weeks, I'll deliver a replacement tree myself" (Alternative). "There's a chance the ficus tree

Figure 4.10. Example of a Blog (continued)

just won't work in your window. If after three weeks the tree doesn't seem to be working, we'll find a new tree that will work for you, or I'll refund your money" (Result).

When you have to give negative feedback, try the BEAR method, channeling positive energy into the alternative so that the result is one that both parties find palatable.

And *now* you can make a joke about how the ficus tree kept losing its leaves because it didn't like the spot in *that particular lawyer's* window.

Contact information:
E-mail: *charlsye.diaz@umit.maine.edu*
Twitter: charlsye
Website: www.charlsyesmithdiaz.com

Figure 4.10. Example of a Blog (continued)

Tweets

Twitter is a messaging tool that restricts messages (called tweets) to 140 characters. It shares some qualities with instant messaging and e-mail, but it is unique in the sense that everyone can read what a user tweets. Make sure your username reflects who you are and your aims. You will need to comment on others' tweets to build a following. You should follow people who are interested in things of importance to your business and respond to their interests in ways that show your favorable intentions. When you follow someone on Twitter, you subscribe to his or her Tweets as a *Follower*. For you to gain *Followers*, you will want to share interesting things in the space your business occupies such as links, tips, and other helpful information that will build up your list of followers.[19]

Here's an example of how Tony Hsieh, CEO of Zappos.com, uses Twitter:

> I was flying in to the Vegas airport, and I twittered "Just landed in Vegas airport." I would have never texted anyone that message, but in the Twitter culture, that's exactly what you're supposed to do. It just so happened that someone on my Twitter network was about to fly out of Vegas, so we met up at the airport bar and had a drink. I would have never known otherwise that this person was at the airport, nor would I have ever sent him a text message or called him that I had just landed.

What Twitter profile mistakes have you seen?

1. **No description of who you are in your profile**: Cheeky 140-character descriptions of your abstract qualities may sound cool, but they make it difficult for others to decide if they want to read your work. Simply describe who you are, what you do, and what you write.
2. **No link to your personal site in your profile**: Readers want to be able to find more about the person behind a Twitter feed—don't leave them guessing. Give them a link to a Facebook page, personal website, or Amazon page.
3. **No picture in your profile**: People are looking for your tweets, not tweets from some generic Twitter logo. Show us what you look like.
4. **No location data in your profile**: Twitter has all sorts of useful features tied to your location. In addition, a simple city and state listing helps people identify with you as well.
5. **Don't protect your tweets**: You can protect your tweets in a personal account—privacy controls are powerful tools in the 21st century. However, if you are submitting your feed to directories and trying to build an audience, protected tweets are frustrating for potential readers.

Source: Twitter Profile Mistakes Writers Should Avoid
By Jason Boog, June 22, 2011
Retrieved from http://www.mediabistro.com/
galleycat/5-twitter-profile-mistakes-writers-should-avoid_b32527

According to Karl Keller of Karl Keller Communication Partners, you can control tone even in brief messages. One-sentence messages can convey a tone. So look at a single sentence in a longer piece that you've written, independent of other sentences. Could it be construed in a different way from what you intended if read separately? If it can't, and it is a thought that needs minimal or no context, it's appropriate to be a text, a tweet, or a brief e-mail through a mobile device.[20]

Instant and Text Messages

Instant messaging (IM) and text messaging are useful in many business environments. IM offers business value—with unified communication, direct contact, improved collaboration, and cost savings. It is a fast way to get coworkers' attention, rapidly resolve issues/questions, and save on phone costs. IM is especially useful for remote workers with whom building a community is essential in helping employees to be more effective.[21] Do use caution, however, when using IM and think about your receiver. Let's consider this situation: A manager is in an airport waiting for a plane and decides to send an IM to a subordinate who has made a decision to have 12 weeks of product in inventory. He sends the following IM:

Bob bad decision on inventory go to 8 weeks not 12.

This manager probably didn't take the time to consider his audience's reaction to his message. He probably should have sent something like this:

Bob on inventory let's do 8 not 12 weeks.

Even in the short world of text messages and tweets, the Aristotelian concept of ethos, logos, and pathos apply. As a business communicator, you must ALWAYS think strategically about every message you write. You can write useful and effective short messages, but do so thoughtfully.[22]

Keep the following suggestions of business writing trainer Lynn Gaertner Johnston in mind when you write your next instant message or text:

- Greet the other person briefly at the start of the IM conversation. Don't do the equivalent of barging in with a business question without saying hello. Be courteous.

- Wait for a response to each of your comments before adding more. Otherwise, you won't be sure which comment the other person is addressing.
- Do your best to use correct grammar, punctuation, and spelling. Mistakes will happen, of course, but don't make them knowingly. They get in the way of quick understanding.
- Use the word "we" cautiously or avoid it. It may refer to you and your team, or you and the other person. Instead write "our team" or "you and I."
- Avoid passive verbs such as "should be downloaded." Passives don't make it clear who should do the action. Instead use "Download," "I have downloaded," or "Your IT administrator will download."
- In IM exchanges with customers, when you use boilerplate text (for example, to respond to common customer questions), edit the boilerplate so it suits the situation. For example, if you have just told the customer, "I will be glad to help," cut the "I will be glad to help" statement from the next boilerplate response. Otherwise, it will be obvious that you are pasting in rote responses.
- As with other business messages, avoid humor unless you are certain the other person will understand and enjoy it.
- Avoid sarcasm. People cannot distinguish between seriousness and sarcasm in brief, flat words on the screen.
- End the conversation with an official sign-off such as "I am signing off now." That way, the other person will know that you believe the exchange is complete, and you won't have a bunch of empty chatter winding down the conversation. But wait a few moments to see whether the other person acknowledges your sign-off or instead says, "Wait—there's more!"[23]

How to Create a LinkedIn Profile That Really Connects

By Jeff Haden

Here's how you can transform your LinkedIn summary into a tool that effectively represents you and your business and allows you to make new connections:

Step 1: Think of your summary as an elevator pitch. If you get 30 seconds to describe your business to your dream client, what three points will you try to make? In essence, that's your summary: Memorable, catchy, descriptive. Since the goal of an elevator speech is to spark a conversation, the goal of your summary should be to make the reader think, "Hmm . . . really? Interesting. Tell me more."

Step 2: Think first-person. Translate accomplishments, achievements, and approaches into personal terms. What have you (or by extension, your company) done, and what does that mean to the person who reads the summary? Experience and background don't just reflect well on you—your accomplishments benefit your customers, too. In short, "Here's what I/we can do for you." Then write using the first person; leave the third-person references to athletes and movie stars.

Step 3: Write it yourself. It's tempting to turn the writing process over to a social media aficionado in your organization. Feel free to delegate implementation, but be careful with the content. Many people who are "skilled at social media" know the nuts and bolts of the applications, but the essence of an effective summary is communication. If you delegate content generation, find someone who is a skilled communicator, not someone who has set up dozens of social media accounts. The difference is huge.

Step 4: Think keywords. Potential clients may find you through mutual connections, but the majority will find you through advanced searches. Make a list of important keywords and use them to build the framework of your summary. But if you're ever in doubt, err on the side of natural rather than keyword: You can bring a client close to your boat with a keyword, but you'll never land them without a summary that makes a real connection.

Step 5: Stick to two or three paragraphs. Be brief, conversational, and engaging. Spark questions. Think in terms of a conversation rather than a presentation. Above all, avoid formal "brochure speak" and write like a real person and not a corporate mouthpiece.

Retrieved from *http://www.bnet.com/blog/small-biz-advice/how-to -create-a-linkedin-profile-that-really-connects/3025?promo=857&tag=n .e857*

Social Media

Social media are the various forms of user-generated content and the collection of websites and applications that enable people to interact and share information online. Social media includes online forums (e.g., DigitalPoint); blogs (e.g., WordPress); social networking sites (e.g., Facebook); social bookmarking sites (e.g., Digg); video sharing sites (e.g., YouTube); photo sharing sites (e.g. Flickr); streaming sites (e.g., Ustream); user reviews (e.g., Amazon); crowdsourcing (e.g., Wikipedia); and content aggregators (e.g., FriendFeed).[24]

For the past four years, the Center for Marketing Research at the University of Massachusetts Dartmouth has tracked social media use among the Inc. 500, a list of the fastest-growing private U.S. companies compiled annually by *Inc. Magazine*. This survey is one of the few longitudinal studies that offer in-depth insight into corporate social media adoption and engagement.

Here are four highlights from the latest Inc. 500 survey, conducted in October and November of 2010:

- **Facebook and Twitter lead the social media pack.** A whopping 87 percent of respondents said they are "very familiar" with the Facebook platform. Forty-four percent say Facebook is the single most effective social networking platform they use. Nearly three-fourths (71 percent) said they are familiar with Twitter—that's up from 62 percent in 2009.
- **Companies in the Inc. 500 are using blogs effectively.** Fifty percent of the 2010 Inc. 500 have a corporate blog (up from 45 percent in 2009 and 39 percent in 2008), and according to the

Center for Marketing Research, there is also clear evidence that companies are using blogs effectively. Inc. 500 companies are engaging consumers by accepting and replying to comments and providing a vehicle for subscriptions. In addition, 34 percent have developed policies to govern blogging by their employees.

- **Most say social media is "very important."** More than half (56 percent) of the Inc. 500 said social media was "very important" to their business/marketing strategy. What's more, 57 percent report using search engines and social networking sites to recruit and evaluate potential employees. Social media is not only used for communication between business and consumers, but for communicating with vendors and partners as well.

- **Social media adoption is skewed by industry.** Even though 83 percent of the 2010 Inc. 500 use at least one of the social media tools studied, the survey showed that adoption continues to vary by industry. For example, government service companies make up 12 percent of the 2010 Inc. 500, but these companies make up 27 percent of those who do not use social media tools. Likewise, energy companies make up 3 percent of the 2010 Inc. 500, but 17 percent of the nonusers. Financial Services companies represent 5 percent of the Inc. 500, but 10 percent of those who have not yet adopted social media.[25]

Given that many organizations are now embracing social media, Figure 4.11 presents some best practices to use in social media.

Conclusion

Texting, tweeting, and other types of social media encourage you to be direct and brief. For those situations when you are limited to a certain number of words, you can use abbreviations such as "4ward." However, you still have to know your audience and determine the purpose of your writing. Laura Wiegert, Strategic Marketing Coordinator for Holy Family Memorial, shared the following:

> What gets scary is when people start incorporating this style of writing into their business communications. Our society's growing

- Do unto others: "Please" and "Thank You" go a long way. If you want to be respected, you first have to give respect.
- Be nice: Remember, what you do on the Internet reflects on you and quite possibly on your business. Be positive and encouraging. No one wants to be associated with a negative individual.
- Don't judge too quickly: You know the old saying "Don't judge a book by its cover?" It still holds true today. When meeting individuals online, you should strike up a conversation, get to know them a bit before you judge who or what they are. In social media and in marketing, relationships matter. Start building yours today!
- Show respect: Just because you are "hiding" behind a computer doesn't give you free rein to act as you please. You still need to treat people properly.
- When marketing, use a first name. If you want someone to respond to you, you need to make your connection more personable. Using their first name is a great way to start!
- Don't be annoying: Don't continue to send e-mails out every hour on the hour. It's annoying and clutters up one's inbox. If you don't hear back from an individual right away, give that person some time. Some people aren't surgically attached to their computers.
- Play by the rules: Respect group and community rules. Follow the *terms of use* of the social platform.
- Don't abuse your network: Use your network the right way. Don't post how your day is going to your network all day long. It's unprofessional and unnecessary. If you must post something, post something of significance that your network can actually use, like a great social media link you just found or some sort of tip, advice, or quote you find significant.
- Add a profile picture: Everyone likes to see who they are talking to. It's easy to do and having a picture on file makes you look more reputable and professional.
- Above all, don't overreact: People are trying to figure out the proper way to communicate electronically, and millions are entering as rookies on a monthly basis. Show patience, kindness, and tolerance.[26]

Figure 4.11. Social Media Best Practices

addiction to instant messaging is starting to flow over into the workplace, slowly chipping away at solid business writing skills. The art of proper writing in the *business* world could become a lost one, whether writing a brochure, a business letter or even an e-mail. In today's fast food world we are always looking for ways to do things faster and more efficiently. But that can often lead to sloppy writing, which in the business world translates into unprofessional. No big deal? Oh, but it is! Keep in mind that for your *customer*, it's all about image—whether it's your logo, how you dress, how clean your building is, how you write, or your website. It is a reflection on YOU and YOUR COMPANY. Make it a good one! Start the process by asking yourself the following questions: Do you know the difference between "that" and "which" . . . "good" or "well" . . . "there," "their," or "they're?" If you don't, it may be time for a refresher on the English language. Better yet, start creating a corporate culture that encourages effective writing utilizing proper grammar, style, and spelling. Become the writing champion at your organization.[27]

Now that you know some basics of business writing, you can become your organization's writing champion. You will improve your writing if you take every opportunity to write and practice the techniques presented in this chapter. Think about the reaction your reader will have to your message and adopt the correct writing strategy. When you start to write, break down the document into pieces and write the easiest section first. You want to write for understanding and not just to impress your audience. Simple writing requires putting ego aside, but it gains you more appreciation. Simplify your language so that you convey your thoughts in a pointed, direct manner. Then edit and revise your document to trim unnecessary words. Think of words as your daily food intake—make sure you get all the essential vitamins and minerals, but trim off the excess fat and calories. Make any passive sentences active and search for any errors in completeness, clearness, concreteness, correctness, conciseness, courtesy, or character. Aim for a final professional document that clearly communicates your message. Use the 7 *Cs* checklist in Figure 4.12 to proofread your document. If you can answer "yes" to every question, you have created an effective business document.

Checking for completeness	Yes	No
Have you given all the facts?		
Have you covered all the essentials?		
Have you answered all the questions?		
Have you organized your writing?		
Checking for clearness		
Have you used familiar words and short sentences?		
Have you presented only one idea in a sentence?		
Have you avoided unfamiliar business or technical terminology?		
Have you written in the reader's language?		
Checking for concreteness		
Have you written with crisp, exact details?		
Have you used words that paint a picture and make the facts vivid?		
Have you avoided using sexist language?		
Have you eliminated vague words?		
Have you presented positive images?		
Checking for correctness		
Have you checked all facts?		
Have you spelled all words correctly, including names?		
Have you verified all numbers and amounts?		
Have you written actively?		
Have you used the grammar checker in your word processing package?		
Checking for conciseness		
Have you identified immediately the subject of the message?		
Have you avoided rehashing the reader's document?		
Have you avoided needless filler words or phrases?		
Have you avoided useless repetition?		
Checking for courtesy		
Will the writing win goodwill?		
Have you used positive, pleasant words?		
Have you used "please," "thank you," or "I appreciate" somewhere in your writing?		
Have you used titles before names?		
Checking for character		
Have you put the reader's needs first?		
Have you highlighted the reader's interest?		
Have you spoken the reader's language?		
Have you incorporated all the Cs into your document?		

Figure 4.12 7 Cs Checklist for Effective Writing

Case for Thinking and Discussing

Instructions: Read the following article and then reflect upon the following questions.

1. What new insights did you gain from this presentation?
2. Compare and contrast the attributes of the various social media.
3. How might social media be used as a political tool within an organization?
4. Discuss potential ethical issues related to the use of social media.
5. What lessons can you apply to your organization?

Business Etiquette | the new rules in a **digital age**

Robert Half®
Excellence in Professional Staffing

Table of Contents

Acknowledgments 1
The New Rules of Etiquette 2
Professional Networking Sites, Including LinkedIn 3
Social Networking Sites, Including Facebook 7
Twitter 11
5 Questions to Ask Yourself About Social and
   Professional Networking Sites 13
E-mail 15
Instant Messaging 18
Mobile Devices 20
Phone, Video and Web Conferencing 22
Sticky Etiquette Questions 24
Conclusion 25
About Robert Half 25

Acknowledgments

Robert Half International would like to recognize the following individuals for providing their time and insights on etiquette in the workplace. Their contributions are greatly appreciated.

Janet Aronica, Community Manager, oneforty inc.

Laura Fitton, CEO and Founder, oneforty inc., Co-author, *Twitter for Dummies*

Vicky Oliver, Author, *301 Smart Answers to Tough Business Etiquette Questions*

Tonia Ries, CEO and Founder, Modern Media, Founder of TWTRCON

Tim Sanders, CEO, Deeper Media, Author, *The Likeability Factor: How to Boost Your L Factor and Achieve Your Life's Dreams*

Clara Shih, CEO and Founder, Hearsay, Author, *The Facebook Era: Tapping Online Social Networks to Build Better Products, Reach New Audiences, and Sell More Stuff*

The New Rules of Etiquette

"Politeness is to human nature what warmth is to wax."
—Arthur Schopenhauer, 19th century philosopher

You've mastered traditional business etiquette, seamlessly reaching for the right fork during a professional dinner while engaging in animated conversation with your dining companions. But at a time in which more business discussions take place via LinkedIn, Twitter or e-mail than over cocktails and hors d'oeuvres, it's just as important – if not more so – to know how to present yourself professionally using digital tools.

Given the newness of social media and other communications vehicles, it's easy to say or do the wrong thing. Unfortunately, missteps in this area can have lasting consequences: An online mistake can show up next to your name in an Internet search for years to come. To help you avoid falling victim to such blunders, Robert Half has created this guide offering insights into digital protocols, as well as advice for handling sticky situations. The information and tips are based on surveys of executives, independent research, input from social media and etiquette experts, and our own experiences working with job candidates and clients throughout North America. We hope you find this guide useful and invite you to contact us at **1.800.803.8367** for more information or help with any of your staffing or employment needs.

Professional Networking Sites, Including LinkedIn

Are you linking in or being left out? Professional networking sites are among the most popular ways of nurturing professional relationships today. Networking online is no different than rubbing shoulders at in-person networking events – it's important to make a positive impression and follow the rules of the road. Here are some ways to get the most out of LinkedIn and similar websites:

▶ Complete your profile. Provide as much information in your LinkedIn profile as you can. This might include your professional summary, work history and education. Be sure to add key accomplishments so other users get a clear picture of your capabilities, and request recommendations from past colleagues and managers. They can highlight and praise your accomplishments in a far richer and more credible way.

▶ Request recommendations individually. Treat each request with the same respect you would in "the real world." A generic message asking all of your connections to endorse you may fall on deaf ears. Think about it: Why create a personal recommendation for someone who can't write personally to request one? When appropriate (and if it's permissible by your company), recommend those whom you know the best and

trust the most. Be careful, however, of what may be perceived as quid pro quo recommendations: If you recommend someone just as he or she has posted some kind words about you, your kudos may be viewed as "payback."

Professional Networking Sites,
Including LinkedIn

▲ Prioritize quality over quantity.
Network envy can make some people
link aimlessly just to build their number
of contacts. Don't invite strangers to
your network merely to make it larger,
and don't be offended when those
you've never met or vaguely know ignore
your requests. Your network is only as
strong as its weakest connection.

▲ Be a joiner. LinkedIn offers many
groups for people who share certain
passions or interests, and these can
be a valuable asset for keeping pace
with new developments in your field.
When participating in professional
groups, provide useful information and
input. Avoid sending direct messages
to fellow group members unless
you have established a personal
connection beforehand.

10 Top LinkedIn Professional Groups

Good business etiquette on LinkedIn includes participating in discussions and
doing small favors for others. The following are the top 10 LinkedIn Groups
ranked by number of members.* To access the LinkedIn Groups Directory,
go to the search box and click on "Groups" from the pull-down menu:

1. Linked:HR (#1 Human Resources Group)
2. Job Openings, Job Leads and Job Connections!
3. eMarketing Association Network
4. Job & Career Network
5. Executive Suite
6. On Startups – The Community For Entrepreneurs
7. Consultants Network
8. Job & Career Network – Professions and Industries
9. Telecom Professionals
10. The Project Manager Network – #1 Group For Project Managers

You also may want to find out if your various alumni and
trade associations have any LinkedIn groups. If so, be sure
to join those you find most appealing.

*Ranked as of Jan. 26, 2011. Top listings subject to change.

Professional Networking Sites, Including LinkedIn

▲ Say 'please' and be respectful. If you would like an introduction to someone in a contact's network, ask politely and explain why you hope to meet the other person. For example, you might point out that the potential contact is in a professional association of interest to you.

▲ Think twice before you say yes. When members of your network request introductions to your other contacts, don't immediately agree, particularly if you don't know very well the person who is making the request. Your reputation is on the line if your contact ends up becoming a nuisance to that individual. It also is common practice now for "hyper networkers" to add as many LinkedIn connections as possible to mine data from your profile and those of your friends.

How to Tend to Your Network in Only Five Minutes a Day:

Networking online doesn't need to be time consuming. You can develop your professional reputation and help others in the process through simple etiquette practices that require only a few minutes each day.

1. Be the first to have a point of view. Share a relevant news article and add value by including an observation that may not be so obvious to others.

2. Let them know they've been heard. Listen to what your network has to say so you can make an informed suggestion or relevant introduction.

3. Establish yourself as the go-to person. Consider connecting your LinkedIn and Twitter accounts to establish more visibility. Tweet your professional ideas and links into your profile using the hash tag #in. (However, think twice before connecting your LinkedIn account to sites such as Foursquare, or other location-based social networks. It's unlikely people in your professional network really need to know where you just ate lunch.)

   4. Try to add at least one new person to your network a week. Growing networks are far more effective than stagnant ones.

5

Professional Networking Sites, Including LinkedIn

▲ Make the connection clear. Too often, people connect without thinking. When seeking to make a new contact, remind a person of how you know him or her if it has been a while since you've talked. For example, you might reference a recent conference you both attended.

▲ Don't be one-sided. An "all-about-me" approach won't get you very far. LinkedIn and similar sites allow you to ask for help from members of your network quickly and easily, but don't abuse this privilege with constant requests. Also, don't forget to thank those who lend you a hand, and always look to return the favor.

▲ Act quickly on requests. Patience is a virtue, but not everyone possesses it. Respond to requests that come via your network promptly – within 24 hours, if possible.

▲ Keep it professional. Think twice before posting on LinkedIn, and don't post too often or on trivial subjects. Your aim should be to become a trusted authority rather than a social gadfly. That said, it's OK to share personal interests such as athletics and hobbies, as well as a profile picture so that others can begin to know you.

▲ Make a big impact with small gestures. Pay attention to what people are saying or working on. You can offer helpful suggestions, send useful articles or just leave comments, letting those in your network know they are heard and understood. You also can share insights and offer introductions to others. This may take you only 45 seconds of effort but could have a profound impact on the people with whom you wish to develop closer professional relationships.

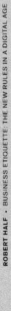

Social Networking Sites, Including Facebook

To friend or not to friend? Social networking websites such as Facebook were initially designed as a way for individuals to connect with friends and family. Today, these tools are increasingly used for professional purposes, particularly in industries such as public relations and entertainment. But for individuals, online social interaction deserves careful thought before deciding to invite your professional contacts to join your friend list.

Many people attempt to keep their Facebook profiles away from the public eye, or create separate profiles for social and professional purposes. Others have decided their work and personal lives are so tightly linked that they have no reservations about friending colleagues as well as pals.

Just as you might share some details about your social life with a client over lunch, you may decide that connecting with colleagues on Facebook allows you to build closer relationships. Depending on your industry, you may even find that

Facebook is a useful way to develop relationships that may lead to new business.

Whatever your decision, it's important to understand the social networking "rules of the road." Even if you determine it's best to keep your personal and business profiles separate, you should know how to handle friend requests gracefully and the actions you can take to protect your privacy. And if you do combine your personal and professional lives, it's always wise to be thoughtful and considerate when

interacting in social communities. Here are a few tips:

▲ Secure a vanity URL. Your name may be more common than you think. A vanity URL will make it easier for people to find you. For instance, instead of a long, unwieldy user name, consider facebook.com/yournameofchoice/. Include it in your e-mail signature file and on your business cards. (Visit Facebook to learn more about usernames and check their availability.)

Social Networking Sites, Including Facebook

Facebook Faux Pas: Don't Make Claims That Your Profile Doesn't Substantiate

A woman who called in to work claiming to be too sick to use her computer got caught updating her Facebook page the same day. She told her employer she was suffering from a migraine and needed to lie down in a dark room. The company said its discovery that she was using Facebook while home sick prompted them to lose trust in her and resulted in her permanent dismissal.

Source: "Ill' Worker Fired Over Facebook," BBC News

▲ Include a profile picture. A picture is worth a thousand words. A personal photo adds legitimacy and confirms that you're the right "Mary Jones." The image you choose can be casual, but make sure it's professional.

▲ Respect the wall. If you wouldn't want to read it on a billboard, don't post it to your Facebook wall – or anyone else's. This holds true even if you use Facebook only to socialize. Remember, anyone you 'friend' can see your comments, photos and YouTube video links. E-mail or use Facebook's messaging feature instead.

▲ Make the call. Are you using Facebook for work or personal use? If you decide to friend coworkers, partners and customers, maintain full business acumen. Avoid posting what you ate today or what bar you are going to tonight for your business contacts to see.

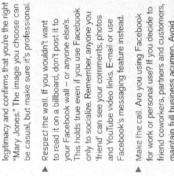

Social Networking Sites, Including Facebook

▲ Keep it focused. Likewise, resist the temptation to post updates about games, quizzes and groups to which you belong if you use Facebook for business. You'll muddy the waters and likely lose the interest of (or even annoy) individuals who want to know about your professional activities. Don't add new applications lightly! Some automatically post your activities on the general RSS feed. Do you really want all of your friends knowing every time you add a sheep to FarmVille? Probably not.

▲ Avoid venting. Big Brother really is watching, yet people continue to make the mistake of posting negative comments or gossiping about their employers, supervisors, colleagues, or any other touchy topic. Don't do it – chances are the wrong set of eyes will stumble upon your remarks. A better approach? Count to 10 and consider the consequences.

▲ Ask before you tag. Check with people before tagging them in photos, especially if you think they might not appreciate it, and don't tag someone else's photo with a

business pitch unless you've asked permission. Remember to check your own photos periodically to make sure you haven't been tagged in one you may not want to be associated with; Facebook has settings that allow you to receive an alert anytime you have been tagged in a photo.

▲ Please, don't poke. Your friends may get a kick out of your "nudges," but it can be interpreted as flirting. Use this feature for personal interactions only. It's never appropriate for professional purposes.

Social Networking Sites, Including Facebook

Thinking About 'Friending' Your Boss on Facebook?

Executives were asked, **"How comfortable would you feel about being 'friended' by the following individuals on Facebook?"** Their responses:

	Your boss	Your coworkers	People you manage	Clients	Vendors
Very Comfortable	15%	10%	10%	6%	5%
Somewhat Comfortable	23%	37%	27%	27%	17%
Not Very Comfortable	17%	15%	18%	21%	25%
Not Comfortable at All	38%	32%	39%	39%	47%
Don't Know	7%	6%	6%	7%	6%

Source: Robert Hall survey of 249 senior executives at the largest companies in the United States and Canada

▲ Take 'no' for an answer. When trying to friend someone, once is enough. There's no need to bombard the person with repeated requests. At the same time, keep in mind that some people may not want to connect with you, including your boss or coworkers. Try not to take it personally; people use different criteria for building their online social networks, or they may not be regular Facebook users.

▲ Keep it private. It's likely you'll find coworkers or other business contacts on Facebook, and not all of them will use the site in a professional way. Respect their privacy, and don't turn their posts into fodder for office gossip.

ROBERT HALF • BUSINESS ETIQUETTE: THE NEW RULES IN A DIGITAL AGE

Twitter

Although you may not know what "twibes" are, most people have used or at least heard of Twitter since it launched in 2006. (FYI: A "twibe" is a group of Twitter users interested in a common topic.) Twitter is perhaps the least understood of all the major social media services. How do you find meaningful information in a stream of tweets? What does RT stand for? And what's a Fail Whale? The following tips can help you interact with the "Twitterverse" (Twitter universe) in a professional manner when exploring this real-time information network:

▲ Introduce yourself. Twitter is not a place for a curriculum vitae. In your biography, you have a limited number of characters to explain what you do and what followers can expect from your feed. This makes it easy for people to decide whether to follow you.

▲ Start by listening. Use Twitter's search function to find feeds that interest you, and then spend some time learning how people in your industry use the platform. Tools like CoTweet, HootSuite and TweetDeck allow you to create saved search terms to track topics of interest.

▲ Be human when tweeting. It's important to use a human voice. Keep your tone real and natural.

▲ Add value. What distinct value do you offer your followers? Be helpful and generous. Share links to relevant articles or online resources. Tweet out information your followers can use, not irrelevant details.

▲ Tweet regularly. Keep your profile current by posting information on a regular basis – a few times a day, if possible, or as often as seems natural. It only takes a

few minutes, and it will help you connect with others who share the same interests. Remember, tweeting is not about a number, and it shouldn't feel forced.

▲ Pay it forward. Retweeting others' posts helps you build rapport with followers, encourage discussion and show people that it's not all about you – others have pertinent things to say, too!

Twitter

▲ Offer thanks. Acknowledge retweets by publicly thanking the people who shared your information. But don't go overboard – it clutters your followers' streams. Consider a direct message (DM) instead.

▲ Keep it light. You only have 140 characters to make a statement, so don't write in too formal a fashion. Consider using fewer than 140 characters to make it easier for others to retweet your posts.

▲ Be open. Twitter offers a privacy feature, and, while it's subject to change from time to time, 90 percent of users don't enable it. Open accounts encourage the most listening, learning and sharing, so think twice before locking an account you use for business. You can easily block individual accounts, if necessary.

▲ But don't be too open. Because of the space limitations, Twitter is not the best place to resolve sticky dilemmas. For sensitive issues, use the DM feature.

▲ Think before you tweet. When using Twitter for business, keep it PG-rated. Avoid posting any information about controversial topics or sharing sensitive information – you could get into hot water.

▲ Connect your LinkedIn and Twitter accounts. You can display select tweets in your LinkedIn profile by using the hash tag #in within your Twitter post. It's a way to gain more traction, further build your reputation and establish yourself as a go-to person, as long as you follow Twitter best practices and use a light hand. It can be annoying when all of a person's tweets indiscriminately show up via LinkedIn.

Social Networking Lessons From the Fatty Paycheck

It's undeniable that one tweet can set off a firestorm, or, in some cases, get you fired. A job candidate was offered a position by Cisco Systems, Inc., but her angst about the opportunity led her to tweet the pros and cons. Someone claiming to be a Cisco employee saw the tweet and responded:

"Cisco just offered me a job! Now I have to weigh the utility of a fatty paycheck against the daily commute to San Jose and hating the work."
– via Twitter

"Who is the hiring manager? I'm sure they would love to know that you will hate the work. We here at Cisco are versed in the web."
– via Twitter

Sources: "A Guide to Protecting Your Online Identity," Mashable; "Social Networking and Your Job: Lessons From the 'Cisco Fatty'," Excelle, A Monster Community

12

5 Questions to Ask Yourself About Social and Professional Networking Sites

Overwhelmed by all of the social media possibilities? Don't worry – you don't have to do it all. Use the following questions to help you determine the best medium for your message:

1

What's your primary goal?

Do you want to connect with friends, business contacts or both? Are you looking to build your professional reputation, relocate to a new city, find a new job, or stay up-to-date on industry news? Knowing your main objective can help you identify the best social networking tool for your needs.

2

Which sites do the people you want to connect with use?

LinkedIn, Facebook and Twitter offer the opportunity to reach a wide audience, but they are used for different purposes and in different contexts. Determine the audience you wish to reach and find out which sites they use and what communication style they prefer.

3

What's your strategy?

Decide how much time you're willing to invest, and then choose specific tasks that will help you achieve your goals. You may decide to join five new LinkedIn groups, follow 10 new people on Twitter each month, or network on Facebook for a set amount of time each day. Change your approach to find out what works best for you. Investing just a few minutes a day can help you manage your time and pay significant returns.

13

5 Questions to Ask Yourself About Social and Professional Networking Sites

4

What can you offer that's different from others?

If you're an expert in your field or just well versed on a particular topic, you can share your knowledge with others. Provide links to relevant articles or videos. Ideally, you can offer insights on industry trends or share some unique expertise of your own.

5

How will you monitor your progress?

The more you participate in your network, the more you'll gain from it. But don't get hung up on the numbers. There are many ways to get more "followers," but those large follower or friend numbers don't necessarily mean you're getting more from your network. Instead, focus on the value of the new relationships you're developing. You'll see a much higher return if you focus on quality versus quantity.

Who's Searching Whom?

- **44%** of adults who are online have searched for information about someone whose services or advice they seek in a professional capacity.

- **31%** of employed Internet users have searched online for information about coworkers, professional colleagues or business competitors, up from 23 percent in 2006.

Who's Sharing What?

- **65%** of adult social networking users have changed the privacy settings on their profile to limit what they share with others online.

- **27%** of employed Internet users now work for an employer that has policies about how they present themselves online – such as what they can post on blogs and websites, or what information they can share about themselves.

Source: Pew Internet & American Life Project, A Project of the Pew Research Center, "Reputation Management and Social Media," by Mary Madden and Aaron Smith, May 26, 2010

ROBERT HALF • BUSINESS ETIQUETTE: THE NEW RULES IN A DIGITAL AGE

E-mail

Although most professionals are well versed in using e-mail, many still struggle with the finer points. It's commonly known that typing in all CAPS is equivalent to "cybershouting" – but here are some other protocol points to consider:

▶ Be kind. Don't use e-mail to say no, argue, criticize or deliver bad news. Pick up the phone or deliver the information face to face.

▶ Make every e-mail fight for its right to be sent. The less you send, the more likely your messages will be read. Don't copy others unless they really need to read it.

▶ Be considerate, not cryptic. Don't expect others to decipher what you mean by reviewing an entire e-mail thread. Just because you are on the go doesn't mean you should expect others to piece together what's being requested.

▶ Use only one account for work. Keep work-related e-mails coming and going from your work account only. Having a single address makes it easy for people to find your messages. And it will prevent business messages from getting tangled with your personal e-mail – and perhaps neglected as a result.

▶ Consider your e-mail account when job hunting. It may go without saying, but don't use your current work e-mail to send resumes to prospective employers. Also, avoid using overly personal e-mail handles when job hunting, such as "partyanimal@_____.com." Not everyone will appreciate your sense of humor and "too much information" can be a turn-off.

▶ Respond in a timely manner. Try to respond to all messages within 24 hours, but don't say you'll reply with a more detailed response at a later date unless you really intend to follow through. If you're in consecutive meetings or away from the office, put an out-of-office message on so people aren't left wondering when you'll get back to them.

▶ Be crystal clear. In your subject line (and you should always have one), explain what you want: Do you need someone to review or approve something, or is the message simply an FYI? In the message itself, get to the point and use bullets, which are easier to scan than large blocks of text.

ROBERT HALF • BUSINESS ETIQUETTE: THE NEW RULES IN A DIGITAL AGE

E-mail

▲ Don't get too fancy. Avoid bright colors, odd fonts or extra-long signature lines. Some people find these distracting or just plain annoying. Include your personal or business links to social and professional networking sites when appropriate.

▲ Watch the size. An e-mail with a mega-attachment might never reach its recipient, and if it does, it could overload the inbox. Consider zipping the file or utilizing a service like YouSendlt that allows you to transmit large files over the Internet. (Be sure to check your company's IT policy first.)

▲ Don't cry wolf. Is it really urgent or are you simply feeling impatient? Resist the temptation to flag your messages with a big red exclamation point when they're really not that time sensitive. The result of doing so constantly? People simply will stop paying attention.

▲ Reply with care. When responding to an e-mail with multiple recipients, think twice about whether you really need to reply to all, and double-check your response before doing so. Bad "Reply to All" threads run rampant throughout organizations.

▲ Think before you send. Always review the distribution list when sending a sensitive message. Many a message has erroneously been sent to the wrong person with disastrous consequences.

Are Tech Etiquette Breaches a Career Killer?

Executives were asked, **"To what extent, if any, can technology etiquette breaches, for example, sending e-mail messages to unintended recipients, checking e-mail on a BlackBerry during meetings, etc., adversely affect a person's career prospects?"** Their responses:

Greatly

Somewhat

15%

61%

23%

Don't know - 1%

Not at all

Source: Robert Half survey of 659 human resources managers in the United States and Canada

ROBERT HALF • BUSINESS ETIQUETTE: THE NEW RULES IN A DIGITAL AGE

16

E-mail

E-mail Mistakes on the Job

Executives were asked, **"Have you ever mistakenly e-mailed someone the wrong message or copied someone on a message without intending to?"** Their responses:

Yes 78%

No 22%

Source: Robert Half survey of 250 advertising and marketing executives in the United States

Among the Most Embarrassing Blunders Reported Were the Following:

- "Someone sent out confidential salary information to the whole firm."

- "An employee sent his resume to me by mistake. It was supposed to go to an outside company."

- "Someone made a nasty comment about a supervisor and it was sent to the supervisor by mistake. It eventually led to dismissal."

- "I once sent a job offer to the wrong person."

- "A person called another employee an idiot in an e-mail to everyone in the company."

- "My receptionist sent a very gossipy and catty e-mail about another employee to the wrong person. It was so unprofessional that she was terminated."

- "We sent an e-mail to a client that was meant for a vendor. It made it difficult when the client had seen our costs."

- "Confidential information about one client was sent to a different client. It was certainly embarrassing."

- "Someone crafted a scathing, sarcastic e-mail about a customer and did not mean to hit 'send.' It caused problems."

17

Instant Messaging

Could it be the "instant" in instant messaging that makes this form of online chat so appealing? It isn't used in every office, but it is becoming more common as a business communication tool. One of the reasons its popularity is growing is because it allows you to send and receive messages so quickly. But before sending your next IM, make sure you follow these etiquette rules:

▶ Be unassuming. When using this medium, remember that your colleagues have their own schedules and deadlines. Don't assume a coworker is available just because the person's IM status indicates he or she is logged on. Your colleague may have forgotten to change the status to "busy" or could simply prefer to concentrate on a different task for the time being.

▶ Restrain yourself. IMs can be distracting because they often pop up in front of other open computer windows and are usually accompanied by a noise trumpeting their arrival. Don't overdo it.

▶ Keep it short and sweet. A good rule of thumb is to consider the length of a "tweet" for your instant messages. IMs are best for quick back-and-forth conversations; many IM programs even limit the amount of text. If you're approaching that limit, it's a sign that you need to switch to e-mail.

And if your overall exchange is taking up too much time or text, a phone call or in-person meeting can yield quicker results.

▶ Avoid pop-ups. There's a time and place for IMs, but not during meetings. Remember to log out of your chat feature before presenting in a meeting using your computer or laptop. Constant IMs popping up, especially if they aren't business-related, can be distracting.

Instant Messaging

▲ Exercise caution. People frequently use IM at work, but it's easy to send a message to someone you didn't intend to contact – particularly when chatting with multiple people at once. When in doubt about the appropriate use of IM at work, check your company's policy.

▲ Watch your tone. Attempts at humor or sarcasm can fall flat or be misinterpreted in an IM. Make sure you are familiar with the recipient's sense of humor before attempting to be funny. Using emoticons can indicate a more lighthearted message, but when used excessively, they can come off as unprofessional. When in doubt, be straightforward.

▲ Go with the flow. After a 10-minute IM exchange with your manager, he writes, "Back to my work" and ends the conversation. Don't take offense at his brevity or perceived tone. Because IM involves quick volleys of conversation, it's easy to appear abrupt or rude when no offense is meant.

▲ Be responsive, not dormant. When chatting on IM, return your reply in a timely fashion. Try to respond to the other person within a few minutes and generally not longer than five minutes. If you are going to be away from your computer temporarily but wish to continue your IM exchange, tell the other person you will BRB (be right back).

▲ Sign off properly. There's nothing more frustrating than having a five-minute IM conversation that ends with someone waiting for a final response. Let the person on the other end know if you must curtail a chat session. It's nice to offer a short reason why you are signing off, such as a scheduled call, or simply a "TTYL" (talk to you later).

Mobile Devices

Mobile devices such as BlackBerrys, Droids and iPods are pervasive, but others can take offense when they're always turned on. As new products are released and these tools become even more ubiquitous, it pays to understand proper workplace decorum. Here's some advice:

▲ Take a break. Give your colleagues the courtesy of keeping your devices out of sight during meetings. Constantly checking and texting tells others that your focus is elsewhere, and it could snowball – when one person uses a device, other people will think it's OK and start using theirs. Step out if you need to respond to an urgent message or make a call.

▲ Turn it off. Are you guilty of a loud ringtone, or a phone vibrating on the conference table? Both will annoy coworkers during a meeting. So, when in doubt, turn it off completely. If you need to be reachable, set the phone to vibrate and keep it in your pocket or bag to muffle the sound.

▲ Know your location. Unless you work in TV, you don't want to be known as the "broadcaster." Too often, conversations that should be confined behind closed doors take place in coffee shops, grocery store lines, airport gates and even restrooms. Would you have the conversation if the guy behind you in line worked for the competition or was related to one of your company's executives? Make – and take – sensitive calls from a private place.

▲ Disconnect the Bluetooth. Always being plugged in doesn't necessarily make you look indispensable, but it may give you the nickname "cyborg." Your "always accessible" demeanor may imply that you can't give your full attention to the matter right in front of you.

▲ Distinguish between 911 and 411. Think about it. Can your question or request wait? If a colleague provides a cell phone number to use in emergencies, honor that request. What's urgent for you might not be so for the company or your contact, so ask yourself honestly: Is this a 911 or a 411 issue?

20

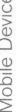

Mobile Devices

▲ Text selectively. Texting a colleague is helpful when sending directions to a lunch meeting or letting the person know you're running late. But it's not the tool for meaningful dialogue.

▲ Identify yourself. Don't assume your recipients have your contact information programmed into their phone. If you text coworkers, be sure to identify yourself.

▲ Go light on the text speak. Cryptic code, such as AFC (away from computer) or CYE (check your e-mail) makes texting shorthand a whole new language, but not everyone is fluent. Don't send messages full of confusing acronyms and abbreviations. Though perfection is not always necessary when texting, remember to remain professional.

Tech Etiquette Outlaws: Are You One of Them?

Chief information officers were asked, **"In your opinion, has the increased use of mobile electronic gadgets – such as cell phones, smartphones, handheld devices and laptops – increased or decreased the number of breaches in workplace etiquette in the past three years?"** Their responses:

Increased significantly

Don't know/no answer - **2%**
Decreased significantly - **2%**
Decreased somewhat - **4%**

21% 29%

Increased somewhat

42%

Remained the same

Source: Robert Half survey of 1,718 chief information officers in the United States and Canada

ROBERT HALF · BUSINESS ETIQUETTE: THE NEW RULES IN A DIGITAL AGE

Phone, Video and Web Conferencing

No doubt about it, today's technology can make distance irrelevant. As the workforce becomes more dispersed and companies recognize the cost savings of connecting remotely, phone, video and web conferencing – and especially, applications like Skype – are growing in popularity. It can be difficult, however, to know how to interact with colleagues and business contacts who are in different locations. Follow these tips to stay on the up-and-up:

▲ Take a trial run. Know how to use the conferencing technology prior to scheduling a meeting. If you're not familiar with the video screen, web-hosting software, webcam or telephone features, plan a practice run so you can troubleshoot issues without wasting others' time.

▲ Watch the clock. Would your colleagues in Asia appreciate a conference call at 3 a.m. their time? When scheduling a meeting that involves individuals from several locations, keep their local times in mind. Websites such as timeanddate.com can help you decipher time zones. Avoid hosting a meeting very early, late or during lunch, if possible.

▲ Get the team ready. In advance of a conference call, give attendees what they'll need for the meeting – dial-in number, pass code, login information and attachments (e.g., presentations, sales reports). If you want them to review the materials in advance, say so. Include a brief agenda so people can come

prepared with some thoughts instead of coming in cold.

▲ Be a good host. Here's your chance to show your true skills as a facilitator. If you're leading the call, make appropriate introductions before giving a brief overview. Keep the discussion moving and have an eye on the clock so you can leave a few minutes at the end to address questions, recap, and confirm next steps and deadlines.

Phone, Video and Web Conferencing

▲ Be inclusive. Out of sight shouldn't mean out of mind. If part of the group is meeting in person, don't forget about those joining via phone or online. Ask them for their thoughts if they seem quiet.

▲ Make the introduction. You may think your voice is distinctive, but it's not always easy to tell who's talking. Encourage everyone to introduce themselves before they speak. Also, be sure to acknowledge someone who joins midway through the call.

▲ Enjoy the silence. It can be a virtue, and who enjoys being interrupted? In virtual meetings, it can be difficult to determine whose turn it is to speak. A lag in the connection may also cause a delayed response. Allow for pauses in the conversation so everyone can weigh in and catch up.

▲ Pay attention. Don't get caught daydreaming. It's easy to let your mind wander during a remote meeting, or you may begin to multitask if you're not being directly addressed.

▲ Don't put people on hold. More than one conference has ended prematurely because on-hold music has prevented the conversation from proceeding. Remind attendees at the beginning of the meeting to hang up if they must attend to something else.

▲ Use mute. It's just common courtesy to limit distracting background noises when you're listening to others. Remember to turn your mute button off before it's your turn to speak.

Conference Call Culprits

Executives were asked, **"When you participate in meetings via teleconference, how frequently do you do other things, like answer e-mail or surf the Internet, during the meeting?"** Their responses:

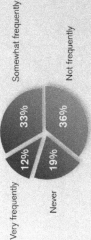

Very frequently — 12%

Somewhat frequently — 33%

Not frequently — 36%

Never — 19%

Source: Robert Half survey of 763 advertising and marketing executives in the United States and Canada

Sticky Etiquette Questions

Occasionally we all come across situations in which we wonder, "Would Miss Manners approve?" But in the digital age of social networking, the etiquette lines can become even blurrier. Following are some common sticky etiquette questions and tips to help tackle them:

Should I personalize my LinkedIn requests to connect with others?

It's perfectly fine to use the form letter, even when connecting with close contacts. But if you wish to connect to someone you haven't seen in a while, take the time to personalize the message.

What's the right way to decline a request to connect with someone?

No response at all might be your best bet. Don't feel pressured to connect with someone you would rather not form a relationship with, and don't feel the need to explain your decision. Simply click "Ignore."

Should I friend my boss or coworkers?

This is the $64,000 question, and those on the receiving end may provide the answer. (See "Thinking About 'Friending' Your Boss on Facebook?" on Page 10.) If you do connect, utilize privacy settings and different friend lists to control how – and with whom – you share content. Be sensitive to how engaged your company is in digital networking.

If someone follows me on Twitter, should I follow him or her back?

No, because you may end up unfollowing the person later. Before following people, check out their feed, bio and previous tweets to get

a sense of them or their organization, and determine if you'll be interested in seeing the kind of content they share. Although it's considered good etiquette to follow someone back, don't do it indiscriminately. It's your feed, and you want to make it valuable to you.

Uh oh. I sent a confidential e-mail to the wrong person. What do I do now?

First, try to use the recall function if your e-mail program offers this option. If this step doesn't solve the problem, contact those who are affected, and explain your error and whether you need their help correcting it. You also may need to inform your manager of the mistake.

For more sticky situations, visit roberthalf.us/BusinessEtiquette.

Conclusion

Social media and other technology tools have created new forums for connecting, sharing and, unfortunately, blundering. Workplace controversies have ensued, but we can learn from our own and others' missteps. The occasional "oops" is inevitable when using a new device or becoming accustomed to an emerging online platform. When that happens, rectify mistakes as soon as possible, apologize to those who may have been affected and forgive others when they make gaffes. Putting yourself in someone else's shoes and forgiving quickly could indeed be the best etiquette lesson of all.

About Robert Half

Founded in 1948, Robert Half is the world's first and largest specialized staffing firm, with more than 350 offices worldwide. The company's professional staffing divisions include Accountemps®, Robert Half® Finance & Accounting and Robert Half® Management Resources, for temporary, full-time and senior-level project professionals, respectively, in the fields of accounting and finance; OfficeTeam®, for highly skilled office and administrative support professionals; Robert Half® Technology, for project and full-time technology professionals; Robert Half® Legal, for project and full-time staffing of lawyers, paralegals and legal support personnel; and The Creative Group®, for interactive, design and marketing professionals. For more information about the specialized staffing and recruitment divisions of Robert Half, visit **roberthalf.com**.

All trademarks contained herein are the property of their respective owners.

25

CHAPTER 5

Sharpening Your Oral Communication Skills

Almost all of us find that speaking before a large audience is not something that comes naturally. On many occasions when I have taught oral presentation modules to EMBA students, MBA students, and executives, I have asked these audiences to identify the top five human fears, and speaking before a group always makes the list. I, too, can remember the first public presentation I had to make and how much anxiety I felt. However, I learned to tackle oral presentations using a systematic approach. This strategy helped me to become more comfortable speaking before a group.

Recently a colleague came up to me after I had spoken to our department. He said, "You are just a natural when it comes to public presentations." I thanked him for his compliment and commented that I still have to do my homework to be confident when I speak. What I have learned is that when I remove the uncertainty surrounding my speaking and replace it with a planned approach, I can be successful and can get the butterflies flying in my stomach to fly in formation. When I follow the three-step strategy of preparing, practicing, and presenting, as shown in Figure 5.1, I can speak confidently to small or large audiences whether those audiences understand English or must rely on translators to understand my message.

Prepare

If you take the time to prepare, you will likely make a successful presentation. The following quotation emphasizes this point: "Few people are born with the gift of public speaking, and most people must work at preparing an effective speech or presentation; however, once mastered, this

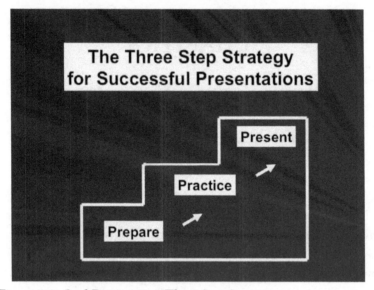

Figure 5.1. Oral Presentation Three-Step Strategy

skill can greatly enhance any professional career."[1] To be effective and to make an outstanding presentation, you must commit to doing the necessary homework. The first step is to begin by determining the general and specific purposes of your presentation.

Determining the General Purpose

As a presenter, you will need to spend some time determining your purpose. In the words of a popular poster, "If you don't know where you are going, you're likely to wind up somewhere else." I often tell individuals to think of PR (**Purpose-Result**). In this case, PR stands for 1) What is your **purpose**? and 2) What is the **result** you want? If you can answer those two questions, you will know whether you need to inform or to persuade, the two common purposes for most business presentations.

Informing. When you try to teach your audience or explain a concept or procedure, you inform. You acquaint your listeners with something completely new and the result you desire is that the audience understands.

Persuading. When you must persuade, you are seeking to change your audience's beliefs, attitudes, or actions. When you persuade, you also inform, but you give a call to action that makes your audience want

Patti Wood, an international speaker, author, and trainer based in Atlanta, is known for her expertise in body language and presentation skills. She makes about 100 presentations each year and I've been honored to be in several of her audiences.

Patti states that "you have to have a clear purpose that outlines what the audience is going to take away from your presentation. When you start, you want to say, 'Today I am going to talk about' and then explain what the subject matter will be so the audience can expect to learn something. Then they will say to themselves, 'I am going to have to be active to receive this information.' Use the word 'you' often. Get rid of 'I' and 'me.' Use phrases like 'Here is something else for you.'"

Patti believes the top tip for making an excellent presentation is connecting with your audience. "That is what distinguishes an OK presentation from a phenomenal one. Afterward, people will talk about it as an experience rather than as a speech."

Source: Presentation Pitfall
By Tonya Laymn
June 3, 2011
Retrieved from: http://www.bizjournals.com/atlanta/print
-edition/2011/06/03/presentation-pitfall.html?page=all

to do something. Your result is a change in direction, in behavior, or in beliefs. Your effectiveness as a persuasive communicator will depend upon how well you can provide facts and logical evidence, be credible, and understand the psychological needs of your audience.

Choosing the Specific Purpose

Although you have only two primary general purposes for making a business presentation, your choices for a specific purpose can be infinite and can vary according to the needs of your audience. Therefore, you should design your specific purpose with both the subject and your audience in mind.

Analyzing and Tailoring Content to the Audience

As we are all aware, audiences in the United States are becoming more diverse. As a presenter, you should know that significant portions of your audience might come from different countries. If you need to do research about the cultures and customs of various countries, I have found Roger E. Axtell's *Essential Do's & Taboos: The Complete Guide to International Business and Leisure Travel* to be a helpful resource for understanding the cultures of other nations.

You want to tailor your message to your audience, so you must find out as much information as possible. When making an internal presentation to your own organization, you should ask the following:

- Who will attend?
- What department or departments will attend?
- Will both employees and managers be present?
- Will the senior leaders be present?

If you are going to present to an audience external to your organization, you will want to find out as much information as you can about

- backgrounds, attitudes, biases, and opinions;
- age range;
- sexual breakdown of the audience;
- racial and ethnic groups;
- occupations;
- national culture; and
- knowledge base about your topic.

You can also ask the individuals who invited you to speak what you need to know about your audience. Other additional steps that you might take include

- asking people who may be representative of the audience what they expect;
- running your agenda by a few people to see what they think; and

- contacting participants by e-mail and asking them a few questions about what they expect.

Then, on the day of your presentation, you should greet audience members at the door and do a quick survey of why they are there and what they expect.[2] I've watched Betty Siegel, the first female university president in Georgia, greet audience members before speaking. Whether she was speaking to an international audience or to an individual department, she would take time to get to know her audience by shaking hands and chatting with individuals. Invariably, she would then incorporate stories about people she had just spoken to within her presentation. She is a master at getting to know her audience, and I once told her I didn't know anyone who could command an audience as effectively as she does. Literally, I have watched people in the audience just hang on her every word. I've known few speakers who were more skilled than Dr. Betty Siegel at getting to know her audience. I would encourage you to learn from Betty's example and start communicating with your audience before making a speech.

As more organizations become global, you will find yourself making presentations to international audiences, and you must really do your homework when you present to culturally diverse groups. It is incumbent upon you to understand the culture as well as to exhibit a willingness to be adaptable and flexible. About two years ago, I was asked to make a workshop presentation in Egypt. I sought out information to understand what a workshop would mean to them. I worked closely with the event planners and did quite a bit of research to understand the culture. However, sometimes even when you do your homework, you have to be open to change. As instructed, I planned for an hour-and-a-half workshop. When I arrived in Egypt, 2 days before my presentation, I learned I would have 45 minutes and that I would be speaking to an audience of 800. As you can imagine, I spent significant time making changes to what I had planned to do and say. If I had not asked questions that first day when I arrived in Egypt, my presentation might not have been as positively received as it was.

Another example of a time when it really paid to do my homework was when I was asked to be the international speaker at a human resources conference in Romania. Working closely with the conference organizers,

I learned that some words would not translate the way I wanted to use them. Together we came up with other words that would relate better to my audience.

Organizing the Presentation

When you organize your presentation, you give it purpose and direction. Therefore, you must examine your topic completely and break down the sections into logical units. You want to remember that old saying "Less is best." You do not want to overwhelm your audience with too many points because they will not be able to retain everything. To organize your presentation, develop your purpose statement, formulate your main ideas, determine support materials, construct your introduction and conclusion, outline your speaking notes, construct the visuals, and think through your Q & A session.

Developing your purpose statement. Gayla Martindale, in her article entitled "Overcoming Your Fear of Public Speaking," states you should ask yourself these questions to determine your purpose:

- Am I interested in the topic?
- Will I enjoy researching this topic?
- Will I enjoy talking about this topic and sharing information with my audience?
- Will my audience be interested in my topic?
- Am I passionate about this topic?[3]

The purpose statement you craft should be a clear single sentence that summarizes your central point.

Forming the three main points. When I am doing training sessions on oral presentation skills, I hold up a cup and pretend that I am pouring something into the cup. I ask the audience what will happen if I keep pouring. Someone shouts out, "It will overflow." I then say, "That's what happens to your audience when you incorporate too much content and why the rule of three works so well." The rule of three, which I learned from my father who was a minister, simply means that you have only three main points regardless of the length of your presentation. You can have as many subpoints as you like to add more depth, but having three main points is the general rule.

Determining the support material. The support material clarifies the main ideas and makes your main points interesting and easier to remember. The bullets present the different types of support you can use:

- Quotations, as support material, take advantage of someone else's memorable wording.
- Analogies, including similes, direct comparisons (using like or as), and implied comparisons (not using like or as) allow you to compare two things.
- Statistics show facts or principles. Cite them exactly as published and identify their sources in the presentation. You must give credit to the original owner of the data or ideas.
- Explanations typically describe the relationship between certain items, make clear the definition of a word, or give instructions on how to complete something or how to get somewhere.
- Comparisons show the similarities or differences between two items.
- An illustration tells a story with such detail it paints a picture in the audience's mind. Illustrations can be factual (based on real incidents) or hypothetical, created for a particular situation or impact.
- Expert opinion refers to the thoughts or ideas of a noted expert in a certain discipline or field. To enhance the credibility of your expert's opinion, be sure to give the expert's name, qualifications, and where and when the individual reported the information.[4] You will probably want to use several examples, illustrations, and visuals to support and reinforce your presentation.

Constructing the introduction. The introduction should include an attention-getter and a preview. The attention-getter captures the audience's attention and leads into the speech. Grab your audience's attention in the beginning and leave them wanting to hear you again. Too many presenters start out by saying, "Hello, my name is Deborah Roebuck." When you only have 20 to 30 seconds to capture your audience's attention, you need a stronger start. Instead of just stating your name, start by reciting a quotation, sharing a startling fact, asking a question, telling a humorous story, describing a specific incident, or demonstrating your point. According to Atlanta consultants Wicke Chambers and Spring Asher, presenters can learn from television. All you have to do is watch the first minutes of any television show to see how quickly that show captures the audience's attention. Regardless of your position, you

Use Structure So the Conclusion Flows Naturally

All too often, presenters create a slide presentation addressing a range of issues and then literally go from one slide to another to tell the story of the slide. The person doesn't necessarily lead up to the next slide or talk about it until the next slide actually appears. Often there's an "um" that accompanies the break between two slides because the presenter may not remember what's on the next slide. The presentation may have a weak impact, because the audience perceives it as a collection of facts that sometimes are and sometimes are not related.

Like any leader, your job is to structure the story so that all the parts are connected. Logically they build to a crescendo. Emotionally they create awareness, interest, and desire; then they resolve the emotional push-backs that come from the fear of taking risks with the product/ service, company and/or buyer, and not feeling certain that the risk is significantly outweighed by the reward. Just as a leader aligns all the people and subgroups so that they are headed in the same direction, supporting one another and creating synergies that add untold extra value, each component of the presentation has to be aligned with the logical and emotional questions that the audience/customer is having at any given moment. Indeed, with a proper structure and balance, "at the end of the date the kiss flows naturally," rather than having objections and challenges to what's been presented.

Source: Presentation Excellence, The Resource Center for Strategic
Business & Leadership Development Services, Enabling Leaders to
Win Deals and Improve Lives
Author: Jerry Cahn, Ph.D., J.D.
July 2011 Newsletter

need an attention-getting introduction so that the audience will want to stay tuned. You want to hook your audience into staying engaged.

After capturing your audience's attention, tell the listeners why they should listen. It's the old "what's in it for them." Tell them how this presentation will benefit them and what they will take away. Following the benefits, tell the audience your name, your qualifications, and why you're the right person to be making this presentation. Then preview your purpose and your three main points. A general rule of thumb is that your introduction should constitute approximately 10–15 percent of your speech.

Making the conclusion. Just as Stephen Covey stated in his second habit of highly effective people, you want to "begin with the end in mind." After crafting your introduction, the next step involves preparing the conclusion. The conclusion reviews your purpose and three main points and gives effective final remarks. These remarks should underscore the substance of the speech in a way that will facilitate the audience remembering it. If you have a Q & A session, be sure to conclude after the last question because you want your audience to remember what you said and not what the person said who asked the question.

Your last statements can enhance or detract from your presentation, so make them count! Your closing should be forceful and not just trail off. Additionally, you should not have to thank your audience. If you have done the job well, the audience will thank you through applause. Your conclusion should comprise approximately 15 percent of your presentation.

Outlining the Presentation

My father, who was a bivocational high school teacher of English, speech, and drama, also served as a pastor of several country churches. He would often tell me that I needed to follow the wise counsel of the preacher who once said, "Tell 'em what you're going to tell 'em. Tell 'em. And then tell 'em what you told 'em." I believe, if you look closely at this statement, you will see that it provides the major sections of your presentation. An outline, as illustrated in Figure 5.2, enables you to present your main points, arrange your support items, and specify what you will say in your introduction and conclusion. The outline unifies all the parts of your presentation.

I. Introduction
- Attention-Getter:
  - Even in times of strife, a leader will be able to pull together his or her team members and keep spirits high. Anyone can manage; only a few can lead.
- Why the audience should listen:
  - Learn how to be one of the few who can lead.
  - Understand the importance of focusing on three key areas
- Credibility:
  - I've managed several people but only consider myself an effective leader about half of the time.
  - I've had to learn to focus on a few key areas to become a leader and not just a manager.
- Purpose: Learn three key areas to increase your credibility as a leader.
- Main Points: 1) Being honest, 2) Delegating and empowering others, and 3) Adapting your leadership style

II. Being Honest
- Honesty
  - Stating the truth no matter how difficult
  - Being authentic in who you are
  - Demonstrating consistency
  - Displaying high standards and ethics

III. Delegating and Empowering Others
- Delegation
  - Understanding it is more than passing on work
  - Finding the right person for the right job
- Empowerment
  - Granting decision making power to employees
  - Letting go of control and giving control away

Figure 5.2. Informative Outline Example

IV. Adapting Your Leadership Style
- Do not assume all employees can be led in the same way
- Get to know your team members

V. Conclusion
- Review of Purpose and Main Points
  - Stand out from the crowd and be a leader, not just a manager.
  - Be an honest leader who willingly gives away power and is adaptable to the needs of his or her followers.
- Final Remarks—learning to lead is a journey
  - Leadership skills are not developed overnight.
  - Be willing to be a lifelong learner who embraces change.
  - Make small wins by remaining consistent and focusing on one of the three areas until you are ready to move to another one.

Figure 5.2. Informative Outline Example (continued)

You will use your outline, like a blueprint, to draft the speaker's notes that you will take to the podium with you. Also note that you prepare your outline before you begin work on your visual aids.

Crafting Effective Visuals

Clearly, most individuals are visual learners and like not only to hear a speaker, but also to see illustrations that support what he or she is saying. In fact, research shows that individuals remember more information when you incorporate visuals into your presentations. Studies also indicate that speakers meet their goals 34 percent more often when they use visuals than when they do not. Group consensus occurs 21 percent more often in meetings with visuals than without, and the time required to present a concept can shrink up to 40 percent with the use of visuals. When visuals supported the teaching of a course on vocabulary, learning improved 200 percent.[5] These statistics demonstrate why you should include visual aids in your presentation.

Today's technology makes the task of creating visual aids quite simple and has led to the phenomenon of "Death by PowerPoint." Review Figure 5.3 for an example of a poor visual that includes too much content. In their book *Wooing and Winning Business*, Spring Asher and Wicke Chambers state, "Corporate America commits death by overheads daily.[6] Audiences have visibly gone to their knees when a presenter reveals a bulleted list."

Figure 5.3. A Poorly Designed Slide

Like a newspaper headline that tells the story (but leaves the detail for the story below it), consider your presentation bullet points like headlines, moving the rest of what's going on to your talking points.

Source: Webinar July 2011

The Masterful Virtual Presenter: 9 Tips You Can't Live Without

Roger Courville Principal,

1080 Group, LLC

Chambers and Asher go on to say that we should learn from television weather forecasters who use symbols or simple pictures for visuals instead of bullet points.

According to research carried out at UCLA, a visual presentation is five times more likely to be remembered after 3 days than a presentation using bullet points.[7]

Think about who benefits from your bullet points and ask yourself the following three questions:

1. Do your bullet points help you remember what you are going to say?
2. Do they provide information that the audience needs to know?
3. Can you present your information in a chart or graph instead of bullet points?

Once you've asked these questions, you'll need to review your two options for creating your slides: (1) the more conventional, bullet point structured slides or (2) the looser, visually-oriented, free-form slides. Structured slides follow the same format throughout the entire presentation and are typically based upon templates found in PowerPoint. Structured slides (Figure 5.4) are what we are probably most used to seeing in corporate settings, but your audience may fall asleep or get bored with slide after slide of bullet points.

Free-form slides do not follow a rigid structure and will have less content on each slide. The free-form slides encourage more whole-brained processing of both text and visuals. Most individuals perceive that the free-form slide design is more dynamic and engaging for an audience and may be well suited for educational and persuasive presentations. In addition, they help to avoid cognitive overload since they limit the amount of

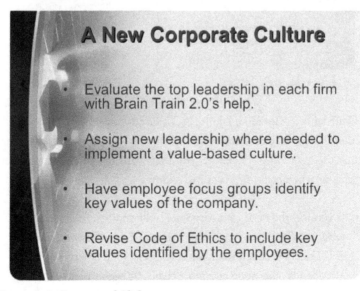

Figure 5.4. Structured Slide

text on each slide and help your audience process information by high-lighting only the most important information.[8] The downside of the free-form slide design is that slides take more time to create.

Keep in mind that because the amount of content varies between the structured and free-form slides, the number of slides varies as well. For example, if you use the structured format, you might have five slides for a 10-minute talk and spend about 2 minutes on each slide. If you use free-form slides, however, you may use 20 slides as you will spend less time on each slide. You will find an example of a free-form slide in Figure 5.5. Please note it would take four free-form slides to create the content contained within the slide shown in Figure 5.4.

Figure 5.5. Free-Form Slide

Courtland L. Bovee and John V. Thill, authors of *Business Communication Today,* state that structured slides may be a practical choice for routine presentations.[9] Therefore, you may want to utilize the following suggestions when creating structured slides:

- If you feel the need to incorporate bullet points, follow the wisdom of Art Feierman, who wrote *The Art of Communicating Effectively.* He stated that, as a rule, every slide deserves at least 10 seconds, and none rate more than 100 seconds.

- The rule of 4 by 5 says four bullet points of five words each. The rule of 33 says a maximum of 33 words per slide. The basic idea is that too many words put your audience to sleep.[10]
- When you use bullet points, use phrases rather than sentences and upper- and lowercase type with a simple typeface. To aid in readability, use serif typefaces instead of sans serif faces. (Serifs are the little lines on the ends of the letters.)
- Keep the lettering style for titles, legends, tables, and other illustrations consistent, and use no more than three type sizes in a single visual.
- For consistency, place the same amount of space at the top of each visual.
- Grab your audience's attention by using color and short words, avoiding clutter, and limiting the amount of text.

Whether you use the free-form or structured design, you want to make your major concepts easy to grasp. Since the human mind thinks and stores information visually, maps, blueprints, machine diagrams, logos, dollar signs, and stock market arrows are parts of our visual memories. The right symbol brings the idea to life and tells the story. If you cannot picture your concept, you have not thought it out.

You should make your visual message simple so that your listeners feel smart. Most importantly, your visuals should emphasize your most important points, and not impress or confuse your audience. Your visuals should focus attention, reinforce your verbal message, stimulate interest, and illustrate difficult concepts. Some experts recommend that you start designing your visuals by creating the last slide first. The idea is that your last slide should emphasize the most important points you plan to make.[11]

You want your visuals large enough for your audience to view them comfortably. If you do not do this, you will have wasted your time as the audience will probably be frustrated and resist your message. Try to incorporate the three "*Bs*"—big, beautiful, and bold.

Using the right colors can also be critical to your presentation's success. Here are some guidelines to remember when using color:

- Match color with the subject and audience while considering the purpose of the visual aid and who will be viewing it. If you want a conservative presentation, you use a blue background instead of yellow. You should keep in mind the moods and themes certain colors can convey.

○ Pale colors, grays, and pinks can convey tranquility.

○ Reds, oranges, pinks, or browns communicate warmth.

○ Black and red can be used together with some gray to show excitement.

○ Green represents growth; blue calms.

○ Red signifies power, danger, loss, or energy; yellow creates dislike; and purple appears spiritual.

- Pick background colors first, before choosing text or data colors. Text and data colors should contrast highly with the background for maximum legibility.

- Try not to allow your colors to clash—they should have a high degree of harmony.

- Avoid the rainbow effect and use no more than three or four colors.

- Assign bright colors to the areas you want to receive the most attention.

- Keep the color theme consistent in all your slides.

- Make the contrast strong between the background and the text. You pick colors with high contrast, such as dark backgrounds with yellow or white text, to make your images more readable. Backgrounds with images can sometimes cause problems, as the text seems to blend in the background instead of floating above it.[12]

If you expect to have an international audience, be careful about using certain colors in your visuals as colors and symbols are deeply ingrained into cultures. For example, you will find that in most of Europe and the Americas, white is associated with purity and marriage. But in Japan, China, and parts of Africa, white is traditionally the color of mourning.[13]

If you use a laser pointer, circle the data or specific area instead of just pointing at it. Making a circle helps prevent the trembling of your hands from showing![14]

PowerPoint is probably the most widely used visual aid, but in some situations, such as training, you might use a flip chart or white board. You can prepare some of your flip charts ahead of time and then reveal them when you present your points. The same principles apply to flip charts and white boards in that you need to write big so that the whole audience can see what you've written. Remember to follow the flip chart pointers given by Katie O'Neil in chapter 3. Use upper- and lowercase letters and darker color markers. Black is still the easiest color to see from a distance. Be careful when using whiteboards and flip charts that you don't talk to them. Point your toes toward your audience when you speak, and establish eye contact before starting to speak.

Studies by educational researchers suggest that approximately 83 percent of human learning occurs visually, and the remaining 17 percent through the other senses—11 percent through hearing, 3.5 percent through smell, 1 percent through taste, and 1.5 percent through touch.[15] Therefore, if you want your audience to remember your presentation, you need to incorporate effective visuals. Use the following questions as a checklist to make sure your visuals are appropriate and reinforce your main ideas:

- Do my visuals help me achieve my objectives?
- Will my visuals clarify my ideas or will they merely support them? If they only support them, should I reconsider using them?
- Have I eliminated complicated typefaces and used serif type?
- Do my visuals communicate directly and to the point?
- Have I planned a logical sequence for my visuals? Do they appear organized so that they add strength and relevance to one another and to my overall topic? Should I use a sequential disclosure or buildup?
- Will they be completely readable?
- Have I used appropriate colors?
- Are they big, bold, and beautiful?
- Have I used a limited amount of animations, clip arts, and special effects so that they do not become distractions to my audience?

Finally, you should remember that your slides are aids and you should be center stage. You should capture the attention of your audience and make sure your slides do not distract your audience's attention away from you. Remember, you should say more than just what is on your slides. If you just repeat what is on the slides, you might want to e-mail everyone the PowerPoint slides in advance and cancel the presentation!

Joey Asher is president of the Atlanta-based communications skills coaching company Speechworks and author of the book *15 Minutes Including Q&A: A Plan to Save the World From Lousy Presentations.* He states that "the best thing to do to engage the audience is leave time for Q&A. One reason people don't build in much time for questions is they really don't want the questions. They are afraid they will be asked something uncomfortable or that they won't know the answer. You have to be prepared for the questions."

Source: Presentation Pitfall
By Tonya Laymn
June 3, 2011
Retrieved from: http://www.bizjournals.com/atlanta/print
-edition/2011/06/03/presentation-pitfall.html?page=all

Think Through the Question & Answer Session

If you are planning to take questions, think about how you will do that. When you speak to executives, you will often find that the Q & A session is the most important aspect of presentation. In fact, the Q & A may be longer than the actual presentation. In my MBA Organizational Communication class, the students deliver competitive team case presentations to senior leaders. Each presentation is 15 minutes in length, but the Q & A session is typically 15 to 20 minutes.

Whether you can establish ground rules for the Q & A session will depend upon your audience. For example, if you are presenting to senior leaders or angel investors, they will typically ask questions whenever they choose. Therefore, you'll definitely need to spend some time thinking through potential questions. The U.S. Army uses a process called the Murder Board in which they brainstorm potential questions; through this process, they can typically plan for about 80 percent of the questions that will be asked.

If you are presenting to a larger audience, you will need to tell your audience when you will answer their questions. You must decide if you will allow the audience to ask questions while you are presenting or if you will ask them to hold their questions until the end. You will need to keep in mind the purpose of your presentation, the size of your audience, and the time constraints to help you decide when you will address questions.

Once you've decided your strategy, you can say something like "I will answer your questions at the end of my presentation. So jot down any questions you have so you don't forgot them." Or you might say, "If you have any questions during the presentation, please raise your hand, and I will address your questions as we go along." The most important factor to remember is that you need to keep control of your question and answer session.

Some experts recommend spending one hour in preparation and practice for each minute of the presentation. You might be thinking that's a significant amount of time. If that seems like too much time for you, ask yourself this question: "How successful do I want to be as a speaker?"

For many speakers—and especially for introverts—preparation is key. Take your time crafting the speech so that it flows logically and is illustrated with stories and examples. Practice it out loud until you're comfortable. If it's an important speech, videotape yourself. The main reason public speaking can be uncomfortable is that you have no idea how you're coming across. If you went to a job interview without fixing your tie or applying your lipstick in front of the mirror, you would *hope* that there's no scarlet lip gloss smeared across your teeth, but how could you know for sure? Better to take the guesswork out of it and do your homework.

Source: 10 Public Speaking Tips (Plus a Few Questions about Your Year of Speaking Dangerously) *Author: Susan Cain* Retrieved from http://www.thepowerofintroverts.com/2011/07/18/ten-public-speaking-tips-this-is-week-two-of-your-year-of-speaking-dangerously/

Practice

You're not alone if you get anxious when you have to make a presentation. Taking a risk, such as speaking before a group, often makes people feel anxious. To a certain extent, being nervous can help you because it makes you alert, full of energy, and "up" for the presentation. By practicing, you can put this anxiety to work for you.

Building Confidence

When you practice your presentation, you'll feel more confident and in control. Renowned psychiatrist Karen Horney conducted extensive study of the development of self-esteem and self-worth. She found that when an individual actually attempts something—intellectually or physically, be it a memory verse, an athletic event, a work promotion, or even a speech—the great majority of the time the individual will succeed. Yet, when a person does not make the attempt, he or she has an impression of failure. The dramatic finding is that for most people, their self-impression is one of failure rather than of success because most of the time they do not take a chance.[16] One of my favorite communication consultants and coaches, Bert Decker, traced the confidence factor in himself and others. He found that about 95 percent of the time, individuals who attempt to speak—to communicate—succeed. Decker often asks this question of his seminar participants: "Why should you jeopardize every performance for the sake of that 5 percent risk?"[17]

Realizing That Practice Is an Important Element

Even the great orator Winston Churchill recognized the importance of rehearsing a presentation. Making public presentations did not come naturally to Churchill, so he had to study and practice. He never gave a speech from memory and would spend days preparing it.[18] Without the ingredient of practice, even a great leader would not be an effective speaker.

Space out your practice into short sessions spread over 6 or 7 consecutive days if possible. Taking this approach is better than trying to practice for 2 hours the day before your presentation. Go through your complete

Here are a few suggestions to make the most of your rehearsal:

- Place rehearsal time on the calendar. Once it's on your schedule, it's harder to take off.
- If you don't like a big crowd, rehearse in front of a smaller group.
- Practice the toughest questions.
- Work on both style and content.
- Use video, even if it's a "flip" type camera, so that you can watch yourself and make adjustments.
- If you don't like the performance or an answer, keep working at it until you get it right.

Source: Why You Can't Skip on Rehearsals
March 31, 2011
Retrieved from: http://smartblogs.com/leadership/2011/03/03/
why-you-cant-skimp-on-rehearsals/

speech each time you practice. You can practice in front of a mirror, in the shower, or in the car as you drive to work. The most important point is to practice!

Practicing as if You Were Making the Real Presentation

When you do practice, say everything as if it were the real presentation. In this way, you will get a feel for the whole message. Remember, you do not want to read your speech, but talk to your audience. You want to make what Bert Decker calls "emotional contact," and you do that by establishing eye contact, which requires that you not read.

You should fear forgetting more than you do speaking. Avoid memorizing your presentation because you might get to the middle and forget. Instead, think through all your points, plan in detail, and use a yellow highlighter to note points where you fear your memory may fail. Use your speaker's notes for the opening, key transitional points, quotes, and the ending, but try not to rely too heavily on your notes.

Photo courtesy flickr user maanow, CC 2.0

Using the Pause

You will want to practice various phrasing by saying the same thing many different ways. This practice will allow you to find the most comfortable way for your style. By practicing 15 minutes a day, you will improve pronunciation, articulation, and inflection. In addition, practice helps you to eliminate your non-words. The way for you to conquer your "ums," "ahs," and "you knows" is to replace them with pauses.

Pausing for two to three seconds does more than just help you overcome using non-words. A brief silence enables your listeners to absorb the point that you just made. It makes listening easy. Pausing gives you the opportunity to take a breath. The more air you have available, the greater the opportunity for your voice to project clearly and with variety. Finally, framing your ideas in silence adds tremendous impact to your words.

You may be wondering how you begin to build more pauses into your spoken communication. First, you must become aware of your favorite non-words, and you do this by listening for them when you speak. As you try to eliminate your non-words and replace them with pauses, make it fun! Ask a friend or colleague to keep track of your non-words and bill you 25 cents for each non-word you use.

I find individuals are surprised by how often they use filler words such as "uh," "um," or "okay." When I do training, I ask participants to get in groups of four. Each group member is given the task of telling a story for one minute. Simple enough, you say, but the catch is that they have to tell this story without using filler words. If they use filler words, the clock starts over. Some individuals never get through the exercise before I have to call time. This experience is often eye opening for some individuals who have never learned how to be comfortable with silence and never realized how often they incorporate filler words when they speak. We all need to learn to be like James Bond, who paused between his first and last name when he introduced himself. He used the pause quite effectively to draw in his audience.

Learning to pause will increase your speaking effectiveness. Your listeners will receive the gift of silence and be able to take in what you have said. You will receive time to generate your next thought and add emphasis to your words. The pause will enable you to take in a full breath of air, which will help you increase your projection and your vocal variety and inflection. In addition, when you pause, you give emphasis to certain words and phrases.[19]

Taking the Final Step

The final step of practicing involves either conducting a dress rehearsal or video recording your presentation. For either a live audience or the camera, you'll want to dress and act as if it were the real presentation. If you record your presentation, place the camera in the back of the room so it will be less of a distraction. You want to be able to move and see your entire body on the recording. You might want to place some chairs throughout the room and place notes with smiley faces on those chairs, or you may choose to do what some of my students have done, and that is to speak to their pets or to stuffed animals!

After the presentation, you'll either ask the audience for feedback or watch the recorded presentation. If you watch the recording tape, you'll want to think about these questions:

- If I were in the audience, would I like what I saw or heard?
- Would I pay attention?
- Would I learn something worthwhile?

If you can say "yes," give yourself a pat on the back. If not, pay attention to weak spots in your delivery. Jot down weak and strong spots on index cards to serve as a reference each time you prepare a speech; then, note needed changes, revise, and continue practicing!

Presentation Tips

1. **Ad lib.** Don't be afraid to throw in a story that might not have been planned. You can mention things you didn't have written down in your notes; you just don't want to go too far on a tangent.
2. **Give more visual cues.** Instead of trying to cram too much text on your slides, use some carefully chosen graphics to let your audience know what's in store. This will also help you keep track of your place during your presentation.
3. **Invite participants to give feedback.** Your participants can really help you figure out where you did great and where you could use improvement. Don't be afraid to ask.

Source: Reading PowerPoint Slides You Should Know Better
By Maranda Gibson
March 30, 2011
Retrieved from http://www.accuconference.com/blog/Reading
-PowerPoint-Slides-e28093-You-Should-Know-Better.aspx

Present

You may experience nervousness when you give a presentation; I must say that I do. Some of us are naturally just more extroverted and comfortable speaking before an audience. Those of us who are more introverted can be just as successful, but we have to acknowledge and work through our natural shyness. Again, the preparation and practice will help tremendously with this fear. I can still remember the time my neighbor asked me to speak to the Georgia National Pest Control Association. As the day drew closer, I started to do my homework by asking questions. I had assumed that this would be a small group of 30 or so, but found out it would be a group of 500. By knowing this information in advance, I could fine-tune my preparation and practice. It took more energy for me to speak to that larger crowd, but I felt that I made an impact because I had put in the necessary time to prepare and practice. My fear of speaking before an audience had not completely disappeared, but I had learned to manage it through my passion for wanting to help others and by concentrating on communicating my message rather than on my fear. I have known others who say that their fear gives them an edge that helps them channel their nervous energy into the process of communicating their message.

Before and during your speech, your body goes through emotional and physical changes, perhaps including a rise in your blood pressure and pulse rate, a slowing down of the digestive system, an increase in perspiration, and irregular breathing. However, you can use your nervous energy to your advantage. If you have too much nervous energy, do simple isometric exercises just before speaking. One exercise simply involves clenching your fists, holding them tight a few seconds, and then relaxing. You will want to repeat this activity two or three times. Another exercise involves pushing down on the arms of a chair for several seconds and then relaxing. Once again, you will want to repeat this or other simple isometrics two or three times just before you speak.[20] When muscles tighten and tense up, you use excess energy. The tighten-and-relax cycle helps to relax other muscles in your body. I've read that Yul Brynner, star of The King and I, and Billy Crystal both did isometric exercises before going on stage. I don't necessarily think you should do push-ups like Billy Crystal before you present, but a few isometric exercises might be in order.

On the Stage

To help with the nerves, first try to make eye contact and smile at three or four people in different parts of the room. When you are expressive and smile, you connect with your listeners, send a consistent message, and look and feel more animated. When you smile, members of the audience smile back at you, and you immediately feel more relaxed. In my coaching of individuals, I often find that at first they resist the notion that smiling is the right thing to do. They perceive they are not being serious enough, but once these individuals see how they look on video, they realize how powerful a smile can be to connect with an audience. A 2002 study in Sweden confirmed the power of a smile. The researchers found that people respond in kind to the facial expressions they encounter.[21] So if you smile at your audience, they will smile back at you.

If you are presenting to a large audience with over 100 individuals, you will probably have to stand behind a podium and use a microphone, but if you are speaking to a smaller audience, move about and use your presentation area. Speakers often stand in one spot as if glued to the floor, which predisposes them to shake or sway. Decker Communications has created what they call the "ready position," which requires you to lean slightly forward with your knees flexed so that you can bounce lightly on the balls of your feet. Using the ready position will help you avoid shaking or swaying. Your posture is an important part of this ready position. You want to stand tall with your shoulders back, which makes you look confident. When you use the ready position, your knees will not shake, as you will have flexed them forward rather than locked them back. It may seem uncomfortable at first, but with practice, you'll feel at ease.

If you are presenting without a podium, the best way to control your nerves is to move. Move in an arc and take at least two steps toward your audience. Decker Communication calls this the "arc and park." You move in an arc or half circle and stop for 10 to 20 seconds at certain spots along that arc. You don't want to step back or take fewer than two steps, as it will appear that you're tentative and unsure. If you've ever been in a play or taken a drama class, you know to keep your body facing the audience, and using "arc and park" allows you to do that.

If you have a podium but a small audience, move to the side or the front to get closer to your audience. Remember, the podium puts a barrier between you and your audience. Most people tend to use the podium as a crutch, which reminds me of a story of a big football player I once had in a class. He was gripping both sides of the podium so tightly that he passed out. Now that's not something you want to do. So just walk away from that podium and you'll find yourself in better control of your nerves.

Your voice is a reflection of you and your way of expressing yourself in this world.

You should vary your voice, taking into consideration your surroundings and the size of your audience. Generally, speakers tend to speak too softly, and this is because one's own voice always sounds louder to oneself than to the listeners. Remember to pay attention to your audience's reactions to have a gauge of whether are you speaking loudly enough.

Source: http://bizcovering.com/education-and-training/
five-tips-on-how-you-can-improve-your-vocal
-delivery-in-a-speech/#ixzz1Sssm1auV

Vocal Delivery

During the speech, you want everyone to hear you or you have wasted their time in coming. If possible, precede your presentation with a sound check. Try to position different individuals in various locations to determine whether your voice will carry throughout the room. "Make your voice work for, not against, your speech. Don't speak so quickly that your audience can't keep up with you or so slowly that they get bored. Articulate each word clearly and distinctly. Remember to be expressive, varying your voice and avoiding a monotone. A boring voice will cause the audience to stop paying attention to your speech. Vary the pitch of your voice for emphasis and variety, and project your voice to all corners of the room."[22]

Pay close attention to your articulation while using a conversational tone. Most importantly, speak at a rate that keeps your listeners interested. Using an appropriate volume, pitch, and rate will also help you maintain audience interest.

You should make sure you are watching your audience's eyes, postures, and facial expressions to see whether they understand you. Your audience's body posture and expression will speak to you. Based on what you see, either go back and repeat, or go on.

Gestures

In business presentations, gestures can help you emphasize your points, just as they do in one-on-one conversations. Your hands are a natural extension of your body, so use them to communicate and to emphasize points you want to make. Become aware of any habitual gestures that you make, as you don't want the audience to focus on your hands instead of listening to your words. Typically, you want to gesture openly with your palms up, as this gesture symbolizes honesty. Rather than put your hands in your pockets, you can just drop them to your sides when not using them. Vary your gestures and switch from hand to hand. You probably don't want to have anything in your hands besides the remote to change your slides. I can remember many years ago, I learned that when speaking, I would swirl rubber bands that I had placed on my wrist. When I found out that those rubber bands had become a distraction for my audience, I learned to remove anything from my hands that I thought might be a distraction. That old saying "a picture is worth a thousand words" rang true for me, and I've never forgotten what I looked like swirling those rubber bands!

Avoid putting your hands in your pockets, handcuffing your hands behind your bank, clasping them in front of you as though they were

Photo courtesy flickr user Imagine Cup, CC 2.0

a fig leaf, clasping them as if you were in prayer, putting them on your hips, crossing your arms, or wringing your hands nervously. If you feel uncomfortable with your hands, keep them at your sides. If your hands make you feel self-conscious, focus on your audience instead of yourself.

Men in particular will often ask me if they can keep one hand in a pocket and gesture with the other hand. I share that they can do that as long as they do not have keys or change in that pocket, but it is better to have your hands at your sides rather than restraining any part of your body, since your body language is an important part of the communication process.

Eye Contact

In the United States, you are expected to establish eye contact with members of your audience as a show of respect. This norm does not apply in some countries, so once again, for international presentations, you'll have to do your homework.

As you present, you should move from one person to another with your eyes. You don't want to go too fast or too slow or to give the impression that your eyes are darting nervously around the room. You want your eye movement to look natural, but intentional. Ensure that you include individuals on the sides as well as at the back of the room. You've probably been told that if you are nervous, you should look over the top of people's heads, but I would encourage you not to follow that advice. Individuals know when someone is looking over rather than at them. It will help your delivery if you think of your audience as individuals rather than as just a group of people.

Dress

Individuals often ask me about how they should dress for a presentation. My advice is to dress one level up from the audience, as you'll make a stronger first impression and maximize your credibility. As you know, it only takes 4 seconds to form a first impression and 4 hours to change that impression. You can always take off your coat or remove a tie to get more comfortable with your audience.

Photo courtesy flickr user Imagine Cup, CC 2.0

Manage Q & A

Encourage your audience to ask questions by using appropriate body language. If you step back from your audience, cross your arms, and appear to be challenging anyone to ask a question, you probably will not get any! Instead, step toward your audience, raise your hand, and ask, "Does anyone have questions for me?" or "What questions do you have?" Your raised hand encourages others to raise their hands when asking questions. Having individuals raise their hands to ask a question helps keep order and encourages shy individuals to participate. You can even help start the questions by saying something like "A question I'm often asked is. . . ."

Assume the audience will ask questions, so you need to give them time to think and to ask. Too often, speakers do not allow the audience time to formulate questions. When listening to questions, do not interrupt, but wait to repeat the question and to respond. While listening, watch the speaker's body language to pick up clues about how the person feels about the question. Consider your own body language, too, as you listen to the question! If you start to back up during a question, you might be communicating that you do not want to answer that question. So instead, stand still and keep your hands in a neutral position with your arms at your sides and your fingers open to show openness and honesty.

Try not to preface your response with "That's a good question." You may forget to preface other questions the same way, and those people asking may wonder why they did not ask a "good question."

Ordinarily you want to repeat the question so the entire audience can hear it. Doing so gives you some time to think about how you want to respond.

Don't avoid answering questions that are difficult or lengthy. If a question requires you to do additional research, tell the individual you will get back to him or her within a certain time and then follow through. Nothing hurts your credibility more than making a promise and not keeping it. If one individual tries to dominate the Q & A, you can tactfully state that you would be more than happy to meet with him or her after the presentation concludes. If you are asked a question designed to get an emotional response from you, try to keep your cool and respond honestly. Sometimes you can defuse the hostility by paraphrasing the question and asking the questioner to confirm you have understood correctly. Using that strategy also allows you to count to 10 and stay in control.

Finally, remember to watch the nonverbal communication of your audience. Yawns might signal a need for a break or for a change or shortening of your presentation. Your goal is to leave the audience wanting a little more rather than sound asleep, frustrated, or irritable!

Team Presentations

You will likely find yourself being asked to present as part of a team. The most successful team presentations are those in which the team truly functions as a team. By that, I mean the team plans the presentation together, determines the purpose and main points, divides the topics into logical and well-balanced divisions, thinks about potential questions, practices together, and then presents. When I coach teams that will be making presentations collaboratively, we sit down and talk through the structure of the presentation. Then we meet again to do a video recorded session, which we watch and review. After the critique, we meet the day before the client presentation for a final run-through.

In preparing your team introduction, make sure the first team presenter hooks your audience, motivates them to listen, and establishes credibility by introducing all the team members. Your team members should be

Rehearse as a group—early and often.

Run through all the presentations. Focus on how each one is structured. Review visuals. Clearly establish everyone's role and how the presentations link to one another. Get used to one another's speaking styles, and strengths and weaknesses. Is there too much content? Too little of the right content? Is there overlap? Do the presentations complement and support one another? Do they flow logically? Are they aligned with your objectives?

The team should also prepare for Q & As as a group. That means anticipating questions that are likely to come up and agreeing as a team on the answers. Also agree in advance on the team member or members who are best suited to respond to a given question.

Source: Ask the Experts
The Total Communicator
Winter 2005
Retrieved from: http://totalcommunicator
.com/vol3_1/expert2.htmlved

introduced as experts in each of their topic areas to add credibility to your team's work. The first team presenter also states the purpose and previews the three main points before transitioning to the second presenter.

A key mistake that teams often make is having individual team members introduce themselves after the first speaker has introduced them. For example, the first presenter has opened and transitions to the next speaker by saying something such as "Now Rob will tell us how we can increase our sales." Then Rob takes the stage and says, "Hi, I'm Rob." In effect, what has happened is that the team presentation has now become four or five individual presentations tacked together. The team presentation has lost its flow and unity. Instead, each presenter should refer to the previous speaker, which connects the individual parts of the presentation into a unified whole. In addition, it clearly demonstrates that the team has practiced together and that each individual presenter is familiar with the whole presentation. You never know when a team member might get sick or have an emergency that prevents him or her from presenting, requiring that the rest of the team take over that section.

Photo courtesy flickr user cogdogblog, CC 2.0

When you present your section, talk to your audience, not to the other members of your team. If you have presented your section, you should listen to the rest of your team as if you are hearing that material for the first time. Nothing distracts an audience more than a team member engaged in other things rather than listening.

Teams should plan for the Q & A session to determine which presenter will respond to various types of questions. What seems to work the best for most teams is to have one team member field the questions and turn the question over to the appropriate team member. If you are the team member who is fielding questions, you may want to repeat the question for two reasons. First, it allows the whole audience to hear the question; and second, it gives the responding team member a bit more time to think and formulate his or her response. Then the individual who is fielding the Q & A session can watch the time and wrap up the presentation with final comments to make an impact on the audience.

In planning your visuals, include color, pictures, and graphics to excite the eye and to invite curiosity. If your team's presentation follows another presentation that made the audience sit through endless bulleted slides, think of how thankful they will be to have interesting pictures and imaginative graphics.[23] Often audiences just want you to have a conversation with them. I can remember hearing a story about an individual who landed an unexpected contract. She had all the latest whistles and bells in her PowerPoint presentation, but she had a computer malfunction. When she couldn't get her computer to work, she just sat down and talked with the potential client. She walked out thinking she would certainly not get the contract. You can imagine her surprise when she received a call stating she had won the contract. She shared her surprise with the CEO, and he stated that she had been a breath of fresh air in a day of endless Power-Point presentations because she simply talked to them.

If you've practiced as a team, you will find it much easier to stay with your time limits. Your team members will become frustrated if they have too much or too little time to present their sections. I recommend that your team establish a minimum 3-hour rehearsal rule. This practice will allow your presentation to flow and to transition from one speaker to the next.

I recommend, once again, that your team video record its presentation and then analyze it. This presentation session will help cut out overlap and reduce logistical problems with presentation order, slides, and the closing. When you make your video recording, you practice with all the visuals, if possible, dressed as if you were making the real presentation and using all the proper equipment in the room where you will present. When you critique your team's presentation, look for mannerisms that could distract from your message and answer the following questions:

- Did we work together well as a team?
- What three things did we do well?
- Did we honor each other's time?
- Did we show interest and listen when our teammates spoke?

Often, I am asked if teams should give a copy of their slides to the audience before they present. My answer is "it depends." To find the answer, you need to once again address the questions of "What is my purpose?" and "What is the result I want?" If you want audience members to take notes, give them something upon which to take notes. I once had a team give their audience a placemat that had all the team members' pictures and lots of space to take notes. The audience of senior execs really liked it and complimented the team on its creativity. If you give your audience a copy of your slides, they may flip through them before you actually make your presentation and then not pay attention. If you want them to stay focused, you may choose to give them a handout with the slides after the presentation.

Spotlight on Today's Managerial Leader

Joe Urbanski is client director for Cisco (http.cisco.com). In his 7-year career with Cisco, Joe has held director and manager roles in sales. In his current role, he is responsible for managing a large multinational team and owns client executive relationships within Cisco's Global Enterprise Theater. Prior to joining Cisco, Joe consulted in the field of technology for Fortune 50 clients. Joe received his master's degree in business administration from the Kennesaw State University in 2006.

The Changing Face of Collaboration on the Global Stage

Five short years ago, my MBA journey came to an end. Online studies were just hitting the MBA market. The BRIC countries were starting to level the competitive playing field against the United States and Europe. *The World Is Flat*, by Thomas L. Friedman, explained how emerging countries gained access to unprecedented opportunity in the global economy via technology. My MBA included international studies. When I partnered with a university in Romania, we exchanged cultural norms and business best practices, and I eventually took a trip to Romania. This was a significant time in Romanian history. Capitalism was new to Romanians, who had been freed from communist rule and a terrible dictator just the decade before. Romanian students focused tremendous energy on understanding the free market.

At the time, Kennesaw State gained international attention for its use of online collaboration tools in classroom teaming. The toolset provided students with a way to share documents, ask and answer questions, and post project results back to faculty. For the culmination of our program, the faculty created international teams comprising

members from both universities. The final international project con-
sisted of a marketing program in which we leveraged our employer's
best practices in delivering a comprehensive marketing plan. Grad-
ing included effectively drawing all team members' best practices into
the final presentation. Our team elected me to take a leadership role
due to my previous leadership experiences in the workplace. However, responsibility escalated when faculty placed a percentage of our
final project grade on how we collaborated via online collaboration
tools, used an audio bridge, and leveraged videoconferencing. All of
our work effort required international collaboration. When the Romanians came to Atlanta, our schedule included one day to practice and
then, literally, stand and deliver our presentation the next morning.

We didn't have the ability or freedom to schedule meetings across
time zones without first calculating the difference in time. Finding a
time that matched various work schedules was nearly impossible.
Videoconferencing offered additional challenges. Adapting to technology we never used before caused delay and frustration. Suddenly,
everyone believed they were the power user, moving the field of view
in and out of focus, causing the audio to disappear, and causing audio
and video to separate. We'd see lips moving and fifteen seconds later,
words followed. Since use of the video equipment meant both sides
travelling to our respective universities, an hour meeting burned 3
hours due to travel time. Some members could not participate regularly because they lived in other parts of the country, meaning we
were limited to meeting on class weekends.

Our experience offered a firsthand view of the challenges of global
teaming. We eventually gave up and reverted to audio-only bridge meetings. However, there were tradeoffs. In a meeting scenario where both
disparate linguistic and cultural norms exist, we lost out by not seeing
the other attendees to validate understanding and gain consensus. In
the end, our project was still a success! However, I didn't realize just how
soon I would leverage the knowledge gained in this experience.

During my MBA journey, Cisco hired me to work in sales. Shortly
afterward, I found myself managing a multinational team. About
this time, Cisco created a video solution to challenge traditional

videoconferencing. Named TelePresence, the solution quickly became my tool of choice for all team meetings.

Cisco recognized everything wrong about the experience I had in my MBA class. Face-to-face meetings generate results because of the experience. We see each other. We hear each other. When we see and hear, we comprehend and retain at a deeper level. If a meeting is conducted over the phone, how do you know the other party is engaged or even awake? The outcome was a solution that allowed participants to be totally **immersed** in a meeting as if they were face-to-face but, in fact, sat a continent apart.

.ı|ı.ı|ı.
CISCO

Pierre-Paul Allard is presently vice president at Cisco Systems, Inc., based in San Jose, California. He is responsible for sales and field operations of Cisco's global industries client segment. His focus is on new market opportunities, accelerated revenue growth, and increased customer satisfaction in one of Cisco's largest market segments. With more than two decades of industry experience, he brings a unique blend of marketing, financial, sales, and systems engineering skills into his role.

Several things come to mind when I think of TelePresence. But I think first and foremost, it's the memories of first-time users. I vividly recall watching the reaction of several clients when they actually sat for the first time, and saw the screen turn on in front of them with real live individuals on the other side. Their eyes light up, their mouth opens, and they remain transfixed for the first several minutes. This happened again recently when we set up a meeting between the head of engineering at Ford Motor Company and Cisco executives.

Cisco was in San Jose, and the client was in Detroit. We had tried to organize the meeting in person for weeks, but were not able to match their calendars. It took 10 minutes to get the client off talking about the reality of the experience, and how overwhelming it was to see the Cisco team so real and vivid on the other side. TelePresence is just a mind-boggling experience. And it's a thrill to introduce someone to it for the first time.

Today, global enterprises know no borders. Increasing demand for speed to market, microinnovation, and multicultural teaming require workplace facilities offering immersive interactions. Leaders of business and government, educators and students, small businesses, and consumers communicate in a face-to-face yet virtual setting regularly now. The trend of video communication into business and home will increase exponentially in the next few years.

Visual Interaction

TelePresence offers leaders and managers an avenue of communication that drives increased associate productivity. With more than 60 percent of communication being nonverbal, results tend to lag when global teams cannot interact visually. In addition, conflicting cultural norms and language barriers hinder effectiveness. An immersive experience breaks constraints, allowing for true team acceleration and solution speed to market.

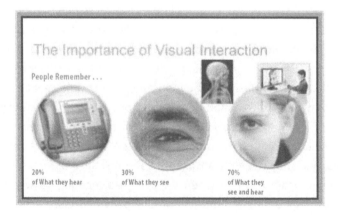

The Importance of Visual Interaction

People Remember . . .

20% of What they hear

30% of What they see

70% of What they see and hear

Matching Experts to Consumers

Working in the retail sector, I'm keenly aware of the changing demographics of available labor resources. Given the number of open hours, retailers find staffing all hours of operation both expensive and difficult. Here are some examples of how TelePresence changes the communication between enterprises and consumers:

- Top international financial services enterprises offer financial portfolio experts to consumers through TelePresence in remote branches.
- Major U.S. home improvement retailer offers design services to consumers via TelePresence.
- Korean auto manufacturer offers sales and leasing assistance to car shoppers via TelePresence.

Global enterprises manage complex sales, supply chain, engineering, or financial organizations. Executives and managers in these organizations are quickly adopting the benefits of eliminating days of travel for meetings that only last a few hours. Employees in these organizations are more productive, enjoy a greater quality of work/life balance, and at the same time generate a smaller carbon footprint. Leaders that command a greater use of collaboration tools improve morale and help both the top and bottom line.

Global Communication

My first use of TelePresence involved a meeting for my client's worldwide supply chain leadership team. Attendees participated from Italy, Mexico, China, India, Canada, and three locations in the United States. The picture on page 313 demonstrates the experience. Imagine six countries, on three continents, all visible at one time. My client simply sat in awe for a few minutes, and then the technology faded to the background, and the meeting agenda started. Global leaders can now drive effective communication directly to internal teams and clients. Leaders of tomorrow will learn to embrace this technology as a differentiator for their teams.

Photo courtesy flickr user eveos, CC 2.0

Conference Room Presentations

Sometimes you may be asked to make a presentation in a conference room. In some situations, you'll be able to follow all of the guidelines that have already been discussed; in other cases, you'll need to adapt. Before you begin your presentation, you may want to shake hands with everyone seated at the conference table. You should walk around the conference table rather than leaning across it to look more professional.[24] If you're part of a team making this presentation, you'll want all of your team members to sit on one side with your audience on the other side of the table. When your team members are presenting, it goes without saying that you should be listening and using nonverbal communication such as nodding and smiling to show you're interested in what your team members are saying.

When presenting while seated, you can still use the ready position. You'll want to sit toward the front of your chair with both feet flat on the floor. If you have one of those conference chairs that you can adjust, you can raise it to its tallest position. Then you'll want to lean forward slightly, put your arms on the table, and use appropriate gestures. Just as in presentations where you stand, you don't want to lean back in your chair until the last question has been asked and you have made your concluding remarks.

Ninety percent of web presentation tool users never receive any formal training or coaching before they present in front of a customer or prospect. Learn the platform so that your brain can relax and allow you to concentrate on your presentation.

Source: How To Give an Online Presentation
By Geoffrey James
February 23, 2011
Retrieved from http://www.bnet.com/blog/salesmachine/how-to -give-an-online-presentation/14630?utm_source=twitterfeed&utm _medium=twitter&utm_campaign=Feed%3A+bnet%2Fsalesmachine +%28BNET+Sales+Machine%29&utm_content=Twitter

---

Online or Webinar Presentations

As the work world continues to become more virtual, we are seeing more online or webcam presentations. Learning to present using a webcam can take some time, as some of the recommendations for live presentations, such as movement, are discouraged for webcam presentations.

Part of your preparation will be setting up your equipment with the correct lighting. You often want to soften the harsh light so you can turn on your desk lamp, but you may need to diffuse that light by covering it with a piece of white paper. Simply tape the paper to the front of the lamp and your lighting is softer. You can also adjust the monitor brightness and/or contrast down to a level where you can just barely see comfortably while you're using your webcam. Doing so helps the color of your skin and allows the audience to see your eyes. It is best to wear white or lighter colors to help with the exposure on your webcam. Finally, you don't want a distracting background to draw attention away from you, the presenter. Therefore, you'll want to take pictures off the wall or use a screen like the one a photographer uses to provide a cleaner and less distracting background.[25]

A common mistake that often happens with webcam or webinar presentations is that someone puts a slide on the screen and then he or she appears later. You'll make more of an impact if your audience sees you first and then your slides. Remember that as the presenter, you, not your visuals, should be center stage. Once you've opened with your attention-getter, then you can move to opening your slides.

Just as in face-to-face presentations, eye contact is critical. However, the biggest change is that you don't see your audience and you're looking at a webcam lens. It may seem awkward at first because you truly can't see your audience, but making eye contact is even more important in this type of presentation. So put a picture of a person on your webcam lens so it reminds you to look there. If you have speaker notes, you'll want to put them right below your webcam, as you don't want to appear to be looking off to the side instead of looking at your audience. Placing your notes there will show less eye movement. You can stand during a webcam presentation, and it can show confidence to do so, but you will have to limit your movement, as it will be blurry. If you choose to present while seated, you should use the seated ready position described in the previous conference room presentation section. Avoid overusing gestures as they typically will blur as well.

Often individuals think they can read their presentation and no one will know, but the reality is that your audience can certainly tell you are reading by your lack of eye contact and your speaking rate. So just don't do it. I've seen individuals do wonderful stand-up presentations and then freeze up and just read when put in front of a webcam. It does take practice to get comfortable with talking to a webcam, but try to be as conversational as you can and only use speaker notes that consist of bullet points to resist the temptation to read!

You should remember that when you're showing your slides or a video, you're technically still on stage. I have noticed during some team webcam presentations that individuals forget that they can still be seen when others are presenting. So they will get up and move around or do something that can distract their audience. That critical element of team practice rings true with this type of presentation. When the team records their practice presentation, they will see what team members do and realize what they should not do! You may find it helpful to turn off the webcam during video clips to avoid drawing attention away from the video and to give you a chance to catch your breath. Just as in the opening, you will want to focus on yourself during the conclusion and not just on the slides. You will make a stronger and more memorable closing if you create a sound bite to use at the end.[26]

Predictions Regarding the Future of Presentations

Nancy Duartes, author of the book entitled *Slideology: The Art and Science of Creating Great Presentations,* has made four predictions regarding the future of presentations.[27] First, she stated that the tablet war will shape the future of presentations. Tablets such as iPads will be passed around the conference table much as individuals used to pass around their notes. Reading what Nancy says reminds me of the television show *Criminal Minds,* in which the characters each have their own tablets that they use around the conference room table. So when you present, you will have to incorporate more stories and short video clips into your presentations. A Harvard Business blog posting stated that "designing documents to be a sensual physical experience and not just a visually cognitive one demands different aesthetics and sensibilities. This nascent transition will be as profoundly important for future interpersonal communications—and branding—as the transition from radio to television. Having the right touch to get the right touch will become a desirable communications competence."[28]

Nancy's second prediction is that authenticity trumps "spin." Audiences want their presenters to be honest and transparent when they communicate. My current university president, Dan Papp, does this so well. We have been challenged with budget cuts and furlough days, but he authentically communicates each month through an e-mail addressing the budget, holds town hall meetings, and delivers a state of the union address each year. He is truly an example of an authentic communicator as you can tell he is sincere. Audiences can pick up when speakers are not being truthful.

Nancy's third prediction is that handmade visuals may be better than computer-generated ones. People have sat through so many PowerPoint presentations that they are hungry to see things done differently. So telling a story through a whiteboard might be more appealing to an audience. The key, of course, is to know your audience so that you can determine what is appropriate.

Her fourth prediction is that we will see fewer slides and that speakers will stand up and talk. She further states that speakers still have to do their homework, but they will do more talking instead of showing slides. She believes this change will occur more at the executive level and that it will filter down through all layers of the business as well. Her prediction is that people will get over the urge to sit behind the security blanket of a badly designed, word-riddled PowerPoint slide. They will either present without slides or put forth more effort to create better slides.

So think about Nancy's predictions as you work on your next presentation. Then review Figure 5.6 for a list of top ten presentation bloopers that were identified by over 200 executive MBA students and 50 Kroger

Number 1	Distracting mannerisms—verbal (slang, cursing, ums and ahs) and physical (body language, gestures, and posture)
Number 2	Poor intonation, inflection, volume, or rate
Number 3	Not being prepared
Number 4	Not connecting with audience
Number 5	Poor visual aids, inappropriate use of a visual aid, or the lack of practice with the equipment
Number 6	Poor presentation structure or fragmented speech; weak openings and closings
Number 7	Not practicing and managing the time
Number 8	Lack of eye contact
Number 9	Reading the presentation
Number 10	Use of inappropriate humor

Figure 5.6. Presentation Bloopers

store managers. You will want to make sure you avoid committing any of these bloopers as you prepare your presentation.

Conclusion

Becoming an effective oral presenter does take the application of the three-step strategy of prepare, practice, and present. In the preparation step, you will need to determine your purpose, analyze your audience, organize your presentation, make your outline, craft your visuals, and think through how you will handle your Q & A session.

Then you will build confidence through practicing with your visuals and rehearsing your presentation. The old adage "practice makes perfect" applies to those who want to become polished speakers.

When the day arrives for your presentation, remember that your audience wants you to succeed, so make emotional contact with them. If you are doing a live presentation, use the ready position and employ the "arc and park." If you are doing a webcam presentation, remember to limit your movement, but to use the seated ready position. You do not want to forget the power of eye contact, facial expressions, and vocal variety. Finally, remember to be you. If you show that you are believable, people will connect with you and you will make an impact.

Case for Thinking and Discussing

Instructions: Read the following article and then reflect on the following questions.

- What lessons from this article can you apply to your organization?
- What can you learn from a leader like Steve Jobs?
- Has your perspective changed regarding preparation and practice?
- How are you doing with what you have to say?

Table of Contents

10 Ways to Sell Your Ideas the Steve Jobs Way! 1
Plan in Analog 2
Create a Twitter-Friendly Description 3
Introduce the Antagonist 4
Focus on the Benefits 5
Stick to the Rule of Three 6
Sell Dreams, Not Products 7
Create Visual Slides 7
Make Numbers Meaningful 8
Use Zippy Words 8
Reveal a "Holy Smokes" Moment 9
One More Thing: Practice, a Lot 10
About Carmine Gallo 11

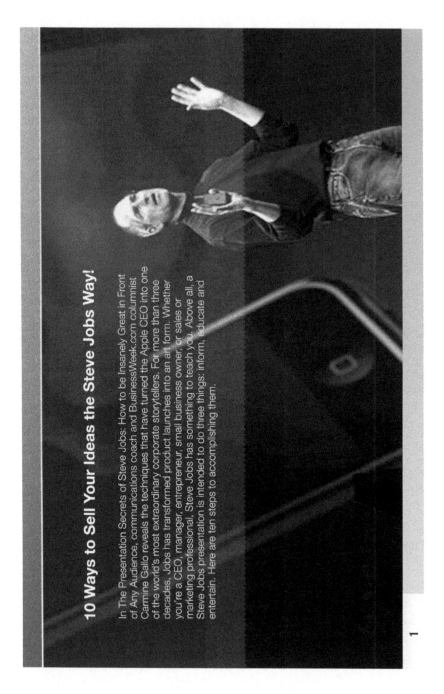

10 Ways to Sell Your Ideas the Steve Jobs Way!

In The Presentation Secrets of Steve Jobs: How to be Insanely Great in Front of Any Audience, communications coach and BusinessWeek.com columnist Carmine Gallo reveals the techniques that have turned the Apple CEO into one of the world's most extraordinary corporate storytellers. For more than three decades, Jobs has transformed product launches into an art form. Whether you're a CEO, manager, entrepreneur, small business owner, or sales or marketing professional, Steve Jobs has something to teach you. Above all, a Steve Jobs presentation is intended to do three things: inform, educate and entertain. Here are ten steps to accomplishing them.

Plan in Analog

Steve Jobs made his mark in the digital world of bits and bytes, but he plans presentations in the old world of pen and paper. A Steve Jobs presentation has all the elements of a great movie—heroes and villains, stunning visuals and a supporting cast. And, like a movie director, Steve Jobs "storyboards" the plot. Before you go digital and open PowerPoint, spend time brainstorming, sketching or whiteboarding in the early stages. Remember, you're delivering a story, the narrative. Slides complement the story. Neuroscientists have found the brain gets bored easily. Steve Jobs doesn't give his audience time to get distracted. His presentations include demonstrations, video clips, and other speakers. All of the elements are planned and collected well before the slides are created.

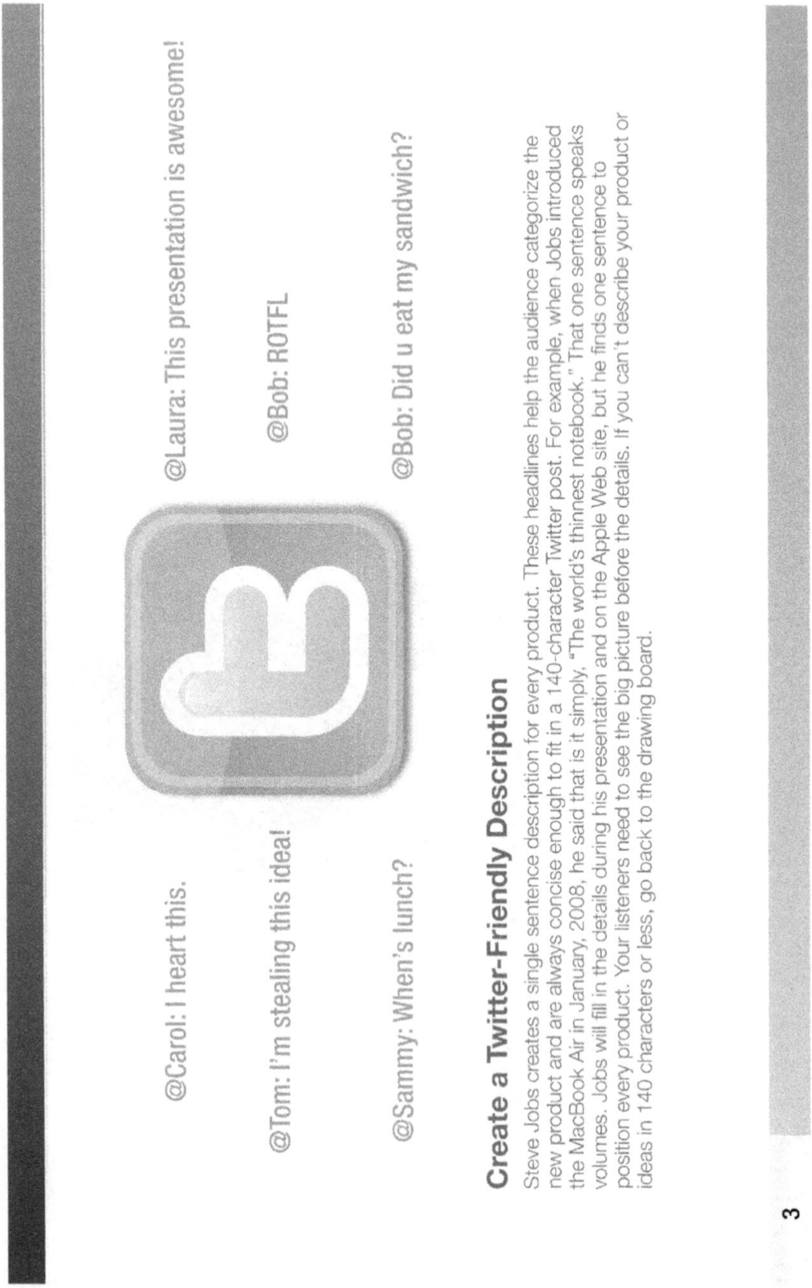

@Carol: I heart this.

@Tom: I'm stealing this idea!

@Sammy: When's lunch?

@Laura: This presentation is awesome!

@Bob: ROTFL

@Bob: Did u eat my sandwich?

Create a Twitter-Friendly Description

Steve Jobs creates a single sentence description for every product. These headlines help the audience categorize the new product and are always concise enough to fit in a 140-character Twitter post. For example, when Jobs introduced the MacBook Air in January, 2008, he said that is it simply, "The world's thinnest notebook." That one sentence speaks volumes. Jobs will fill in the details during his presentation and on the Apple Web site, but he finds one sentence to position every product. Your listeners need to see the big picture before the details. If you can't describe your product or ideas in 140 characters or less, go back to the drawing board.

3

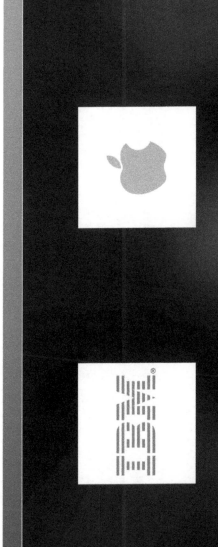

Introduce the Antagonist

In every classic story, the hero fights the villain. The same holds true for a Steve Jobs presentation. In 1984, the villain was IBM, known as "Big Blue" at the time. Before Jobs introduced the famous 1984 television ad to a group of Apple salespeople, he created a dramatic story around it. "IBM wants it all," he said. Apple would be the only company to stand in its way. It was very dramatic and the crowd went crazy. Branding expert Martin Lindstrom says that great brands and religions have something in common: the idea of vanquishing a shared enemy. Create a villain that allows the audience to rally around the hero—you and your product.

A "villain" doesn't necessarily have to be a direct competitor. It can be a problem in need of a solution. When Steve Jobs introduced the iPhone in January, 2007, his presentation at Macworld focused on the problems mobile phone users were experiencing with the current technology. The iPhone, he said, would resolve those issues. Setting up the problem opens the door for the hero to save the day.

4

Why should I care?

Focus on Benefits

Your listeners are asking themselves one question: Why should I care? Steve Jobs sells the benefit behind every new product or feature—and he's very clear about it. Why buy an iPhone 3G? Because "it's twice as fast at half the price." What's so great about Time Capsule? "All your irreplaceable photos, videos and documents are automatically protected and easy to retrieve if they're ever lost." Even the Apple Web site focuses on benefits with top ten lists like, "10 Reasons Why You'll Love a Mac." Nobody cares about your product. They only care about how your product or service will improve their lives. Make the connection for your customers. Don't leave them guessing.

> **Three stories from my life.**

Stick to the Rule of Three

Nearly every Steve Jobs presentation is divided into three parts. When Jobs returned from a health-related absence on September 9, 2009, he told the audience he would be talking about three products: iPhones, iTunes and iPods. Along the way he provides verbal guideposts such as "iPhones. The first thing I wanted to talk about today. Now, let's move on to the second, iTunes." The number "three" is a powerful concept in writing. Playwrights know that three is more dramatic than two; comedians know that three is funnier than four, and Steve Jobs knows that three is more memorable than six or eight. You might have twenty points to make about your product, but your audience is only capable of holding three or four points in short term memory. Give them too many points and they'll forget everything.

If three is such an important number, why does this e-book have ten points? Because it's a written reference tool that is not intended to be delivered verbally. If this information were delivered verbally, we would only stick to three key takeaways. Remember, Steve Jobs will send his audience to the Apple Web site for more information, but he only delivers three points in a conversation.

6

Sell Dreams, Not Products

Charismatic speakers like Steve Jobs are driven by a nearly messianic zeal to create new experiences. Steve Jobs doesn't sell computers. He sells the promise of a better world. When Jobs introduced the iPod in 2001, he said, "In our own small way we're going to make the world a better place." Where most people see the iPod as a music player, Jobs sees it as a tool to enrich people's lives. Of course, it's important to have great products. But passion, enthusiasm and a sense of purpose beyond the actual product will set you and your company apart.

Jobs is also passionate about his customers and he's not afraid to wear that passion on his sleeve. During a presentation in 1997 he concluded by saying, "Some people say you have to be a little crazy to buy a Mac. Well, in that craziness we see genius and that's who we make tools for." Cultivate a sense of mission. Passion, emotion and enthusiasm are grossly underestimated ingredients in professional business communications and yet they are powerful ways to motivate others. Steve Jobs once said that his goal was not to die the richest man in the cemetery. It was to go to bed at night thinking that he and his team had done something wonderful. Do something wonderful. Make your brand stand for something meaningful.

Create Visual Slides

Apple products are easy to use because they eliminate "clutter." This design philosophy applies to every Steve Jobs presentation. There are no bullet points in his presentations. Instead Jobs relies on photographs and images. Where the average PowerPoint slide has forty words, it's difficult to find seven words on ten of Jobs's slides. The technique is called "Picture Superiority:" information is more effectively recalled when text and images are combined. For example, when Steve Jobs unveiled the Macbook Air, Apple's ultra-thin notebook computer, he showed a slide of the computer fitting inside a manila inter-office envelope. That image was worth a thousand words. "Simplicity is the ultimate sophistication," Jobs once said. Be sophisticated. Keep it simple.

Make Numbers Meaninful

In every Apple presentation, big numbers are put into context. On September 9, 2009, Apple VP Phil Schiller said that 220 million iPods had been sold to date. He placed that number into context by saying it represented 73% of the market. He broke it down even further—and took a jab at the competition—by saying Microsoft was "pulling up the rear" with its 1% market share. Schiller learned his technique from Jobs who always puts large numbers into a context that's relevant to his audience.

The bigger the number, the more important it is to find analogies or comparisons that make the data relevant to your audience. For example, when the United States government bailed out the U.S. economy to the tune of $700 billion, it was too huge a number for most people to comprehend. Journalists tried to put it into context. The one example that seemed to capture the attention of the press—$700 billion is like spending one million dollars a day since the day Christ was born. Now that's a big number!

Use Zippy Words

Steve Jobs speaks in plain English. In fact, he has fun with words. He described the speed of the new iPhone 3G as "amazingly zippy." Where most business presenters use words that are obtuse, vague or confusing, Jobs's language is remarkably simple. He rarely, if ever, will use the jargon that clouds most presentations—terms like "best of breed" or "synergy." His language is simple, clear and direct. Legendary GE CEO Jack Welch once said, "Insecure managers create complexity." Exude confidence and security; speak simply.

Reveal "Holy Smokes" Moment

Every Steve Jobs presentation has one moment that neuroscientists call an "Emotionally Charged Event." The emotionally charged event is the equivalent of a mental sticky note that tells the brain, "Remember this!" For example, at Macworld 2007, Jobs could have opened the presentation by telling the audience that Apple was unveiling a new mobile phone that also played music, games, and video. Instead he built up the drama. "Today, we are introducing three revolutionary products. The first one is a widescreen iPod with touch controls. The second is a revolutionary mobile phone. And the third is a breakthrough Internet communications device....an iPod, a phone, an Internet communicator... an iPod, a phone, are you getting it? These are not three devices. This is one device!" The audience erupted in cheers because it was so unexpected and very entertaining.

The world's thinnest notebook.

One More Thing: Practice, a Lot

Steve Jobs spends hours rehearsing every facet of his presentation. Every slide is written like a piece of poetry, every presentation staged like a theatrical experience. Yes, Steve Jobs makes a presentation look effortless but that polish comes after hours and hours of grueling practice. Steve Jobs has improved his style over time. If you watch video clips of Steve Jobs's presentations going back twenty years (available on YouTube) you will see that he improves significantly with every decade. The Steve Jobs of 1984 had a lot of charisma but the Steve Jobs of 1997 was a far more polished speaker. The Steve Jobs who introduced the iPhone in 2007 was even better. Nobody is born knowing how to deliver a great PowerPoint presentation. Expert speakers hone that skill with practice.

10

About Carmine Gallo

Carmine Gallo is the communication skills coach for the world's most admired brands. He is a sought-after keynote speaker, seminar leader, media training specialist, crisis communication specialist, presentation expert and communications coach. His clients appear in the news every day and many would not think of launching a new product without his insight. Gallo is a former CNN business journalist and a current columnist for BusinessWeek.com. He is the author of several books including his latest, *The Presentation Secrets of Steve Jobs: How to be Insanely Great in Front of Any Audience* and *Fire Them Up! 7 Simple Secrets of Inspiring Leaders.*

Contact Information

Email Carmine directly at carmine@gallocommunications.com

Email Carmine's assistant at vanessa@gallocommunications.com (phone: 925-963-7958)

Web site: http://www.carminegallo.com

Webzine: http://www.talkingleadership.com

APPENDIX A

Barbara S. Gainey (PhD, University of South Carolina) is Associate Professor of Communication, Public Relations, at Kennesaw State University, Georgia. She is coordinator of the public relations concentration and a member of the KSU Honors Program faculty. Dr. Gainey's research interests include crisis communication/crisis management (particularly in educational settings), public relations, public engagement through new media, and leadership. Dr. Gainey has more than 20 years of professional communication experience.

Crisis Leadership for the New Reality Ahead

Reprinted with permission from the *Journal of Executive Education*

In this post–September 11 and post–Virginia Tech era, it may seem foolish to ask if crisis planning is something in which you should engage, spending precious time, financial, and personnel resources. The realities of a 24/7 news cycle can make any organization's crisis headline news, enhancing a sense of vulnerability among stakeholders. The new demands and pressures faced by today's organizations underline the need for planning and preparation for the unknown ahead.

Need for Crisis Planning

Why is formal crisis management important for today's organizations, private and public sector alike? What are the challenges that may confront business leaders just around the bend? According to Coombs, the need to protect organizational reputations, respond to stakeholder activism and advances in communication technologies, take a broader viewer of crises that have a ripple effect, and concerns about charges of negligence if companies fail to plan are driving many organizations to make crisis preparations.[1]

Today's crises pose geographic, social, and political threats of increasing complexity, according to Devitt and Borodzicz.[2] Crises ahead may be increasingly "transboundary" in nature, Boin proposes, due in part to new technologies, international terrorism, climate change, demographic shifts, and shifts in global power arrangements that present threats as well as opportunities.[3] Buckle[4] warns of transnational (across borders or outside of jurisdiction, such as in space, in the ocean, or in the Antarctic) and transgenerational issues that extend far into the future. More immediately, business leaders must respond to the decline in trust in relationships between organizations and stakeholders—employees and customers—which have hit significant bumps in the road with the recent economic recession.[5] Trust is an essential ingredient in crisis situations; stakeholders will adapt more confidently if they have a trusted source of communication in a crisis.[6]

Multiple voices echo the need for ongoing crisis planning. The reality is that business may be moving slowly in another direction. Without the sense of urgency of a 9/11-scale event, the number of organizations without current crisis plans in place is slowly decreasing, according to a 2005 American Management Association study. The AMA study in August and September of 2005 found that, while more than half of the United States companies surveyed had crisis management plans, the percentage with crisis plans had dipped from 64 percent in 2003 to 60 percent in 2005. Only 38 percent of AMA respondents had provided crisis management training for key personnel ("AMA 2005 Crisis Management & Security Issues Survey").[7] 79 percent of American small businesses indicate that they do not have a disaster recovery plan in place.[8] At the same time, the private sector passed a crisis milestone. The so-called discipline of crisis management[9] marked its 25th anniversary in 2007. Business has moved from the Johnson & Johnson first crisis of product tampering to environmental disasters of the Gulf oil spill, from natural disasters such as Hurricane Katrina to the more recent concerns of an influenza pandemic, from financial upheaval to threats of terrorism within the United States and abroad. Leaders are needed who recognize the threats and opportunities ahead, rather than simply being driven by the dictates of the moment. We must acknowledge today's inclination to live only in the moment and push our creative and intuitive abilities to project and imagine the challenges ahead.

Best Practices

Crisis events facing the corporate sector have the potential to

- affect and disrupt the entire organization;
- negatively affect the organization's publics, products, and services;
- jeopardize the organization's reputation, future profitability, and even its survival;
- dramatically redefine an organization, affecting its business and culture;
- violate the vision of what the organization is set up to accomplish;
- inflict long-term damage on the organization and its relationships with its stakeholders.[10]

On the other hand, crisis management and crisis communication propose strategies and processes for preparing for, preventing, responding to, managing, recovering from, and learning from crisis events. A number of best-practice models have been proposed. Most address activities that should take place (1) in a pre-crisis environment, when day-to-day business is conducted in a normal climate; (2) during a crisis situation or as a crisis is unfolding; and (3) in a post-crisis environment[11] as the crisis cycle comes to a close. To be crisis-ready in a communication sense, organizations should (a) evaluate the organization's communications climate and whether the organization is open or closed to sharing information; (b) identify stakeholders crucial to the organization's success; (c) create a written communication map or network of stakeholders that could be relied on in a crisis; (d) develop ongoing, two-way communication between the organization and these key stakeholders; (e) incorporate a mix of traditional and new media in an established communication program; (f) develop new ways of meaningfully engaging stakeholders in areas of shared interest and concern; (g) anticipate the demands that users of traditional and new media will place on the organization in times of crisis.[12]

Before a Crisis Hits

Many steps should be considered before hints of a crisis appear on the horizon. The first is to develop a signal detection or early warning system to identify issues that may develop into a crisis in the future. Coombs recommends focusing on threats or vulnerabilities that have the greatest likelihood of occurring and would cause the most damaging impact.

According to Weiner, "Research shows that the vast majority of crises arise when companies fail to identify a potentially contentious issue at an earlier, more benign, stage, and to develop a plan of action to manage the issue before the issue manages them."[14] An issues management program, for example, can assist an organization in identifying emerging issues early. Organizations should track media articles, industry reports, and legislative actions on these potential issues and conduct a vulnerability audit to identify internal weaknesses.[15] Some researchers even reference organizations that have proactive cultures of "looking for problems" in their respective environments.[16]

Gaining top management support for the integration of crisis management into corporate planning is also a key pre-crisis step.[17] Making crisis planning a priority and embedding the crisis management process into organizational policies and processes must be supported and championed from the top. Dodd, in addressing crisis planning in higher education, notes that crisis preparedness must be owned by someone with direct responsibility and accountability; the resources of time and money must be committed to maintain crisis preparedness.[18]

Other pre-crisis activities should include the following:

- Create and maintain a formal (written) crisis management plan to serve as a framework for the organization's response in a crisis and a trained crisis team to lead the response effort.[19] Even when companies have crisis plans and crisis teams identified, they tend to fall short on crisis planning. In one study, the most frequent crisis team training activity involved review of the crisis management plan. Training lagged far behind other planning activities and was used by fewer than half of the study's responding companies.[20]

- Develop and maintain an ongoing media relations program. Seeger advocates engaging the traditional mass media "as a strategic resource to aid in managing the crisis."[21] Crisis spokespersons should be identified and trained in this pre-crisis environment. Organizations may wish to consider using diverse spokespersons to enhance credibility with diverse stakeholder audiences and to reflect differing types of expertise that may be called on in an actual crisis.[22] Commit to being the first and best source of information;[23] remember that silence is often perceived as guilt or arrogance and that an information vacuum is likely to be filled by others, often your critics.

- Expand your organization's online presence by emphasizing content and interactivity with stakeholders.[24] Telsa Motors used the CEO's blog to explain employee layoffs; the organization found the blog "helped frame the story for the media, minimizing the chance for inaccurate articles."[25]

- Develop a pre-crisis network of strategic partnerships that can provide expertise and support in a crisis and assist with the dissemination of consistent messages.[26] These partners may include subject area experts, grassroots organizations, or others that have relationships with stakeholders at various levels.

- Take proactive steps to develop a regular and systematic two-way process of communication with key stakeholders in a pre-crisis environment to enhance relationships between the organization and its stakeholders. "It is nearly impossible to build a relationship and credibility with stakeholders in the middle of a crisis."[27] Establishing good relationships and good-will before a crisis can be important to successful management of a crisis.[28] Key messages should reinforce (1) competency, accessibility, openness, transparency, and honesty;[29] (2) a willingness to listen and engage stakeholders with a goal of mutually beneficial outcomes;[30] and (3) compassion, concern, and empathy.[31] Finally, consider messages of self-efficacy when appropriate. These messages may instruct people on what they can do to protect themselves, help others, or take actions that may be meaningful in more abstract or social contexts.[32]

Responding to the Crisis

Activities that should be taken in a crisis environment, where the crisis is unfolding, include the following:

- Take action quickly after the crisis event.[33] With traditional media, organizations were expected to have a window of 45 minutes to 12 hours to communicate. That window is much smaller today because of the new media. Cell phones, digital cameras, and personal digital devices can be used to capture a breaking crisis and post video or photos online as the crisis happens. Cell phone images after the London bombings or from the U.S. Airways Flight 1549 landing on the Hudson River in New York were captured by citizens, posted online, and then used in traditional media outlets.[34] This adds pressure on organizations to be prepared to respond almost immediately in a crisis.
- Implement the crisis plan, and engage the crisis team. Recognize that a crisis exhibits the characteristics of time pressure, control issues, threat level concerns that vary in magnitude, and constraints regarding response options.[35] Having a well-constructed crisis management plan that includes training and simulations will help your organization manage these crisis characteristics.
- Be prepared to rely on a mix of media to communicate with internal (primarily employees) and external audiences. Face-to-face meetings may be appropriate in some situations, while in others, reliance on web page updates, RSS feeds, e-mail,

Twitter, and interactive web features may be more beneficial. Take note of where your stakeholders go for information; for example, millennials spend more time with e-mail, texting, and on social media networks than on the telephone, watching television, or reading magazines, according to one study.[36] Identify the key messages that should be communicated to your key stakeholders.[37] These key messages should include statements of concern for those injured or killed and what your organization is doing to manage the crisis.[38] Don't assume your stakeholders know what you are doing—always tell them and keep reminding them what your plans are to prevent a similar crisis in the future.

Post-Crisis Activities

The primary actions to take as a crisis is resolved are to continue the communication efforts with internal and external stakeholders (including media), evaluate the effectiveness of the crisis response, update the crisis management plan and perhaps the crisis team based on the evaluation, and incorporate what the organization has learned into organizational processes and policies. Your organization will want to return to business-as-usual, to the pre-crisis environment, as soon as possible.[39]

Leadership Challenges

Caponigro stated the following:

> Effective crisis management is a process, not an event. It is an ongoing, systematic, and disciplined process that a business should follow to help identify vulnerabilities, prevent crises from occurring, plan for those most likely to occur, communicate effectively during and after a crisis, monitor and evaluate the situation, and make adjustments as necessary.[40] The problem actually begins when they [executives] think of *crises* only as the high-profile, spectacular ones that cause catastrophic results, and they forget about the ones that—like termites—weaken and gnaw away at the foundation that underlies the company's success. When the damage

is finally identified and confirmed as something to be taken seriously, it's often much too late to fix the problem without lengthy, costly repairs to the cornerstone of the foundation—its credibility, reputation, loyalty, and trust.[41]

Today's crisis-laden environment creates challenges for organizations and their leaders. Quirke recommended that leaders get out and about, seeking visibility among employees. "Contact equals familiarity, familiarity builds trust."[42] Messages should be clear and consistent, engaging to connect with people emotionally, and focused on what they need to communicate and how the business plans to move forward. Champy said, "Real leadership requires relationships and personal engagement. Nothing I see in technology has yet to replace these qualities. I believe that technology will enable new business models, but not 'new leadership'."[43] Threats on the road ahead vary, depending on the researcher, politician, consultant, or person on the street. Potential catastrophes include explosion of a nuclear weapon in a major city; natural disasters such as hurricanes, floods, earthquakes, or tsunamis; health threats such as viruses and influenza pandemics; financial crises; technology attacks in cyberspace; unrest that transcends political and geographic boundaries; terrorism; workplace violence; infrastructural and organizational decline; sabotage; and industrial and environmental disasters.[44] Buckle suggests the following:

> [P]erhaps we need to be more imaginative and more resourceful in looking at the hazards we face . . . This may well require us to develop a much longer temporal perspective for risk management—looking at generations rather than a few years into the future; looking more broadly at regional and global consequences rather than national consequences; and examining ways in which we can share knowledge—vertically from governments with communities; across different disciplines; and from formal disciplines to traditional knowledge.[45]

The test for new leadership may be the degree to which managers can step forward to identify and plan for new and emerging crises that may not have been considered in the previous century. We are indeed a global society, with deep and numerous connections. A localized crisis in a rural community in one corner of the world can become the next breaking story, generating headlines around the globe and affecting us in ways we are still learning to understand. Some crisis incidents will "cause disruption and enormous pain," while others will have legal and ethical implications, causing a different kind of trauma.[46] Some will have limited effects on specific locations, while other crisis incidents will cause destruction and upheaval for months or years to come. Whether the next crisis affects our oceans, our economy, or the well-being of our children's children, we need businesses with leaders who can adapt to the challenges ahead. Only some crises create a sense of urgency; threats that don't appear to pose immediate problems don't tend to induce a sense of crisis.[47] However, the warning signs are clearly present. Leaders can prepare for crises, but they must be willing to learn from their own experiences and the crisis experiences of others. Boin et al. maintained that developing lessons learned is one of the most underdeveloped aspects of crisis management.[48]

As consultant Barton noted, there are no safety gear for organizations. The seat belts that prevent severe injuries or death for individuals offer no comfort for organizations. Businesses and their leaders must rely on crisis management plans to prepare for the hazards that lie ahead. Preparation and planning—and learning from our own experiences—will help equip organizations to respond to future threats. We will look to leaders who can use creativity and the resources at hand to manage new and emerging threats in the reality ahead.

Common Errors Found in Written Documents

Completeness

Completeness means including only the necessary details and excluding the unnecessary. Answer the following questions: Who? What? Why? How? Where? When?

1. Too much, too little, misplaced, or omitted information or words.

You included either too much information, too little information, or information altering the meaning of the message. Some examples of altered meanings include generalizations, misleading statements, and contradictions.

2. Incorrect writing strategy is employed.

Given the anticipated audience's reaction to your message, you did not use the correct writing strategy. Remember you have three primary writing strategies—direct, indirect persuasive, and indirect bad news.

Clearness

Clearness involves using familiar words, avoiding technical jargon, and checking for readability.

3. Simpler, shorter, more familiar words.

Much of the time, big words distance you from your audience and increase the risk of miscommunication. Therefore, use simpler, more familiar words.

4. Technical jargon, cliché, and business slang.

Use technical jargon sparingly and eliminate business slang. Jargon creates a sense of unity among the in-group, but distances people in other units. Some business slang (as per your request, enclosed please find, please do not hesitate) was common years ago, but no longer. Only business writers used these expressions. Writers had the impression they ought to use a specialized terminology. Today writers call these terms *dead wood* because they are no longer living words. A cliché is an overused expression. If you use a cliche, you may give the impression that you have not thought much about your writing. This link will give you the Encyclopedia of Business Cliches: http://www.squidoo.com/businesscliches.

5. Awkward sentence structure, awkward organization, or difficult readability.

The sentence seems difficult to read and requires rereading. Remember, long words and long sentences make the reading difficult.

Concreteness

Skillful business writers avoid words that are vague in meaning, create disagreeable mental pictures, or express general ideas.

6. Word choice.

Avoid using abstract words. Words like *very, good, a lot, nice, important, bad, thing,* and *fine* are a few examples of vague words to avoid. Use specific words to paint pictures in the mind.

7. Bias-free language.

Avoid words and phrases that unfairly refer to people in ways related to gender, race, ethnicity, age, or disability.

To avoid gender bias use generic pronouns that refer to groups of persons. When you use plural pronouns such as *they* or *their,* you do not indicate the sex of the group members. Alternatives you can use include

    a. eliminating the pronoun;
    b. changing from singular to plural;
    c. using words that do not indicate gender (you, individual, person, one);
    d. using job titles instead of the pronoun;
    e. changing the pronoun to an article;
    f. changing to passive voice;
    g. adding names to eliminate generic usage;
    h. repeating the noun instead of using the pronoun.

To avoid racial and ethnic bias, do not identify people by race or ethnic origin unless the situation requires you to do so.

To avoid age bias, do not identify individuals by age unless the age is relevant to the situation.

To avoid disability bias, no label should be used within business writing unless the conditions directly relate to the subject.

Correctness

Correct writing involves using proper format, spelling, grammar, and punctuation. It also involves writing actively and allowing the doer to do the action.

8. Ending in a preposition (in, on, of, for, into).

Prepositions indicate relationships. The end of a sentence (like the beginning) emphasizes, and a preposition may not be worth emphasizing. When readers see a preposition, they expect something to follow it. At the end of a sentence, nothing follows. In job application letters, reports, and important presentations, avoid ending sentences with prepositions.

9. Misspelled word or lack of proofreading.

Always remember to proofread. Read your work aloud to help avoid costly mistakes. The *i* before *e* except after *c* rule applies to 1,000 words in the English language. Doubling the final consonant rule governs 3,000 words. *Offered* does not double the *r* because the accent falls on the first syllable; do not double the last consonant before adding the ending. *Referred,* with the accent on the second syllable, does double the final *r.*

10. Subject and verb agreement.

Subject-verb agreement errors often occur when other words come between the subject and the verb. Edit your drafts by finding the subject and the verb of each sentence. Subjects and verbs must both be singular or plural. Compound subjects require plural verbs. Example: *The president, as well as his staff, was able to attend;* or *The president and his staff were able to attend.*

Don't be confused by words that come between the subject and its verb. For example, *The price of the computers keeps some businesses from having access to the Internet.*

Indefinite pronouns such as *anybody, everybody, everyone, everything, somebody, each,* and *no one* use singular verbs.

11. Faulty parallelism.

Parallel construction requires using the same parts of speech for items in a series. Compare like nouns and avoid shifts in tense.

12. Dangling modifiers.

Modifiers give more information about the subject, verb, or object in a clause. Your modifiers dangle when the words they modify are not in the sentence. Whenever you use a verb or adjective ending in *ing,* check to see which word in the main clause it modifies. Modifiers used as introductory phrases must modify the grammatical subject of your sentence. Use adjectives to modify nouns and pronouns. Use adverbs to modify verbs, adjectives, and other adverbs. Examples: *The flowers look beautiful;*

not *The flowers look beautifully. She filed the reports quickly;* not *She filed the reports quick.*

13. Incomplete thoughts.

You must have a subject and a verb for a sentence to be complete. To fix the problem, add whatever parts of the sentence you need.

A sentence fragment occurs when a piece of a sentence, such as a phrase or dependent clause, is erroneously punctuated as if it were a complete sentence. When you discover a fragment in your writing, either (1) attach the fragment to an independent clause or (2) rewrite the fragment to form a sentence by itself. Even a statement with a subject and a predicate can be a fragment if it follows a subordinate conjunction such as *if, when,* or *because.*

14. Paragraphing and paragraph coherence.

A typical paragraph has these elements: the topic sentence, details, and words binding paragraphs together. The topic sentence contains the central idea, details support the main idea, and binding words provide coherence. Coherence ties the thoughts together smoothly. Transitional expressions and repetition aid coherence. Your paragraphs should have organization and not seem like scattered ideas.

Paragraphs should usually have at least two sentences. You may have just one sentence in a closing paragraph. Generally, business documents have more than just one paragraph. Using only one paragraph makes the document look unbalanced.

15. Effective sentences.

A well-written sentence reflects clear thinking. If your sentence appears clumsy, you have not thought through your ideas. Consider not only what you want to say, but how you can best say it. A well-written sentence has unity, coherence, and emphasis. Unity and coherence make it logical and clear; emphasis makes it forceful.

Always edit sentences for tightness. Even a 17-word sentence can be wordy. When you use a long sentence, keep the subject and verb close together.

16. Pronoun-antecedent agreement.

The pronoun must agree with the antecedent—the noun, noun phrase, or other pronoun to which the pronoun refers. Pronouns must correspond to their antecedents in number (singular or plural). Errors in noun-pronoun agreement occur when the pronoun reflects a different number or person from the word to which it refers.

When antecedents are joined by *or* or *nor,* the pronoun must agree with the antecedent closest to it if one is singular and the other is plural.

17. Numbers.

- Use the same form (figures, words, or combined figures and words) within each set of numbers. Sets of numbers relate to one another.
- Write the numbers one to nine in words; express larger numbers in figures.
- If the month follows the day or if the writer does not state the month, use ordinal numbers (1st, 2nd, 3rd, etc.) or ordinal words (first, second, third, etc.).
- If a sentence begins with a figure, spell out the number or reword the sentence.
- Write approximate amounts in words.
- Write amounts of money and percentages as figures.
- Use figures with nouns.
- Use figures with distances of more than one mile.
- Use figures to express numbers in a series.
- Write house numbers and building numbers in figures, except for the number one.
- Use figures for quantities and measurements.

18. *a.m., p.m., and o'clock.*

- Times of day should be written as *a.m.* or *p.m.* in lowercase letters.
- Use *o'clock* with spelled-out numbers (it adds formality) and *a.m.* or *p.m.* with numerals.

19. *Spacing.*

Follow the spacing guidelines given in your text. Remember to double-space between paragraphs.

20. *Pronouns cannot be interchanged.*

Person	Singular	Plural
First [person(s) speaking]	I, my, mine, me	we, our, ours, us
Second [person(s) spoken to]	you, your, yours	you, your, yours
Third [person(s) spoken about]	he, his, him, she, her; hers, it, its	they, their, theirs, them

The case of a pronoun refers to the form it takes in a particular use in a sentence (subject, direct object, etc.). English has three cases: nominative, possessive, and objective. Pronouns with different nominative and objective forms cause the most confusion: I/me, he/him, she/her, we/us, they/them, who/whom.

	Nominative case (Subject forms)	Possessive case (Possessive forms)	Objective case (Object forms)
Singular	I, he, she, it	my, mine, his, her	me, him, her, it, hers, its
Plural	we, they	our, ours, their, theirs	us, them
Singular and plural	you, who	your, yours, whose	you, whom

21. *Who, whom, which, and that (relative pronouns).*

Use *who*, not *which*, when referring to people. *Who* replaces the noun or *he, she,* or *they* as the subject of a sentence. *Whom* takes the place of a noun or *him, her,* or *them* as the object in a sentence. *Which* refers to things. *That* can refer to people or things. *Who* may introduce either a restrictive or nonrestrictive clause. *That* introduces restrictive clauses.

22. Capitalization.

- The first word of each item in a formal outline and in a sentence should be capitalized.
- The first and last words in the salutation of a letter and the first word in the complimentary close should be capitalized.
- Do not capitalize points of the compass, seasons, words denoting a family relationship, names of academic disciplines, and common nouns.
- All personal names should be capitalized.
- Days of the week, months of the year, personal titles, abbreviations, acronyms, languages, and nationalities should all be capitalized.

23. Commas.

Use a comma in the following situations:
- *Parenthetical*—word or phrase not necessary to complete a sentence but gives emphasis.
  Example: *Furthermore, the report did not meet the guidelines.*
- *Apposition*—word, phrase, or clause that explains other terms.
  Example: *Our representative, Mr. Black, attended the meeting.*
- *Introductory Subordinate Clause*—Main clause follows introductory subordinate clause, which may begin with the words *as, if, when, while, after, although,* or *because.*
  Example: *As you know, the meeting started at noon.*
- *Long Introductory Phrases*—Use a comma after a long introductory phrase, but not after a short one.
  Example: *During the last two months of every year, executives search for ways to decrease company taxes.*
- *Introductory Verb Phrase*
  Example: *After checking the numbers for accuracy, the manager handed the report to her superior.*
- *Conjunctions*—Use a comma to separate two independent clauses joined by one of the following conjunctions: *and, but, or, for, nor.*

>   **Example:** *We have no record of a school by that name in Wood-stock, nor do we have a record of anyone by the name of Heart in our files.*

- *Series*—When the last member of a series of three or more items comes before *and* or *or,* place a comma before the connective as well as between the other items.

    Example: *The shipment included a large selection of combs, brushes, and hair supplies.*

- *Omission of and between consecutive adjectives*—When two or more adjectives modify the same noun, separate them by a comma.

    Example: *Our well-trained, efficient staff will do a top-notch job for you.*

- *Use a comma if the sentence would be confusing without it.*

    Example: *The day before, I borrowed George's calculator; not The day before I borrowed George's calculator.*

- Do not use a comma to separate subject and verb or verb and complement. Also, do not use a comma to join two independent clauses in place of a coordinate conjunction (*and, but, or, nor, for, yet, so*). If you use a comma this way, you create a comma splice.

- Always use *which* (instead of *that*) to introduce nonessential clauses: *The bay, which was full of small sailing craft, was rough.* A comma should precede *which.*

- In a month-day-year date, place the year within commas. Do the same with the state or country in an address.

24. Apostrophe.

Use an apostrophe to form the possessive case of nouns. Almost all singular nouns require an apostrophe, then *s*. Plurals ending in *s* require only the apostrophe. Apostrophe with *s* (*'s*) should never be used to form plurals except to avoid confusion (*CPAs,* not *CPA's;* but *dot your i's*).

Use an apostrophe to form contractions (when one or more letters have been intentionally omitted).

Do not use an apostrophe to form the plurals of nouns, including acronyms (example: *PCs*).

Do not use an apostrophe to form the possessive of personal pronouns (*his, hers, ours*).

25. Percent.

Express percentages in figures and spell out the word *percent* within the text of a document. The percent sign may be used within graphs and charts.

26. Comma splices and fused sentences.

A comma splice occurs when you erroneously join independent clauses with a comma rather than a conjunction or semicolon.

A fused sentence occurs when you join independent clauses with no conjunction punctuation at all.

To avoid such errors (both also called run-ons or run-togethers) be sure you can recognize an independent clause. Use the following four ways to correct run-ons. Choose the solution best fitting your purpose and your paragraph.

  a. Separate the clauses into two sentences.
  b. Join the clauses with a coordinating conjunction.
  c. Join the clauses with a semicolon.
  d. Join the clauses by making one of them a dependent (subordinate) clause. Join them with a subordinate conjunction such as *because, if, when, since, after, although,* or *unless* or with relative pronouns such as *who(m), which,* or *that.* Subordinating can be the best way to eliminate run-ons, since the kinds of words listed here show the precise relation between ideas.

27. Its versus it's.

The possessive form of *its* does not include an apostrophe. The apostrophe indicates the contraction of *it is.*

28. Words with similar meanings.

Writers often misuse these words. Although the differences may be subtle, you should use these words correctly to make sure your message conveys the meaning you intend.

between	used with only two elements
among	used with three or more objects or persons
anxious	fearful, worried
eager	enthusiastic
disinterested	impartial, detached
uninterested	indifferent, not interested
fewer	refers to items individually counted
less	refers to bulk or volume
good	desired or right qualities
well	satisfactory manner
than	used in making comparisons
then	at that time (when)
conscience	inner sense of right and wrong
conscious	knowing, aware
human	people
humane	having the best qualities of human beings
incidence	degree of occurrence
incidents	events

29. Words sounding alike.

Writers use many words incorrectly because they sound alike. The incorrect use of the following words may make a negative impression on your reader. The most commonly confused pairs of words are listed and defined here.

affect	(v) to influence
effect	(n) result, (v) to bring about
accept	(v) to receive
except	(v) to exclude or leave out, (prep) other than
adapt	(v) to adjust or alter, to make suitable
adept	(adj) skilled
adopt	(v) to take as one's own
advice	(n) suggestions, recommendations
advise	(v) to give advice or make suggestions
all ready	(adj) prepared
already	(adj) previously
capital	(n) money
capitol	(n) government building
compliment	(v) to praise or flatter
complement	(n) that which completes or makes whole
council	(n) a group
counsel	(n, v) advice
ensure	(v) to make certain
insure	(v) to protect against financial loss
everyday	(adj) commonplace, usual
every day	(adj, n) two separate words
farther	(adj) at a greater distance (measurable)
further	(adj) additional, extending beyond, (adv) additional, a greater extent, (v) to promote or advance
later	(adj) after the proper time
latter	(adj) the second of two things mentioned
loose	(adj) not fastened
lose	(v) to fail to keep or to misplace
moral	(n, adj) generally accepted principle of right or wrong
morale	(n) mental and emotional condition
overdo	(v) to exaggerate
overdue	(adj) delayed beyond an appointed time
passed	(v) to go by
past	(n) time gone by or time ended
personal	(adj) of a particular person
personnel	(n) persons employed
perspective	(n) point of view

prospective	(adj) likely
principal	(adj) main, most important, (n) a sum of money, administrator
principle	(n) rule, law
rational	(adj) in possession of one's reason
rationale	(n) explanation of reasons
respectively	(adv) in order named
respectfully	(adv) with due regard
sight	(v) to see or to take aim, (n) a view
site	(n) a location
stationery	(n) letterhead or writing materials
stationary	(n) permanent, not movable
their	(pron) possessive of they, in the predicate
there	(adv) in, at, or to that place
too	(adv) excess and also
to	(prep, adv) toward
two	(n, adj) number
your	(pron) possessive pronoun
you're	(contraction) contraction for you are

30. Gerunds (verb + ing), used as noun.

Whenever a noun or a pronoun comes before a gerund, the possessve form should be used.

Example: *I am concerned about your taking the job.* (Common error: *I am concerned about you taking the job.*)

Example: *Did you find any record of the customers' being notified?* (Common error: *Did you find any record of the customer being notified?*)

31. Hyphens.

A compound adjective should be hyphenated when used immediately before a noun.

Hyphenate fractions and the numbers twenty-one through ninety-nine.

32. Format errors.

A problem occurred with the standard format for letters, memos, or reports. See your professor if uncertain where the problem occurred.

33. Semicolons and colons.

- A semicolon may be used to replace a coordinating conjunction between independent clauses. (Coordinating conjunctions are *and, but, for, or, nor,* and *so.* Independent clauses have a subject and verb and can stand alone as sentences.)
  Example: *The sun rises earlier and the days are warmer.*
  The sun rises earlier; the days are warmer.
- Use a semicolon between independent clauses joined by a conjunctive adverb (*therefore, however, nevertheless, thus, moreover, also, besides, consequently, meanwhile, otherwise, then, also, furthermore, likewise, in fact, still*):
  Example: *On weekdays we close at eleven; however, on weekends we stay open until one.*
- Use a semicolon between independent clauses joined by a coordinate conjunction when commas occur within the clauses.
  Example: *Today, people can buy what they need from department stores, supermarkets, and discount stores; but in colonial days, when such conveniences did not exist, people depended on general stores and peddlers.*
- Use a semicolon between items in a series when commas occur within the items.
  Example: *At the high school alumni dinner, I sat with the school's best-known graduate, Harper White; the editor of the school paper; two stars of the school play, a fellow and a girl who later married each other; and Tad Trump, the class clown.*
- Use a colon to separate independent clauses when the second clause explains or amplifies the first.
  Example: *Carl seemed proud of his wife: She had been promoted to manager.*
- Use a colon before a list, a long quotation, or an explanation.
  Example: *You may be required to bring many items: staples, pencils, pens, and disks.*

34. Verb tense.

- The first principal part of the verb (the present tense) expresses present time, makes true statements, and uses *shall* or *will* to express future time.

  Example: *We fill all orders promptly.* (present time)

  Water seeks its own level. (true statement at all times)

  We will order new stock next week. (future time)

- The second principal part of the verb (the past tense) expresses past time. (No auxiliary verb is used with this form.)

  Example: *We filled the order yesterday.*

- The third principal part of the verb (the past participle) can be used to

  a. form the present perfect tense. This tense indicates action starting in the past that has recently been completed or will continue up to the present time. It has the verb *have* or *has* plus the past participle.

  Example: *We have filled the order.*

  b. form the past perfect tense. This tense shows action that will be completed before a certain time in the future. It has the verb *shall have* or *will have* plus the past participle.

  Example: *We will have filled the orders by that time.*

- The fourth principal part of the verb (the present participle) is used to

  a. form the present progressive tense. This tense indicates action still in progress. It takes the verb *am, is,* or *are* plus the present participle.

    Example: *We are filling all orders as fast as we can.*

  b. form the past progressive tense. This tense indicates action in progress sometime in the past. It consists of the verb *was* or *were* plus the present participle.

    Example: *We were waiting for new stock at the time your order came to the store.*

  c. form the future progressive tense. This tense indicates action that will be in progress in the future. It consists of the verb *shall be* or *will be* plus the present participle.

  Example: *We will be working overtime for the next two weeks.*

d. form the present perfect progressive, the past perfect progressive, and the future perfect progressive tenses. These tenses appear like the simple perfect tenses, except the progressive element suggests continuous action. These tenses consist of the verbs *has been, have been, had been, shall have been,* and *will have been* plus the present participle.

Example: *We have been filling these orders with Model 212A instead of 212.* (present perfect progressive) *We had been filling these orders with Model 212A until we saw your directive.* (past perfect progressive) *By next Friday, we will have been working overtime for two straight weeks.* (future perfect progressive)

35. Terminal punctuation: periods, question marks, and exclamation points.

Use a period at the end of a sentence. Many abbreviations have periods following each letter or word. Do not space after periods within an abbreviation. Space after the final period, as though the abbreviation were a word and the period were the final letter in that word.

Use a question mark to end a sentence that is a direct question.

Use an exclamation point to indicate strong emotion or urgency at the end of your sentence.

36. Delayers and false starts.

Some examples include *there is, there are, it is, this is,* or *this will.* You want your writing to be active. Delayers encourage passive writing that creates longer sentences.

37. Helping verbs and passive writing.

Some examples include *is, are, can, will be, had, has, was,* and *were.* Try to replace helping verbs with an action verb. An action verb does the action the verb describes. To change a passive verb to an active verb, you must make the agent (that is, the person taking action) the new subject. If you do not specify an agent, you must supply one to make the sentence active.

- **Active:** *The plant manager approved the request.*
- **Passive:** *The request was approved by the plant manager.*

38. Italics.

- Words to be defined in a sentence are usually set in italics.
- Italicize foreign expressions.
- Italicize words when you are calling attention to them as words.
- Don't underline; use italics.
- Use italics for titles of books, newspapers, magazines, and periodicals.

39. Quotation marks.

Use quotation marks to enclose an exact repetition of someone else's spoken or written words. Use quotation marks to set off a word used in a special sense.

40. Abbreviations.

Abbreviations such as *etc.* are generally not used in business writing. When you cannot list all items, use and *so on* or *and the like* rather than *etc.* Or, you can choose to begin the list with *for example.*

Conciseness

A concise writer avoids wordy expressions, trite phrases, and useless repetition.

41. Wordiness.

Avoid filler words that add nothing to the meaning of the sentence. Use gerunds (the *ing* form of verbs) and infinitives to make sentences shorter and smoother. Combine sentences to eliminate unnecessary words. Reword sentences to cut the number of words. When you eliminate unnecessary words, you save time for your reader.

If you included information the reader did not need to know, omit the unnecessary information.

42. Redundancy or inflated wording.

Redundancy means needless repetition. Remember, careful planning can help eliminate rambling and repeating ideas.

You inflate words when you use elaborate modifiers and unnecessary Latinate diction (words with endings such as *-tion, -ity, -ize,* or *-ify*). Avoid useless suffixes (as in *zealousness* for *zeal*); unfamiliar foreign phrases; and needless, unexplained jargon.

Express your ideas in clear, direct language. Try to increase your vocabulary, but use words with accuracy and intent to convey meaning, not merely to impress your reader. Otherwise, your writing may appear affected, and you may even obscure your ideas.

Courtesy

When you write with courtesy, you express an attitude of friendliness and goodwill. Focus on the positive, not the negative. Use the "you-attitude," and avoid negative words such as *delay, can't, impossible, inconvenience,* or *trouble.*

43. Expressing the "you-attitude."

Focus on what the receiver receives or can do. Using second-person pronouns (*you*) rather than third-person (*he, she, one, they*) gives your writing more impact. You can refer to a single person or to every member of your organization.

44. Starting some sentences with "I" and others with "we."

Using *I* too often can make your writing sound self-centered. Using it unnecessarily makes your ideas seem tentative. If you write, "I think we should adopt this plan," you imply that it's really only your idea. When you write, "We should adopt this plan," you sound more confident.

Your writing should be consistent from sentence to sentence or paragraph to paragraph. One paragraph should not be all *I* sentences and the next paragraph all *we* sentences. Ask yourself this question: "Am I writing for myself or the company?" When you answer that question, you will know when to use *I* or *we*.

However, when you write a document such as a self-improvement memo or a review of your performance, you use first-person "I" instead of the more formal third person or awkward phrases such as "this writer" or "the undersigned."

45. Positive rather than negative words and positive tone.

Eliminate negative words and words with negative connotations. Focus on what the reader can do instead of what you won't or can't let the reader do.

Tone refers to your attitude toward the subject and your reader. Regardless of the situation or the subject, you strive to paint a positive picture with your writing even if the information is negative. You want your writing to be perceived by your reader as courteous and professional so that you will project strength and confidence.

Character

Character combines all the principles of effective business writing. You give your document character when you avoid all stereotyped words and worn-out clichés. You gain character when your document shines with courtesy and clear writing.

Notes

Chapter 1

1. Martin (2009).
2. Allen (2011).
3. Allen (2011).
4. Gandossy (2010).
5. Gallo (2009).
6. Middleton (2011).
7. Hopkins (2010).
8. ScienceDaily (2008).
9. Brown (2011).
10. Winston Churchill quotes (n.d.).
11. Editor (2010).
12. Goby (2009).
13. Communication barrier—prejudging and filtering. (n.d.)
14. Covey (1989).
15. Wilson (n.d.).
16. Brock (2004).
17. Dalton (2000, September).
18. Weinstein (2006).
19. Catton (2010).
20. Clark (2010).
21. Lips (2009).
22. Goman (2010).
23. LaMarr (2010).
24. Lowen (2005)."
25. Hammill (2005).
26. Lang (2008).
27. Soroptimist International of the Americas (2010).
28. Chick-fil-A (n.d.).
29. Hartman and DesJardins (2008).
30. Workforce (2008).
31. 2010's 100 most influential people in business ethics (2011).
32. Welch (2008b).
33. Steiner (2006).
34. Welch (2008a).

35. Workforce (2003).
36. Harshman and Harshman (1999).
37. Lewis (2007).
38. Collins (2001).
39. Block (1996).
40. Collins (2001).

Chapter 2

1. Blanchard (2011).
2. Raina (2010).
3. Colquitt et al. (2011).
4. Zia et al. (2010).
5. Prabhakar et al. (2005).
6. Prabhakar et al. (2005).
7. Alsop (2004).
8. Gratton (2008).
9. Bracey (2002).
10. Asmus (2008).
11. Goldsmith (n.d).
12. Buckingham (2008).
13. Lawler (2008).
14. Krug (1998).
15. Asmus (2008).
16. Krug (1998).
17. Foster (2002).
18. Berry et al. (1996).
19. Boe (n.d.).
20. Timm and DeTienne (1980).
21. Amazing face: It can lie, tell truths, express emotion (2006).
22. Axtell (2011).
23. Ekman (2003).
24. Hay (2009).
25. Lane (2009).
26. Bremer (2009).
27. Hamilton (2011).
28. 4. Non-verbal communication (n.d.).
29. Marwijk (2009).
30. What your body language says about your business savvy (2011).
31. Wolfe (2011).
32. Laura (2008).
33. Baskin and Arnoftt (1980).

34. What is paralanguage? (n.d.).
35. Boe (2009).
36. Anderson (2010).
37. Decker (2006).
38. Essi Systems, Inc. (n.d.).
39. Barrett (2006).
40. Segal and Smith (2010).
41. Segal and Smith (2010).
42. Gary (2002).
43. Mejak (2009).
44. Iftikhar (2010).
45. Vollmer (2004).
46. Clifford (2009).
47. Shwom and Gueldenzoph (2012).
48. Ross (2009).
49. Ross (2009).
50. Ross (2009).
51. Paggi (2010).
52. Sandberg (2007).
53. Lencioni (2002).
54. Paggi (2010).
55. Paggi (2010)
56. Edelson (2008).
57. Thomas and Kilmann (n.d.).
58. Collins (2001).
59. Goldsmith and Morgan (2004).
60. Miller (2001).
61. Braddick (2003).
62. Wright and Tao (2001).
63. Ryan (2009).
64. Ryan (2009).
65. Scott (2004).

Chapter 3

1. Moore (n.d.).
2. Elbin (2010).
3. 3 communication mistakes leaders make (and how to avoid them) (2011).
4. Kouzes and Posner (2003).
5. Zia et al. (2010).
6. Beslin and Reddin (2004).
7. Bracey (2002).

8. Katenzenbach and Smith (1993).
9. Musselwhite (2007).
10. Timm and DeTienne (1986).
11. Hamilton (2011).
12. Deems (1994).
13. Deems (1994).
14. Scannell (1992).
15. Thomas (2010).
16. Bovee and Thill (2012b).

Chapter 4

1. Kwablahs (2009).
2. Web writing that works (n.d.).
3. College Board, The National Commission on Writing for America's Families, Schools and Colleges (2004).
4. Bowers (2010).
5. Bowers (2010).
6. *Module 4 planning, writing, and revising* (n.d.).
7. Sabah (2010).
8. Walinskas (2011).
9. Strunk and White (1999).
10. Gallo (2009).
11. Roberts (1992).
12. Why should I avoid capital letters in email addresses and other online forms? (n.d.).
13. Why should I avoid capital letters in email addresses and other online forms? (n.d.).
14. Lanham (2006).
15. eHow.com (n.d.).
16. Markowitz (2010).
17. Bovee and Thill (2010).
18. Krakoff and Wakeman (2009).
19. Porter (n.d.).
20. Keller (2009).
21. Advantages of instant messaging in the enterprise (n.d.).
22. Keller (2011).
23. Gaertner-Johnston (2010).
24. Scocco (2009).
25. Paige (2011).
26. Kievman (2010).
27. Wiegert (2010).

Chapter 5

1. Presentation tips and tricks (n.d.).
2. Podmoroff (n.d.).
3. Martindale (n.d.).
4. Hamilton (2010).
5. Decker (1992).
6. Asher and Chamber (1997).
7. The seven sins of visual presentations (n.d.).
8. Bovee and Thill (2012a).
9. Bovee and Thill (2010).
10. Harris (2008).
11. Feierman (n.d.).
12. Paradi (2003).
13. Swallow (2010).
14. McKenzie (2008).
15. Schultz (2010).
16. Homey (1970).
17. Decker (1992).
18. Tomich (2009).
19. Decker (2008).
20. Peterson (2011).
21. Snopes.com (2007).
22. A guide to public speaking (n.d.).
23. Asher and Chamber (1997).
24. Rossin (2010).
25. Strobist.com (2007).
26. Byrd (2008).
27. Duarte (2011).
28. Schrage (2010).

Appendix A

1. Coombs (2007).
2. Devitt and Borodzicz (2008).
3. Boin et al. (2005).
4. Buckle (2003).
5. Quirke (2010).
6. Longstaff and Yang (2008).
7. American Management Association (2005).
8. *Study: Most firms unprepared for disaster (2005). Duhé, S. F. (2005).*
9. Rudolph (1986); Burnett (1998).

10. Coombs (2007); Fearn-Banks (2007); Coombs and Holladay (1996); Lerbinger (1997); Silva and McGann (1995); Murphy (1996).

11. Coombs (2007).

12. Gainey (2007), p. 414.

13. Coombs (2007).

14. Weiner (2006), p. 1.

15. Weiner (2006); Heath (1998).

16. Boin (2009), p. 372.

17. Pauchant and Mitroff (1992); Dodd (2006).

18. Dodd (2006), p. 7.

19. Lee et al. (2007).

20. Lee et al. (2007).

21. Seeger (2006), p. 240.

22. Duhe' (2005).

23. Heath (2006).

24. Kent et al. (2003).

25. Kolek (2009).

26. Seeger (2006).

27. Stocker (1997), p. 197.

28. Seeger (2006).

29. Quirke (2010); Seeger (2006).

30. Covello (2003).

31. Seeger (2006); Covello (2003).

32. Seeger (2006); Heath (2006).

33. Lerbinger (1997); Burnett (1998).

34. Owen (2005); Noguchi (2005); Hannah (2009).

35. Burnett (1998).

36. Loechner (2009).

37. Fearn-Banks (2007).

38. Boin (2009).

39. Dodd (2006).

40. Caponigro (2000), p. 29.

41. Caponigro (2000), p. xii.

42. Quirke (2010), p. 26.

43. Champy (2010), p. 2.

44. Barton (2008); Know your enemy (2006); Boin et al. (2005);

45. Buckle (2003), p. 121.

46. Barton (2008).

47. Boin et al. (2005).

48. Boin et al. (2005).

References

2010's 100 most influential people in business ethics. (2011, January 31). *Ethisphere*. Retrieved from http://ethisphere.com/2010s-100-most-influential-people-in-business-ethics/#15

3 communication mistakes leaders make (and how to avoid them). (2011, February 7). [Web log post]. Retrieved from http://www.leadershipandinfluenceblog.com/3-common-mistakes-leaders-make-and-how-to-avoid-them/

4. Non-verbal communication. (n.d.). [Web log post]. Retrieved from http://www.zeromillion.com/business/management/non-verbal-communication.html

A guide to public speaking. (n.d.). Online Publications. Retrieved from http://www.ca.uky.edu/agc/pubs/fcs1/fcs1206/fcs1206.htm

Advantages of instant messaging in the enterprise. (2009). NETID CHATSURE. Retrieved from http://www.chatsure-enterprise.com/advantages.html

Allen, F. E. (2011, March 13). Google figures out what makes a great boss. *Forbes*. Retrieved from http://blogs.forbes.com/frederickallen/2011/03/13/google-figures-out-what-makes-a-great-boss/

Alsop, R. (2004, September 4). How to get hired. *The Wall Street Journal* Online. Retrieved from http://leeds-faculty.colorado.edu/Bhagat/How%20To%20Get%20Hired.pdf

Amazing face: It can lie, tell truths, express emotion. (2006). *Business Communication Headline News*. Retrieved from http://www.businesscommunicationblog.com/blog/2006/05/07/amazing-face-it-can-lie-tell-the-truths-express-emotion/

American Management Association. (n.d.). 2005 AMA survey: Crisis management and security issues. Retrieved from http://www.amanet.org/research/pdfs/Crisis-Management05%20.pdf (password protected)

Anderson, M. (2010). How to communicate with power and influence. *Special Report from Maggie Anderson, Words that Work, Executive Communications* Retrieved from http://www.wordsthatwork.com.

Asher, S., & Chamber, W. (1997). *Wooing and winning business*. New York, NY: Wiley.

Asmus M. (2008). Performance appraisal interviews: Preference organization in assessment sequences. *Journal of Business Communication, 45*(4), 408–429. doi:10.1177/0021943608319382

Axtell, R. (2011). Roger Axtell: Profile. Speaking.com. Retrieved from http://www.speaking.com/speakers/roger-axtell.php

Barrett, D. J. (2006). Leadership communication: A communication approach for senior-level managers. *Handbook of Business Strategy, 7*(1), 385–390. doi:10.1108/10775730610619124

Barton, L. (2008). *Crisis leadership now.* New York, NY: McGraw-Hill.

Baskin, O., & Arnoftt, C. (1980). *Interpersonal communication in organizations.* Glenview, IL: Scott Foresman.

Berry, D., Cadwell, C., & Fehrmann, J. (1996). *Coaching for results: A skills-based workshop participant workbook.* Amherst, MA: HRD Press.

Beslin, R., & Reddin, C. (2004, Nov./Dec.). How leaders communicate to build trust. *Ivey Business Journal Online, G1.* Retrieved from ProQuest: mhtml:file://E:\PVAMU\how leaders communicate.mht

Blanchard, J. (2011). Workplace communication failures—Secrets revealed. *eConferencing News.* Retrieved from http://econferencingnews.com/workplace-communication-failures-secrets-revealed/635159/

Block, P. (1996). *Stewardship: Choosing service over self interest.* San Francisco, CA: Berrett-Koehler.

Boe, J. (2009). Actions speak louder than words. *BizCommunity.com Daily Industry News.* Retrieved from http://www.bizcommunity.com/Article/196/20/31448.html

Boe, J. (n.d.). People skills quiz. John Boe International. Retrieved from http://www.johnboe.com/people_skills_quiz.html

Boin, A. (2009). Introduction to the special issue. The new world of crises and crisis management: Implications for policymaking and research. *Review of Policy Research, 26*(4), 367–377.

Boin, A., 't Hart, P., Stern, E., & Sundelius, B. (2005). *The politics of crisis management: Public leadership under pressure.* Cambridge, England: Cambridge University Press.

Bovee, C., & Thill, J. (2010). *Business communication today* (10th ed.). Upper Saddle River, NJ: Prentice-Hall.

Bovee, C., & Thill, J. (2012a). *Business communication essentials* (5th ed.). Upper Saddle River, NJ: Pearson Education.

Bovee, C., & Thill, J. (2012b). *Business communication essentials: A skills-based approach to vital business English.* Upper Saddle River, NJ: Pearson Education.

Bowers, T. (2010, January 11). Tech pros: Don't forget to develop writing skills. Tech Republic. Retrieved from http://www.techrepublic.com/blog/career/tech-pros-dont-forget-to-develop-writing-skills/1645

Bracey, H. (2002). *Building trust: How to get it! How to keep it!* Taylorsville, GA: HB Artworks.

Braddick, C. (2003). The ROI (Return on Investment) of executive coaching: Useful information or a distraction? Part Two. The Coaching and Mentoring Network. Retrieved from http://coachingnetwork.org.uk/ResourceCentre/Articles/ViewArticle.asp?artID=79

Bremer, J. (2009). Personal communication.

Brinkman, R. (2011). Email, will you go with the devil or the angel? Conscious Communication. Retrieved from http://www.rickbrinkman.com/enews/

Brock, S. (2004). Personal communication.

Brown, M. (2011, February 5). Southwest Airlines social media strategy lessons for all organizations. Blogging Innovation. Retrieved from http://www.business-strategy-innovation.com/wordpress/2011/02/southwest-airlines-social-media-strategy/

Buckingham, M. (2008). Four design principles. *People & Strategy, 31*(3), 8.

Buckle, P. (2003, March). Some contemporary issues in disaster management. *International Journal of Mass Emergencies and Disasters, 12*(1), 109–122.

Burnett, J. J. (1998). A strategic approach to managing crises. *Public Relations Review, 24*(4), 475–488.

Byrd, D. (2008). 10 tips for powerful presentations. *Ezine Articles*. Retrieved from http://ezineartilces.com/?10-Tips-For-Powerful-Presentations&id=1279572

Caponigro, J. R. (2000). *The crisis counselor*. Chicago, IL: Contemporary Books.

Catton, K. (2010, December 6). Her inform: On another planet? Retrieved April 11, 2011, from Her Business, http://www.herbusinessmagazine.com/Articles/December+06.html

Champy, J. A. (2010, May 4). Does leadership change in a Web 2.0 world. *Harvard Business Review*. Retrieved May 7, 2010, from http://blogs.hbr.org/imaginingthe-future-of-leadership/2010/05/does-leadership-change-in . . . , Accessed 5/7/2010

Chick-fil-A. (n.d.). *Company fact sheet*. Retrieved from http://www.chick-fil-a.com/Company/Highlights-Fact-Sheets

Clark, N. (2010, January 23). Differences between men and women: An interview with Martha Barletta. Women's Media. Retrieved from http://www.womensmedia.com/work/207-differences-between-men-and-women-an-interview-with-martha-barletta.html

Clifford, T. (2009). The importance of being a good listener. Workscape Institute. Retrieved from http://www.workscape.com/blogs/blog1.php/the-importance-of-being-a-good-listener

College Board, The National Commission on Writing for America's Families, Schools and Colleges. (2004, September). Writing a ticket to work or a ticket out: A survey of business leaders. Retrieved from http://www.collegeboard.com/prod_downloads/writingcom/writing-ticket-to-work.pdf

Collins, J. (2001). *Good to great*. New York, NY: HarperCollins.

Colquitt, J. A., Lepine, J. A., & Wesson, M. J. (2011). *Organizational behavior.* New York, NY: McGraw-Hill/Irwin.

Coombs, W. T. (2007). *Ongoing crisis communication: Planning, managing, and responding* (2nd ed.). Thousand Oaks, CA: Sage.

Coombs, W. T., & Holladay, S. J. (1996). Communication and attributions in a crisis: An experimental study in crisis communication. *Journal of Public Relations Research, 8*(4), 279–295.

Covello, V. T. (2003). Best practices in public health risk and crisis communication. *Journal of Health Communication, 8*, 5–8.

Covey, S. R. (1989). *The 7 habits of highly effective people.* New York, NY: Fireside.

Dalton, F. (2000, September). The eight classic types of workplace behavior. *HR Magazine.* Retrieved from http://findarticles.com/p/articles/mi_m3495/is_9_45/ai_65578688/

Decker, B. (1992). *You've got to be believed to be heard.* New York, NY: St. Martin's Press.

Decker, B. (2006). *Communication skills for leaders: Delivering a clear and consistent message* (3rd ed.). Boston, MA: Thomson/Course Technology. Retrieved from http://cengagesites.com/academic/assets/sites/Axzo/1418864900pv.pdf

Decker, B. (2008, December 21). Why Caroline Kennedy needs speaking game. Decker Blog. Retrieved from http://decker.com/blog/?s=Why+Caroline+KEnnedy+needs+speaking+game

Deems, R. (1994). *Interviewing: More than a gut feeling.* West Des Moines, IA: American Media Publishing.

Devitt, K. R., & Borodzicz, E. P. (2008, December). Interwoven leadership: the missing link in multi-agency major incident response. *Journal of Contingencies and Crisis Management, 16*(4), 208–216.

Dodd, D. W. (2006). Have we learned the lessons of disaster preparedness. College planning and experimental study in crisis communication. *Journal of Public Relations Research, 8*(4), 279–295.

Duhe', S. F. (2005, Spring). The sources behind the first days of the anthrax attacks: What can practitioners learn? *Public Relations Quarterly, 50*(1), 7–12.

Duarte, N. (2011, January 3). Four presentation predictions for 2011. Duarte. Retrieved from http://blog.duarte.com/?s=Four+presentation+predictions+for+2011

Edelson, C. (2008). Are you an effective communicator. E-mail newsletter.

eHow.com. (n.d.). How to write an executive summary. Retrieved from http://www.ehow.com/how_16566_write-executive-summary.html

Ekman, P. (2003). *Emotions revealed: Recognizing faces and feelings to improve communication and emotional life.* New York, NY: Times Books.

Elbin, S. (2010). Three communication mistakes leaders make (and how to avoid them). Michael Hyatt Intentional Leadership. Retrieved from http://

michaelhyatt.com/three-common-mistakes-new-leaders-make-and-how-to
-avoid-them.html

Essi Systems, Inc. (n.d.). *Emotional intelligence professional certification program Instructor's guide*. San Francisco, CA: Essi Systems.

Fearn-Banks, K. (2007). *Crisis communications—A casebook approach* (2nd ed.). Mahwah, NJ: Lawrence Erlbaum.

Feierman, A. (n.d.). *The art of communicating effectively: On preparing for a presentation*. Retrieved from http://www.glaciers.pdx.edu/fountain/Advice _SpeakingWriting/TheArtofCommunicatingEffectively.pdf

Foster, P. (2002). Performance documentation. *Business Communication Quarterly, 65*(2), 108–114.

Gainey, B. S. (2007). Crisis communication evolves in response to new public engagement constructs in educational settings and beyond. In S. C. Duhe' (Ed.), *New media and public relations* (pp. 411–422). New York, NY: Peter Lang.

Gallo, C. (2009, May 6). Delta CEO seeks leaders with strong communication skills. Gallo Communications. Retrieved from http://gallocommunications.com/ talking-leadership/delta-ceo-seeks-leaders-with-strong-communication-skills/

Gandossy, R. P. (2010). *Ten principles for leadership communication*. AON. Retrieved from http://www.aon.com/human-capital-consulting/thought -leadership/leadership/article_leadership_communication.jsp

Gary, L. (2002). Quoting Goleman in "Becoming a Resonant Leader." *Harvard Management Update, 7*(7), 4–6.

Goby, V. P. (2009). Primacy of personal over cultural attributes demonstrating receptiveness as a key to effective cross-national interactions. *Canadian Social Science, 5*(3), 91–108.

Goldsmith, M. (n.d). The FeedForward Tool. Marshall Goldsmith FeedForward. Retrieved from http://www.marshallgoldsmithfeedforward.com/

Goldsmith, M., & Morgan, H. (2004). Leadership is a contact sport. The "follow-up factor" in management development. *Strategy and Business, 36*, 70–79.

Goman, C. K. (2010, July). 10 body language mistakes women leaders make. *Financial Post*. Retrieved from http://www.financialpost.com/body+language +mistakes+women+leaders+make/3281723/story.html

Gratton, L. (2008). Counterpoint. *People & Strategy, 31*(3), 9.

Hamilton, C. (2010). *Communicating for results: A guide for business and the professions* (8th ed.). Belmont, CA: Wadsworth.

Hamilton, C. (2011). *Communicating for results: A guide for business and the professions* (9th ed.). Boston, MA: Wadsworth Cengage Learning.

Hammill, G. (2005, Winter/Spring). Mixing and managing 4 generations of employees. *Edu Magazine.* Retrieved from http://www.fdu.edu/newspubs/magazine/05ws/generations.htm

Hannah, M. (2009, February 5). In Hudson River landing, PR pros were not first responders. Media Shift. Retrieved from http://www.pbs.org/mediashift/2009/02/in-hudson-river-landing-pr-pros-were-not-first-responders/036.html

Harris, R. (2008, October 2). PowerPoint tips and techniques. Virtual Salt. Retrieved from http://www.virtualsalt.com/powerpoint.htm

Harshman, E. F., & Harshman, C. L. (1999). Communicating with employees: Building on an ethical foundation. *Journal of Business Ethics, 19*(1), 319.

Hartman, L. P., & DesJardins, J. (2008). *Business ethics decision making for personal integrity and social responsibility* (2nd ed.). New York, NY: McGraw-Hill/Irwin.

Hay, S. (2009, April 8). Personal interview: Nonverbal communication in the workplace.

Heath, R. L. (1998). New communication technologies: An issues management point of view. *Public Relations Review, 24*(3), 273–288.

Heath, R. L. (2006, August). Best practice in crisis communication: Evolution of practice through research. *Journal of Applied Communication Research, 34*(3), 245–248.

Homey, K. (1970). *Neurosis and human growth: The struggle toward self-realization.* New York, NY: Norton.

Hopkins, T. (2010, November 2). The feel, felt, found strategy. Tom Hopkins International. Retrieved from http://www.tomhopkins.com/blog/presentation/the-feel-felt-found-strategy

Iftikhar. (2011, January 17). Lecture 08 Listening. Interculture Communication. Retrieved from http://bcwithanjum.blogspot.com/

Gaertner-Johnston, L. (2010, October 13). Tips for efficient instant messaging at work. Business Writing Blog. Retrieved from http://www.businesswritingblog.com/business_writing/2010/10/tips-for-efficient-instant-messaging-at-work-.html

Katenzenbach, J., & Smith, D. (1993). *Wisdom of teams.* Boston, MA: Harvard Business School Press.

Keller, K. (2009). *Twitter presentation at ABC International Conference.* Chicago, IL.

Keller, K. (2011, January 20). Personal communication.

Kent, M. L., Taylor, M., & White, W. J. (2003). The relationship between Web site design and organizational responsiveness to stakeholders. *Public Relations Review, 29*(1), 63–77.

Kievman, N. (2010). Social media etiquette: 10 commonly overlooked best practices in social media. Linked Strategies. Retrieved from http://www.linkedstrategies.com/social-media-etiquette-10-commonly-overlooked-best-practices-in-social-media/

Know your enemy: Why we contemplate catastrophe. (2006, Fall). *Harvard International Review, 36.*

Kolek, J. (2009, Summer). Managing a crisis—and becoming a stronger organization. *The Public Relations Strategist, 15*(3), 36–37.

Kouzes, J., & Posner, B. (2003). *Credibility.* San Francisco, CA: Jossey-Bass.

Krakoff, P., & Wakeman, D. (2009, November 21). Top 10 blog writing tips: Write a blog you'd want to read. Website 101. Retrieved from http://website 101.com/social-media/how-write-blog-writing/

Krug, J. (1998). Improving the performance appraisal process. *Journal of Management in Engineering, 14*(5), 19–20.

Kwablahs, E. (2009, March, 2). *Do you want to be a CEO? The Charles Cofie recipe.* MC Modern Ghana.com. Retrieved from http://www.modernghana .com/news/204512/1/do-you-want-to-be-a-ceo-the-charles-cofie-recipe.html

LaMarr, B. (2010). Feminine leaders. *Leadership Excellence, 10*(2), 1.

Lang, D. (2008). Personal communication.

Lanham, R. (2006). *Revising prose* (5th ed.). New York, NY: Macmillan.

Laura. (2008). *Kinesics* [Web log post]. Retrieved from http://speaking-without -words.blogspot.com/2008/11/kinesics.html

Lawler, E. (2008). Counterpoint. *People & Strategy, 31*(3), 8–9.

Lee, J., Woeste, J. H., & Heath, R. L. (2007, September). Getting ready for crises: Strategic excellence. *Public Relations Review, 33*(3), 334–336.

Lencioni, P. (2002). The 5 dysfunctions of a team. Table Group.com. Retrieved from http://www.tablegroup.com/books/dysfunctions/

Lerbinger, O. (1997). The crisis manager: Facing risk and responsibility. Mahwah, NJ: Lawrence Erlbaum.

Lewis, J. J. (2007, May 14). Ten basics of ethical communication. North Virginia Ethical Society. Retrieved from http://www.esnv.org/web/ ten-basics-ethical-commun

Lips, H. (2009, April 2). Women and leadership: Delicate balancing act. Women's Media. Retrieved from http://www.womensmedia.com/lead/88 -women-and-leadership-delicate-balancing-act.html

Loechner, J. (2009, October 28). Probing GenY'ers. *Research Brief.* Retrieved from http://www.mediapost.com/publications/?fa=Articles.showArticle&art _aid=116067

Longstaff, P. H., & Yang, S. (2008). Communication management and trust: Their role in building resilience to "surprises" such as natural disasters, pandemic flu, and terrorism. *Ecology and Society, 13*(1), 3. Retrieved from http:// www.ecologyand society.org/vol13/iss1/art3/

Lowen, L. (2005). Qualities of women leaders. About.com. Retrieved from http://womensissues.about.com/od/intheworkplace/a/WomenLeaders.htm

Markowitz, E. (2010, September 15). How to write an executive summary. *Inc.* Retrieved from http://www.inc.com/guides/2010/09/how-to-write-an-executive-summary.html

Martin, M. C. (2009, June 9). Management qualities for today's manager from communication skills to motivation. Associated Content from Yahoo. Retrieved from http://www.associatedcontent.com/article/1827243/management_qualities_for_todays_manager.html

Martindale, G. (n.d.). Overcoming your fear of public speaking. State University.com College and University Blog. Retrieved from http://www.stateuniversity.com/blog/permalink/Overcoming-Your-Fear-of-Public-Speaking.html

Marwijk, F. (2009). Body language during a job interview. Self Growth.com. Retrieved from http://www.selfgrowth.com/articles/Marwijk1.html

McKenzie, I. (2008). Tips on using a pointer when giving a presentation. Ian's Messy Desk. Retrieved from http://www.ismckenzie.com/tips-on-using-a-pointer-when-giving-a-presentation/

Mejak, R. (2009, October 5). Stages of the listening process explained. Articles Factory. Retrieved from http://www.articlesfactory.com/articles/communication/stages-of-the-listening-process-explained.html

Middleton, D. (2011, March 3). Students struggle for words: Business schools put more emphasis on writing amid employer complaints. *The Wall Street Journal* Online. Retrieved from http://online.wsj.com/article/SB10001424052748703409904576174651780110970.html?mod=wsj_share_twitter

Miller, L. (2001). Designate an internal manager to slash unscheduled absences. *HR Magazine, 46,* 18.

Module 4 planning, writing, and revising. McGraw-Hill. Retrieved from http://highered.mcgraw-hill.com/sites/dl/free/0070958262/462504/loc958262_module04.pdf

Moore, W. (n.d.). Top four mistakes leaders make. Mentoring. Retrieved from http://www.mentoring-disciples.org/Mistakes.html

Murphy, P. (1996). Chaos theory as a model for managing issues and crises. *Public Relations Review, 22*(2), 95–113.

Musselwhite, C. (2007). Building and leading high performance teams. *Inc.* Retrieved from http://www.inc.com/resources/leadership/articles/20070101/musselwhite_Printer_Friendly.html

Noguchi, Y. (2005, July 8). Camera phones lend immediacy to images of disaster. *The Washington Post,* A16. Retrieved from http://www.washingtonpost.com/wp-dyn/content/article/2005/07/07/AR2005070701522

Owen, J. (2005, July 11). London bombing pictures mark new role for camera phones. *National Geographic News.* Retrieved from http://news.nationalgeographic.com/news/2005/07/0711_050711_londoncell.html

Paggi, R. (2010). Managing conflict at work. Bakersfield.com. Retrieved from http://www.bakersfield.com/news/business/economy/x534569910/ROBIN -PAGGI-Managing-conflict-at-work

Paige. (2011, February 17). Study of *Inc.* 500 finds most companies blog, tweet, and friend. Social Media Paige. Retrieved from http://socialmedia paige.wordpress.com/2011/02/17/study-of-inc-500-finds-most-companies -blog-friend-and-tweet/

Paradi, D. (2003). HELP! My presentation display looks awful, five common problems with poor display on computer presentations. Communicate Using Technology.com. Retrieved from http://www.thinkoutsidetheslide.com/ articles/poor_presn_display.htm

Pauchant, T. C., & Mitroff, I. I. (1992). *Transforming the crisis-prone organization.* San Francisco, CA: Jossey-Bass.

People Communicating. (n.d.). Communication barrier—Prejudging and filtering. Retrieved from http://www.people-communicating.com/communication -barrier-prejudging.html

Peterson, E. (2011). Turn your anxiety into productive energy. Speech and Voice Enterprises. Retrieved from http://www.speechandvoice.com/Turn_Your _Anxiety_into_Productive_Energy.htm

Podmoroff, D. (n.d.). Managing presentation nerves: Coping with the fear within. Mind Tools.com. Retrieved from http://www.mindtools.com/pages/ article/PresentationNerves.htm

Porter, D. (n.d.). How to use Twitter for business. ehow.com. Retrieved from http://www.ehow.com/how_4705014_use-twitter-business-reasons.html #ixzz1B3AT0e57

Prabhakar, B., Litecky, C. R., & Arnett, K. (2005). IT skills in a tough job market. *Communications of the ACM, 48*(10), 91–94.

Presentation tips and tricks. (n.d.). MeetingTomorrow.com. Retrieved from http:// www.meetingtomorrow.com/cms-category/presentation-tips-and-tricks

Quirke, B. (2010, December/January). Steering leaders out of a crisis using effective communication. *Strategic Communication Management, 14*(1), 24–27.

Raina, R. (2010). Timely, continuous and perceived organizational effectiveness. *The Indian Journal of Industrial Relations, 46*(2), 11–13.

Roberts, S. (1992). Writing tips. The Roberts Group. Retrieved from http:// www.editorialservice.com/11ways.html

Ross, J. (2009, May 6). How to ask better questions. Blogs HBR.org. Retrieved from http://blogs.hbr.org/hmu/2009/05/real-leaders-ask.html

Rossin, J. (2010, August 2). How to make a successful presentation at the conference room table. All Business.com. Retrieved from http://www.allbusiness .com/media-telecommunications/14877893-1.html?utm_source=fe.

Rudolph, B. (1986, February 24). Coping with catastrophe: Crisis management becomes the new corporate discipline. *Time*. Retrieved from http://crisis management.com/time.html

Ryan, J. (2009, September 30). Every CEO must be a chief listening officer. *Forbes*. Retrieved from http://www.forbes.com/2009/12/30/chief-listening -officer-leadership-managing-ccl_print.html

Sabah. (2010, July 23). Exclusive interview with Yahoo! managing editor Chris Barr. The AC Week. Retrieved from http://theacweekly.wordpress.com/2010/07/23/ exclusive-interview-with-yahoo-managing-editor-chris-barr/

Sandberg, R. (2007). The cost of conflict. Conflict Coaching.com. Retrieved from http://www.conflictcoaching.com.au/conflictarticle.pdf

Scannell, E. E. (1992). We've got to stop meeting like this. *Training and Development*, *46*(1), 70–71.

Schrage, M. (2010, December 16). The top six innovation ideas of 2011. HBR Blog Network. Retrieved on from http://blogs.hbr.org/schrage/2010/12/the-t

Schultz, M. C. (2010, June 28). Subrogation trials and multimedia support— Why it's vital. Schultz Law. Retrieved from http://www.mschultzlaw.com/ subrogation-trials-and-multimedia-support-why-its-vital.

ScienceDaily. (2008, June 4). Instant messaging proves useful in reducing workplace interruption. Science News. Retrieved from http://www.sciencedaily .com/releases/2008/06/080603120251.htm

Scocco, D. (2009). What is social media? Daily Blog Tips. Retrieved from http:// www.dailyblogtips.com/what-is-social-media/

Scott, S. (2004). *Fierce conversations: Achieving success at work and in life one conversation at a time*. New York, NY: Berley.

Seeger, M. W. (2006, August). Best practices in crisis communication: An expert panel process. *Journal of Applied Communication Research*, *34*(3), 232–244.

Segal, J., & Smith, M. (2010, September). Emotional intelligence (EQ): Five key skills for raising your emotional intelligence. HelpGuide. Retrieved from http://www.helpguide.org/mental/eq5_raising_emotional_intelligence.htm

Shwom, B., & Gueldenzoph, L. (2012). *Business communication: Polishing your professional presence*. Upper Saddle River, NJ: Pearson Education.

Silva, M., & McGann, T. (1995). *Overdrive*. New York, NY: Wiley.

Snopes.com. (2007, July 21). Happiness is only a grin deep. Retrieved from http://www.snopes.com/science/smile.asp

Soroptimist International of the Americas. (2010). Communicating across generations. Retrieved from http://www.soroptimist.org/members/membership/ MembershipDocs/RecruitReten/CommAcrossGen-May2010.pdf

Steiner, L. M. (2006). Best Buy goes 100% flextime. *The Washington Post*. Retrieved from http://voices.washingtonpost.com/onbalance/2006/12/draft _best_buys_flextime_exper.html

Stocker, K. P. (1997). A strategic approach to crisis management. In C. L. Caywood (Ed.), *The elements of style (4th ed.). New York, NY:* (pp. 189–203). New York, NY: McGraw-Hill.

Strobist.com. (2007, May 22). How to improve your cheapo webcam's picture quality. Retrieved from http://strobist.blogspot.com/2007/05/how-to -improve-your-cheapo-webcams.html

Strunk, W., & White, E. B. (1999). *The elements of style* (4th ed.). New York, NY: Macmillan.

Study: Most firms unprepared for disaster. (2005, November 18). *The Central New York Business Journal,* 11.

Swallow, E. (2010, November 1). 5 tips for marketing online to an international audience. Mashable.com. Retrieved from http://mashable.com/2010/11/01/ international-marketing-online/

The seven sins of visual presentations. (n.d.). *Presentation Magazine.* Retrieved from http://www.presentationmagazine.com/7sinsvisual.htm

Thomas, F. (2010). 5 tips for conducting a virtual meeting. *Inc.* Retrieved from http://www.inc.com/guides/2010/12/5-tips-for-conducting-a-virtual-meeting .html

Thomas, K., & Kilmann, R. (2010). Conflict and management styles. Retrieved from http://www.kilmann.com/conflict.html

Timm, P., & DeTienne, K. (1980). *Managerial communication: A finger on the pulse* (3rd ed.). Englewood Cliffs, NJ: Prentice-Hall.

Timm, P., & DeTienne, K. (1986). *Managerial communication: A finger on the pulse* (4th ed.). Englewood Cliffs, NJ: Prentice-Hall.

Tomich, J. (2009, September 27). Practice, practice, and practice some more. Janice Tomich Calculated Presentations. Retrieved from http://janicetomich .com/blog-post-2

Trendsetters. (2010, July 12). Beat business burnout with frequent communication. Communication Trendsetters. Retrieved from http://blog.hopehealth .com/?s=Beat+business+burnout+with+frequent+communication

Vollmer, L. (2004, December). *Mulcahy took a no-nonsense approach to turn Xerox around.* Stanford GBS News. Retrieved from http://www.gsb.stanford.edu/ news/headlines/vftt_mulcahy.shtml

Walinskas, K. (2011, January 10). Persuasive business writing: 5 step formula for success. Articlesbase.com. Retrieved from http://www.articlesbase.com/ non-fiction-articles/persuasive-business-writing-5-step-formula-for-success -4106766.html

Web writing that works. (n.d.). Plain Language.Gov. Retrieved from http://www .plainlanguage.gov/webPL/web_writing/index.cfm

Weiner, D. (2006, March/April). Crisis communication: Managing corporate reputation in the court of public opinion. *Ivey Business Journal, 70*(4), 1–6.

Weinstein, M. (2006, November). The differences between boys and girls . . . Gender talk works at the office. Connie Glasser. Retrieved from http://www .connieglaser.com/article_tm.html

Welch, M. (2008a). The mystery of the workforce revolution: Women and millennials leading the work/life movement. *Atlanta Woman, 7*(2), 42–44.

Welch, M. (2008b). Women's leadership development UPS program for retention—and business. *Atlanta Woman, 7* (2), 45.

What is paralanguage? (n.d.). Win3 Bacal and Associates. Retrieved from http:// work911.com/communication/nonverbparalanguage.htm

What your body language says about your business savvy. (2011). Business Insider War Room. Retrieved from http://www.businessinsider.com/ body-language-is-half-of-business-communication-2010-12#eye-contact-1

Why should I avoid capital letters in email addresses and other online forms? (n.d.). Wise Geek. Retrieved from http://www.wisegeek.com/why-should-i -avoid-capital-letters-in-email-addresses-and-other-online-forms.htm

Wiegert, L. (2010, November 18). The lost art of writing. htrnews.com. Retrieved from http://www.htrnews.com/article/20101118/MAN0301/311190019/0/ MAN010301/The-lost-art-writing?odyssey=nav|head

Wilson, L. (n.d.) Wilson's newer views of learning: Personality and learning styles materials. Wilson's Newer Views of Learning: Personality and Learning Styles Material. Retrieved from http://www.uwsp.edu/education/lwilson/learning/ kirby4.htm

Winston Churchill quotes. (n.d.). Right Wing News. Retrieved from http://right wingnews.com/quotes/churchill.php

Wolfe, L. (2011). Business etiquette: 10 tips on how to shake hands with confidence. About.com Women in Business. Retrieved from http://wom-eninbusiness.about.com/od/businessetiquette/tp/10-Tips-on-How-to -Shake-Hands.htm

Workforce. (2003, November). Five standards of excellence practiced by ethical leaders. Retrieved from http://www.workforce.com/section/hr-management/ article/five-standards-excellence-practiced-by-ethical-leaders.html

Workforce. (2008, February 8). Kudos . . . to Wal-Mart! Retrieved from http:// www.workforce.com/section/01/feature/25/35/50/index.html

Wright, P., & Tao, F. (2001). The missing link: Coaching as a method of improving managerial skills in smaller businesses in Asia. *Career Development International, 6*(4), 218–226.

Zia, A., Shields, F., White, R., & Wilbert, J. (2010). Managerial communication: The link between frontline leadership and organizational performance. *Journal of Organizational Culture, Communications and Conflict, 14*(1),107–127.

Index

A

abbreviations, errors in written documents and, 359

accommodating mode, in conflict management, 113

accuracy, in written communication, 217–221

achiever personality type, 31–32

action, in persuasive writing, 193

adaptor gestures, 87

ad libs, for oral presentations, 298

agenda
 guidelines for development of, 164–165
 identification, in Model of Helping Relationships, 122–123
 sample agenda, 164

AIDA approach in persuasive writing, 191–193

Allard, Pierre-Paul, 311–314

Alston & Bird, 53–54

alternative behavior, feedback focus on, 79

American Management Association, 75, 334–335

analogies, as oral communication support material, 281

analytical personality type, 31

apostrophe, errors in written documents and, 351–352

appropriate language, intercultural differences and, 46

"Arc and Park" movements, for oral presentations, 300

articulation, in oral presentations, 301

Art of Communicating Effectively, The, 288–289

Asher, Joey, 292

Asher, Spring, 282, 286

Asmus, M., 71, 74

AT&T, 53, 66

attacker personality type, 30

attending, listening and, 102

attention, in persuasive writing, 191–192

audience
 oral communication tailoring for, 278–280
 for written communication, 186–187

authenticity, in webinar presentations, 317–318

avoider personality type, 31

avoiding mode, in conflict management, 114

awareness
 of intercultural differences, 46
 of personality differences, 29

Axtell, Roger E., 86, 278

B

baby boomers
 communication with, 44
 defined, 39–42

back, 302

bad news, written communication of, 189–191

BEAR (behavior, effect, alternative, result) feedback model, 78–81
 promotion of, in team leadership, 151

behavior, feedback focus on, 77–78

BellSouth, Connect for Success Initiative at, 66–69

Berger, Jennifer Garvey, 175–177

Berry, D., 77

best practices, in crisis leadership, 335–336

BET (behavior, effect, thank you) feedback model, 77–78, 80–81
    promotion of, in team leadership, 151

bias-free language, in written documents, 345

Blackbaud company, 36

Blanchard, Ken, 125

Block, Peter, 57

blogs
    crisis management using, 337
    example of, 234–236
    writing guidelines for, 232–236, 241–242

body movement
    interpersonal communication skills, 88–89
    in nonverbal communication, 96

Boe, John, 82

Boston Consulting Group, 53

bottom-line messaging, communication quality and, 20

Bovee, Courtland L., 288

Bracey, Hyler, 70–71, 138–140

brain anatomy and function, communication strategies and, 26–27

brainstorming model, problem solving at meetings and, 162–163

Bremer, Jill, 87

Brinkman, Rick, 223–225

Brynner, Yul, 299

Buckingham, Marcus, 73–74

Buffalo Wild Wings, 143–144

Building Trust (Bracey), 70–71, 138–140

bullet points, visual presentations and, 286–287

Business Communication Today (Bovee-Thill), 288

C

Cadwell, C., 77

capitalization, errors in written documents and, 350

Center for Creative Leadership, 129

Center for Marketing Research, 241–242

chairing of meetings
    people duties for, 169–171
    task duties for, 163–168

Chambers, Wicke, 282, 286

channel or medium in communication process, 12–16

character
    errors in written documents and negativity in, 361
    managerial ethics and, 48–49
    in written communication, 213

Chevron Corporation, lawsuit against, 32

Chick-fil-A, 49

choice, for behavioral changes, 29

Chrysler Corporation, 57

Churchill, Winston, 16, 294

Ciancutti, Arky, 136–141

Cisco systems, 309–311

clarity, in written communication, 217–221

clearness
    common errors in written documents involving, 343–344
    in written communication, 195–199

Clifford, Tim, 105

closed-ended questions, in interpersonal communication, 108

closing phase, in interviews, 153

coaching, interpersonal communication skills in, 119–124

Cofie, Charles, 183

collaboration
    communication and, 149–150
    in conflict management, 114
    ethics in, 56
    globalization and, 309–311

Collins, Jim, 57, 115

colons, errors in written documents and, 356

color selection, in visual presentations, 289–290

Colquitt, J. A., 64

commander personality type, 30

commas, errors in written documents and, 350–352
communication
    crisis management and development of systems for, 337–338
    definition and types of, 2–6
    ethics in, 54–56
    gender differences in, 32–36
    generational differences in, 36–45
    intercultural differences in, 46–48
    leadership communication, 2
    managerial communication, 2
    managerial leadership communication, 3–6
    personality differences in, 29–32
    See also miscommunication
communication process
    basic principles of, 9–17
    channel or medium, 12–16
    environmental factors, 17
    feedback in, 17
    frequency and use of multiple channels, 16–17
    message, 11–12
    receiver, 10–11
    sender, 9–10
comparisons, as oral communication support material, 281
competing mode, in conflict management, 113
completeness
    common errors in written documents involving, 343
    in written communication, 195
compromise, in conflict management, 114
conciseness
    errors in written documents and, 359–360
    in written communication, 208–211
conclusions, in oral presentations, 282–283
concreteness
    common errors in written documents involving, 344–345
    in written communication, 199–200

conference calls, communication process in, 14
conference room presentations, 314–315
confidence
    in communication, 60
    in oral presentations, 294
conflict management
    interpersonal communication and, 108–115
    in meetings, 169–171
"Connect for Success" programs, interpersonal communication and, 66–69
connectivity, in communication, 61
connotative work meanings, 19
consensus decision making, 163
correctness
    common errors in written documents involving, 345–346
    in written communication, 200–208
counseling, interpersonal communication skills in, 119–124
courtesy
    errors in written documents and, 360–361
    in written communication, 212–213
Covey, Stephen, 49, 283
"cranial divide," communication strategies and, 26–28
creativity
    business leaders' suspicion of, 27–28
    stress management and, 100
Creativity Training Institute, 25–26
Credibility (Kouzes/Posner), 135
Crincoli, Dom, 59–62
crisis leadership
    best practices in, 335–336
    challenges in, 339–341
    guidelines for, 333–341
    planning strategies for, 334–335
    post-crisis activities, 339
    response strategies, 338
Crystal, Billy, 299

cue matching, in nonverbal communication, 95–96
culture
  communication and, 46–48
  nonverbal communication and, 22

D

Dalton, Francie M., 29–30
dangling modifiers
  errors in written documents and, 346–347
  in written communication, 201–203
day-to-day situations, communication in, 129–182
  collaboration and, 149–150
  meeting effectiveness guidelines, 160–173
  one-on-one meetings and interviews, 152–160
  for performance review, 154–155
  trust building in, 131–141
  virtual vs. face-to-face team building, 141–151
De Angelis, Barbara, 140–141
"Death by PowerPoint" phenomenon, visual presentations and, 286–292
decision-making meetings, 161
  mechanisms for, 163
  participant selection for, 166
Deck, Jeff, 202
Decker Communications, 300
defensiveness, miscommunication and, 24–25
delayers, errors in written documents and, 358
denotative word meanings, 19
descriptive ethics, defined, 49
desire, in persuasive writing, 192
differences, smoothing over, 100
direct writing, organization and logical order for, 187–193
disagreement, rules for constructive agreeable disagreement, 116
disaster recovery plans, importance of, 334–335

Do's and Taboos Around the World: A Guide To International Behavior and Gestures (Axtell), 86
Do's and Taboos Around the World for Women (Axtell), 86
Do's and Taboos of Body Language Around the World (Axtell), 86
draft, written communication and construction of, 193–194
dress, for oral presentations, 303
drifter personality type, 30
Duartes, Nancy, 317
Duke, Mike, 51

E

early warning systems, crisis planning and, 336–338
echo boomers, defined, 39–42
effect of behavior, feedback focus on, 77, 79
8th Habit, The (Covey), 49
Eisenhardt, Kathy, 111–112
Ekman, Paul, 86
Elements of Style (White), 193
e-mail
  communication process in, 14
  writing guidelines for, 220–225
Emanuel, Rahm, 60
emblem gestures, 86
emotional appeal, in persuasive writing, 192
emotional intelligence
  coaching in, 178–182
  interpersonal communication and, 97–101
emotions
  connection with, 99
  miscommunication and, 24–25
  in nonverbal communication, 96
employment interview, guidelines for, 155–156
energizing techniques, 100
environmental factors
  in communication process, 17
  personality and, 28
Essential Do's and Taboos: The Complete Guide to International Business and Leisure Travel (Axtell), 278

ethics
    classification of, 49–54
    for managerial leaders, 48–54
    standards of excellence and, 54–57
evaluation, listening and, 102
exclamation points, errors in written
    documents and, 358
executive summaries, writing guide-
    lines for, 231–232
expert opinion
    matching consumers to, 313–314
    as oral communication support
        material, 281
external noise, miscommunication
    and, 22–23
eye contact
    interpersonal communication
        through, 87–88
    in oral presentations, 303
    in webinar presentations,
        316–319

F
Facebook, 241–242
face-to-face meetings
    communication process in, 12–13
    day-to-day communication and,
        141–151
    for feedback sessions, 73–74
facial expressions, interpersonal com-
    munication through, 88
facilitators, for meetings, 169–170
false starts, errors in written docu-
    ments and, 358
familiar words, in written communi-
    cation, 195–196
feedback
    BET model of, 77–78
    in communication process, 17
    generational differences in need for,
        37–38
    interpersonal communication and,
        69–77
    training for, 75–77
feedforward system of feedback,
    71–72
feel-felt-found communication strat-
    egy, 10

Fehrmann, J., 77
Festa, Chris M., 139
15 Minutes Including Q&A: A Plan to
    Save the World From Lousy Presen-
    tations (Asher), 292
filtering, miscommunication and, 23
"fish hand," in handshakes, 90
5 Dysfunctions of a Team (Lencioni),
    111
Flesch-Kincaid Grade Level, 198
Flesch Reading Ease, The, 198
flexible work environments, 53
flipcharts, guidelines for using, 157–
    160, 291
forgetting, in oral presentations, 295
format errors, in written documents,
    356
forward and backward movements, in
    nonverbal communication, 91
Foster, P., 76
free-form slides, in oral presentations,
    287–292
full block letter style, 227–228
fused sentences, errors in written
    documents and, 352
Futren Corporation, 117–119

G
Gandossy, Robert P., 4
gender issues
    differences in communication and,
        32–36
    ethics and, 51–53
Gender Talk Works: 7 Steps for Crack-
    ing the Gender Code at Work
    (Grasser), 32
generational differences
    classification of, 39–42
    in communication, 36–45
    feedback guidelines and, 73–74
Generation Xers
    communication with, 44
    defined, 39–42
Generation Yers
    communication with, 44
    defined, 39–42
    generational differences in commu-
        nication and, 36–37

genetics, personality and, 28
gerunds, errors in written documents
 and, 356
gestures
 interpersonal communication
  through, 86–87
 in nonverbal communication, 96
 in oral presentations, 302–303
Gibbs, Robert, 60
global communication, TelePresence
 technology and, 314
globalization, crisis leadership and,
 334–335
goal setting, team building and,
 145–146
Goldsmith, Marshall, 71–72
*Good to Great: Why Some Companies
 Make the Leap . . . and Others
 Don't* (Collins), 57, 115
Google, managerial leadership communication research by, 4–6
Goman, C. K., 34
grammatical mistakes, in written communication, 200–211
Grasser, Connie, 32
Gratton, Lynda, 69–70
*Great Typo Hunt: America's 10 Most
 Common Typos* (Deck and Her-
 son), 202
Gunning Fog Index, 198

H
Haden, Jeff, 240–241
Hall, Edward T., 92
handshakes, interpersonal communication through, 89–91
hardships, management of, 100
Hay, Steward, 87
hearing, listening and, 102
Herson, Benjamin D., 202
honesty, trust and, 135–141
Hoppe, Michael, 101
humanity, in communication,
 61–62
humor, interpersonal communication
 and, 100
hyphens, errors in written documents
 and, 356

I
Iacocca, Lee, 57
"I" as sentence-starting word, errors in
 written documents and, 360–361
IBM, 53
idea meetings, 161
illustrations, as oral communication
 support material, 281
illustrator gestures, 86
incomplete thoughts, errors in written
 documents and, 347
indirect writing
 bad news writing, 189–191
 organization and logical order for,
  187, 189–193
 persuasive writing, 191–193
individual decision making, 163
inference, miscommunication based
 on, 18
inflated wording, errors in written
 documents and, 360
informational meetings, 161
information overload
 miscommunication and, 21
 in written documents, 343–344
information purpose, in oral communication, 276–277
instant messaging
 communication process in, 14–15
 writing guidelines for, 238–239
interactive effectiveness, promotion
 of, in team leadership, 151
intercultural differences, communication and, 46–48
interest, in persuasive writing, 192
internal noise, miscommunication
 and, 22–23
international audiences, oral communication strategies for, 279–280
interpersonal communication skills
 case study of, 127
 conflict management strategies,
  108–115
 Connect for Success Initiative,
  67–69
 emotional intelligence and, 97–101
 eye contact, 87–88
 facial expressions and, 88

giving and receiving feedback and, 69–77
kinesics and, 86–97
listening skills, 101–106
for managerial leaders, 6–7, 63–115
mentoring, coaching and counseling and, 119–124
nonverbal communication and, 81–85
posture and body movement and, 88–89
questions and paraphrasing in, 106–110

interviews
employment interview, 155–156
guidelines for, 152–160
organization of, 153–154

intimate zone, in proxemics, 92

introduction, in oral presentations, 281–282

introverts, oral presentation preparation for, 293

isometric exercises, before oral presentations, 299

italics, errors in written documents and, 359

its *vs.* it's, errors in written documents and, 352

J
jargon
miscommunication and, 19–20
in written communication, 196–197, 344

K
Kalb, Nathan, 117–119
Katzenbach, J., 141
Kilmann, Ralph H., 113–114
kinesics, interpersonal communication skills and, 86–97
knowledge acquisition, promotion of, in team leadership, 150
Kouzes, James, 135
Krug, J., 75

L
Lafley, A. G., 124
Lamb, Warren, 91

Lane, George, III, 87
Lanham, Richard, 213–214
Lawler, Edward E., III, 73
leadership communication, 2
in crisis response, 339–341
gender differences in, 33–34
team building and, 150–151
learning mechanisms, visual presentations and, 285–292
left-brain thinking, communication strategies and, 26–28
Lencioni, Patrick, 111
Lepine, J. A., 64
letters, writing guidelines for, 226–227
like words, errors in written documents and, 354–356
LinkedIn Profiles, guidelines for, 240–241
listening
in interpersonal communication, 101–106
in interviews, 153
logical appeal, in persuasive writing, 192–193
Long, Candace Lowe, 25–26
loyalty, generational differences in expectations for, 38

M
majority-based decision making, 163
managerial communication, 2
managerial leaders
as communication receivers, 10–11
as communication senders, 9–10
crisis leadership guidelines for, 333–341
ethics for, 48–54
generational differences in, 36–45
inferences by, 18
interpersonal communication skills for, 6–7, 63–115
listening skills in, 101–106
oral communication skills, 8
written communication skills, 7–8
managerial leadership communication, 3–6
Mansour, Rebecca, 61

Martin, Chris M., 2
Martin, Jonathan, 60
Martindale, Gayla, 280
McElvy, Paul, 216–221
media relations program
  crisis management and, 337
  crisis response and, 338–339
meetings
  agenda guidelines for, 164–165
  case studies for, 175–182
  facilitators for, 169–170
  guidelines for effective meetings,
    160–173
  leaders' introduction for, 167–168
  online meetings, 173
  participant selection guidelines,
    165–166
  people responsibilities during, 171
  problem solving techniques for,
    162–163
  summary of meeting notes,
    171–172
  time and location guidelines for,
    166–167
  types of, 161
memos, writing guidelines for,
    225–226
Menkin, Randi, 51–52
mental pictures, written creation of,
    199–200
mentoring, interpersonal communica-
    tion skills in, 119–124
message, in communication process,
    11–12
millenials, defined, 39–42
miscommunication
  causes of, 18–48
  defensiveness and emotions and,
    24–25
  differing perceptions as cause of, 20
  inferences as cause of, 18
  information overload and, 21
  noise and, 22–23
  word-meaning confusion and,
    19–20
mission statement, team building and,
    145

mistakes, courage in face of, 61
mistrust, guidelines for avoiding,
    137–141
Model of Helping Relationships,
    121–124
modified block letter style, 227, 229
Moody, Dwight, 48
motivation, generational differences
    in, 37
movement pattern analysis, 91
Mulcahy, Ann, 103–105
multichannel communication
  crisis leadership, 334–335
  frequency and use of, 16–17
Myers-Briggs Type Indicator, 29–32,
    133

N
Napier, Pam, 66
Nardelli, Bob, 124
negative feedback, guidelines for, 74
negative words, errors in written
    documents and, 361
nervous habits, in nonverbal commu-
    nication, 96
neural activity, communication strate-
    gies and, 26–28
Now Discover Your Strengths (Bucking-
    ham), 72–74
New York Times Magazine, 60, 62
noise, miscommunication and, 22–23
nominal group model, problem solv-
    ing at meetings and, 162
nonverbal communication
  in face-to-face meetings, 13
  intercultural differences in, 46–47
  interpersonal communication skills
    and, 81–85
  kinesics, 86–97
  miscommunication and, 22
  paralanguage, 93–94
  proxemics in, 92–93
  strategies for, 94–97
normative ethics, 50–51
normative perception, miscommuni-
    cation and, 20
norms, in team building, 146–147

note taking
in interviews, 153
for meetings, 171–172
number presentation, errors in written documents and, 348

O

objectives, team building and, 145–146
O'Neil, Kathryn, 157–160, 291
one-on-one meetings, guidelines for, 152–160
online meetings
crisis management and, 337
guidelines for, 173
webinar presentations, 315–319
open-ended questions, in interpersonal communication, 107
opening, in interviews, 153
open-mindedness, interpersonal communication and, 67
oral communication skills
case study in, 319–332
conference room presentations, 314–315
confidence building for, 294
dress guidelines for presentations, 303
eye contact and, 303
gestures in presentations and, 302–303
improvement of, 275–332
for managerial leaders, 8
organization of presentation, 280–283
pauses in presentations, 296–297
practice guidelines, 294–295
preparation strategies, 275–298
presentation bloopers and, 318–319
presentation tips, 298–305
purpose identification, 276–277
Q & A sessions, 292–293
rehearsals for presentations, 294–295
team presentations and, 305–309
video recording of rehearsals, 297

visuals in, 285–292
vocal delivery, 301
webinar presentations, 315–319
oral introduction, interpersonal communication, 89–91
Organizational Behavior (Colquitt, Lepine, and Wesson), 64
organizational structure, team building and, 144
orphans and widows in proofreading, 216
outline
for interviews, 152–153
in oral presentations, 283–285
Overcoming Your Fear of Public Speaking, 280

P

Palin, Sarah, 59–62
palm-to-palm contact, in handshakes, 89–91
paragraph coherence, errors in written documents and, 347
paralanguage, in nonverbal communication, 93–94
parallel structure
errors in written documents and faults in, 346
lack of, in written communication, 203–204
paramedic method, in written communication, 213–214
paraphrasing
errors in written documents and, 347
interpersonal communication and use of, 106–110
participant feedback, in oral presentations, 298
participant selection for meetings, guidelines for, 165–166
participation, interpersonal communication and, 67
partnerships, pre-crisis network of, 337
partner system for proofreading, 215–216

passive voice
  errors in written documents and,
    358–359
  in written communication,
    205–208
pauses, in oral presentations,
  296–297
People Skills Quiz, 81–85
percentage expressions, errors in written documents and, 352
perception, miscommunication and
  differences in, 20
performance review, guidelines for,
  154–155
performer personality type, 31
periods, errors in written documents
  and, 358
persistence, in communication, 60–61
personality differences
  classification of, 30–32
  communication strategies and,
    28–32
personal zone, in proxemics, 92
persuasion
  in oral communication, 276–277
  in written communication,
    191–193
phone calls, communication process
  in, 14
planning meetings, 161
play, interpersonal communication
  and, 100
pleaser personality type, 30–31
podiums, for oral presentations, 300
positive words
  errors in written documents and,
    361
  in written communication,
    212–213
Posner, Barry, 135
posture
  interpersonal communication skills,
    88–89
  in nonverbal communication, 96
PowerPoint, in visual presentations,
  290–291
Prabhakar, B., 65

practice guidelines, for oral presentations, 294–295
pre-crisis activities, crisis planning
  and, 336–338
prepositions, avoidance in written
  documents of, 345
presentation tips for oral communication, 299–305
  future predictions for, 317–319
probing questions, in interpersonal
  communication, 108
problem solving, at meetings,
  162–163
progressions, generational differences
  in expectations for, 38
promotions, failure rates for, 129–130
pronoun-antecedent agreement, errors
  in written documents and, 348
pronoun cases, errors in written documents and, 349
proofreading
  errors in, 346
  partner system for, 215–216
  in written communication,
    214–221
proxemics, in nonverbal communication, 92–93
public zone, in proxemics, 92
punctuation, errors in written documents and, 358
purpose result, in oral communication, 276–277
purpose statement
  in oral communication, 280
  team building and, 145
  in written communication, 185
Puzo, Mario, 193

Q

question & answer sessions
  management guidelines for,
    304–305
  in oral presentations, 292–293
question marks, errors in written
  documents and, 358
question–response phase, in interviews, 153

questions
  interpersonal communication and
    use of, 106–110
  as oral communication support
    material, 281
quotation marks, errors in written
  documents and, 359

R

rapport, in Model of Helping Relationships, 122
readability, in written communication, 197–199, 344
"ready position," for oral presentations, 300
receiver, in communication process,
  10–11
redundancy, errors in written documents and, 360
reflecting questions, in interpersonal
  communication, 108
reflective thinking, problem solving at
  meetings and, 162
regionalisms, miscommunication
  based on, 18
regulator gestures, 86
rehearsals
  for oral presentations, 294–295
  for team presentations, 305–309
relationship management, interpersonal communication skills and,
  98
relative pronouns, errors in written
  documents and, 349
relaxation techniques, 100
remembering, listening and, 102
repetition, in written communication,
  avoidance of, 210–211
reports, writing guidelines for, 227,
  229–230
response, listening and, 102
results, feedback focus on, 79–80
results-only work environment
  (ROWE), 53
right-brain thinking, communication
  strategies and, 26–28
Roosevelt, Theodore, 48

rule of 4 by 5, in visual presentations,
  289
rule of 33, in visual presentations, 289
rule of three, points in oral communication and, 280–281

S

Sarbanes-Oxley Act, 52
Scott, Lee, 50–51
self-awareness, interpersonal communication skills and, 97
self-management, interpersonal communication skills and, 97
self-reflection, feedback sessions and,
  73–74
semiblock letter style, 227
semicolons, errors in written documents and, 356
sender
  in communication process, 9–10
  nonverbal communication by, 22
sensitivity, to intercultural differences,
  46
sensory perception, miscommunication and, 20
sentence structure
  errors in written documents and,
    347–348
  in written communication, 344
session planning, in Model of Helping
  Relationships, 123–124
7 Cs (completeness, clearness, concreteness, correctness, consice-
  ness, courtesy, and character)
  in written communication,
    194–213
  common errors in, 343–362
7 Habits of Highly Effective People
  (Covey), 49
side-to-side movements, in nonverbal
  communication, 91
Siegel, Betty, 279
signal detection systems, crisis planning and, 336–338
silent generation, defined, 39–42
similar words, errors in written documents and, 353

simplified letter style, 227

skip level meetings, communication in, 13

Slideology: The Art and Science of Creating Great Presentations (Duarte), 317

slide presentations, in oral presentations, 287–292

SMART (specific, measurable, assignable, realistic, time period) goals, team building and, 146

Smith, Andy, 178–182

Smith, D., 141

Smith, Sally, 143–144

social awareness, interpersonal communication skills and, 98

social media
  case study in, 59–62
  communication process in, 15
  crisis response using, 338–339
  writing guidelines for, 241–242

social zone, in proxemics, 92

spacing, errors in written documents and, 349

specific purpose, in oral communication, 277

spelling errors, in written documents, 346

stage setting, for oral presentations, 299–300

standards of excellence, ethics and, 54–57

STAR (situation or task, action, result) feedback, interpersonal communication and, 67–69

statistics, as oral communication support material, 281

stress reduction, guidelines for, 98–99

structured slides, in oral presentations, 287–292

subject-verb agreement
  errors in written documents and, 346
  in written communication, 204–205

succession planning, ethics in, 56–57

Sun Microsystems, Inc., 53

support material, for oral communication, 281

sweaty hands, in handshakes, 90

T

Tannen, Deborah, 33

team building
  ABCs of, 142
  collaboration and, 149–150
  communication protocol in, 145–149
  for crisis management, 338
  interpersonal communication and, 65
  leadership roles and, 150–151
  for oral presentations, 305–309
  organizational structure and, 144
  virtual *vs.* face-to-face teams, 141–151

technology
  generational differences in management of, 38–39
  information overload and, 21
  visual presentations and, 285–292

TelePresence, for videoconferencing, 310–314

television
  oral communication tips from, 282
  visual tips from, 286–287

tenacity, importance of, 29

tenses, errors in written documents and, 357–358

tenure, ethics in, 58

terminal punctuation, errors in written documents and, 358

Tesla Motors, 337

text messaging, writing guidelines for, 238–239

thank you, feedback focus on, 78

therapy, counseling *vs.*, 120–121

Thill, John V., 288

Thomas, Kenneth W., 113–114

Thompson, Jody, 53

Thornton, Grant, 52–53

three Bs (big, beautiful, and bold), in visual presentations, 289–290

time management
  in interviews, 153
  for meetings, 166–167

time-of-day designations, errors in written documents and, 349
tone
  errors in written documents and negativity in, 361
  in interviews, 152
  in written communication, 217–221
TOP (trust, open-mindedness, participation) values, interpersonal communication and, 67
traditionalists
  communication with, 42–43
  defined, 39–42
  technology expectations of, 39
training programs, for feedback, 75–77
trite phrases, in written communication, avoidance of, 211
trust
  in day-to-day communication, 131–134
  guidelines for building, 135–141
  interpersonal communication and, 67
  team building and, 148
Tucci, Joseph, 184
Turner, Dee Ann, 49
tweets, writing guidelines for, 236–238, 241–242
Two Truths and a Lie trust game, 132–134
typos, in written communication, 202

U
understanding
  listening and, 102
  promotion of, in team leadership, 150
Unilever Ghana Ltd., 183
upbringing, generational differences in communication and, 36–37
UPS Corporation, ethics at, 51–52
Urbanski, Joe, 309–311

V
vague words, written communication, avoidance of, 200

valuing difference, intercultural communication and, 47–48
Van Flein, Thomas, 61
verbs, errors in written documents and, 358–359
verb tenses, errors in written documents and, 357–358
vertical movements, in nonverbal communication, 91
veterans generation, defined, 39–42
videoconferencing
  communication process in, 13–14
  TelePresence technology for, 310–314
videotaped rehearsals, for oral presentations, 297
virtual teams, day-to-day communication and, 141–151
visual cues, for oral presentations, 298
visual interaction, TelePresence technology for, 312–314
visuals
  handmade *vs.* computer-generated visuals, 318
  in oral presentations, 285–292
vocal control, interpersonal communication, 96–97
vocal delivery, in oral presentations, 301
vocal differentiators, in nonverbal communication, 93
vocal identifiers, in nonverbal communication, 93
voice mail, communication process in, 14
voice tones, in nonverbal communication, 93

W
Wall Street Journal, 65
Walmart, normative ethics at, 50–51
Walton, Ron, 50
Warlick, Rebecca, 130–134
Watson, Thomas, 129
"We" as sentence-starting word, errors in written documents and, 360–361

we-attitude, in written communication, 212
webcam conferencing, communication process in, 13–14
webinar presentations, guidelines for, 315–319
Weiner, Anthony, 57
Wesson, M. J., 64
White, E. B., 193
why-questions, in interpersonal communication, 107–110
Wisdom of Teams, The (Katzenbach and Smith), 141
women, communication skills in, 32–36
Wooing and Winning Business (Asher and Chambers), 286
word choice, in written documents, 344
wordiness, errors in written documents and, 359–360
word length, in written documents, 344
word-meaning confusion, miscommunication and, 19–20
wordy expressions, in written communication, avoidance of, 209–210
WorkPlace Big Five personality assessment, 10
Workscape, 105
World is Flat, The (Friedman), 309
writer's block, guidelines for, 194
written communication
    audience identification in, 186–187
    blogs, 232–236
    case studies in, 246–274
    categories of, 220–242
    checklist for, 245
    crisis management plan guidelines, 337
    direct *vs.* indirect writing, 187–193
    draft construction guidelines, 193–194
    editing and polishing in, 194–213
    e-mail guidelines, 220–225
    errors found in, 343–362
    executive summaries, 231–232
    instant and text messages, 238–239
    letters, 226–229
    LinkedIn Profiles and, 240–241
    managerial leaders' skill in, 7–8
    memos, 225–226
    paramedic method in, 213–214
    proofreading in, 214–221
    purpose identification in, 185
    reports, 227, 229–230
    skills development for, 183–246
    social media, 241–242
    tweets, 236–238

Y
Yeater, Paige, 36
you-attitude
    errors in written documents and, 360
    in written communication, 212
You Just Don't Understand! (Tannen), 33

Z
Zia, A., 64–65

Announcing the Business Expert Press Digital Library

Concise E-books Business Students
Need for Classroom and Research

This book can also be purchased in an e-book collection by your library as

- a one-time purchase,
- that is owned forever,
- allows for simultaneous readers,
- has no restrictions on printing,
- can be downloaded as PDFs from within the library community.

Our digital library collections are a great solution to beat the rising cost of textbooks. E-books can be loaded into their course management systems or onto students' e-book readers.

The **Business Expert Press** digital libraries are very affordable, with no obligation to buy in future years.

For more information, please visit **www.businessexpertpress.com/librarians**. To set up a trial in the United States, please contact **Sheri Dean** at sheri.dean@globalepress.com; for all other regions, contact **Nicole Lee** at *nicole.lee@igroupnet.com*.

OTHER TITLES IN OUR CORPORATE COMMUNICATION COLLECTION

Series Editor: **Debbie DuFrene**, *Stephen F. Austin State University*

Corporate Communication and Media Relations: Tactical Guidelines for Strategic Practice
by Michael B. Goodman and Peter B. Hirsch

Managing Virtual Teams by Debbie DuFrene and Carol Lehman

Fundamentals of Writing for Marketing and Public Relations by Janet Mizrahi

Managing Investor Relations: Strategies for Effective Communication by Alexander Laskin

Lightning Source UK Ltd.
Milton Keynes UK
UKHW020635110921
390336UK00005B/156